THE PERMANENT REVOLUTION?

CONSERVATIVE LAW
AND THE
TRADE UNIONS

THE PERMANENT REVOLUTION?

Conservative Law and the Trade Unions

John McIlroy

S P O K E S M A N
for the
SOCIETY OF INDUSTRIAL TUTORS

First published in Great Britain in 1991 by
Spokesman
Bertrand Russell House
Gamble Street
Nottingham, England
Tel. 0602 708318

British Library Cataloguing in Publication Data

McIlroy, John 1955-
The permanent revolution?: Conservative law and the trade unions.
1. Great Britain. Trade unions. Law
I. Title
344.104188

ISBN 0-85124-527-7
ISBN 0-85124-528-5 pbk

Printed by Russell Press Ltd., Nottingham. (Tel. 0602 784505).

Contents

The Permanent Revolution?

". . . an excellent book, a first class resource for trade union activists."
Frank Cosgrove, Director of Education, TGWU

". . . learned, lucid and useful . . . it will be very well received — and not simply in trade union classes."
Professor Royden Harrison

". . . a valuable contribution and a must for any student's reading of social history."
Peter Heathfield, General Secretary, NUM

". . . a very timely book . . . essential reading. It gives an excellent step by step account of the enactment of Tory legislation and the reaction to it of the Labour and Trade Union movement. If the Labour movement is to tackle the task of undoing the worst effects of Tory legislation it will need the information and guidance of John McIlroy's book. . . . There is little time for the informed discussion, that McIlroy's book demands, to begin. In that urgent discussion John McIlroy's book will play a major and essential role."
Professor Paul O'Higgins

"This comprehensive guide to Britain's employment legislation is worthwhile and exhaustive in its content without being exhausting in its style. Informative and accessible, it will no doubt become a valuable asset to stewards representatives and union officers at all levels of the movement."
Val Stansfield, Head of Organisation and Education, CPSA

"A vividly written, meticulously documented, well argued book . . . an indispensable tool for both union activists and students of the labour movement."
Maureen Toomey, TUC General Council Education Committee

"McIlroy's book is a timely and detailed review of the Thatcher experiment in industrial relations but which also casts a coolly radical eye on the Labour Party's alternatives. A first in the field, this is a must."
Professor Brian Towers

Foreword

After 12 years of the Thatcherite regime industrial relations in the United Kingdom have been turned upside down. From being the country where the law had least of any to do with labour relations, Britain has become the one with the most all embracing legal constraints on the exercise by trade unions and employers of their industrial relations functions. In a succession of increasingly repressive acts of legislation, trade union power has been effectively corraled. By the summer of 1989 it did not seem unreasonable for a left of centre trade union leader to ask whether it was still "possible to call a strike and remain within the law". What legislation had initiated the judges completed. Taking the unions to the courts with injunctions and the threat of sequestration for contempt had become the norm for employers facing industrial action.

John McIlroy has written a book which provides a layperson's guide through the six major acts of 1980, 1982, 1984, 1988, 1989 and 1990 and the mass of ancillary legal measures introduced by the Thatcher governments. He sets the assault on trade union power firmly within the general framework of the Thatcherite appeal to personal responsibility and against collective action and of the radical, albeit ultimately unsuccessful, restructuring of British industry. He scrutinises thoroughly and very fairly the largely abortive policy responses of the TUC and the several individual unions. We are reminded of the major confrontations of this decade — the attack on Eddie Shah's *Stockport Messenger*; the NUJ's dispute with Dimbleby and Sons; the Miners' strike of 1984-85; the GCHQ affair; the battles of SOGAT with Murdoch at Wapping; the Seafarers' dispute with Sealink; the NUR's strike against London Underground; the T&G's defence of the dockers over the repeal of the Dock Labour Board scheme; NALGO's rolling strikes; and a host of minor skirmishes.

All the issues which legislation sought to address are examined in the book — the closed shop, union ballots, secondary action, union democracy, fair wages, essential services, political funds — and the multiple complexities unravelled. The book ends with a thoughtful study of the TUC and Labour Party attempts to elaborate an alternative programme of employment legislation, leading up to the Labour Party's latest Policy Review. This is given a critical assessment, which leads up to the author's judgment on the question posed in the title of the book — will the revolution prove to be a permanent one? This is something which politicians as well as tutors, students, and practitioners in industrial relations will greatly benefit from studying.

John McIlroy has presented the material in the book in a form which can be used equally well by trade union officials, by personnel managers, and by tutors and students in trade union studies, industrial relations and political and economic studies. Legal and other technical terms are clearly defined when they are introduced. The story, which covers more than a decade, is broken up by boxes outlining key judgments, case study chronologies, a complete list of injunctions, and major historical developments in trade union and employment law. Each chapter ends with a set of five or six questions which can be developed by tutors for group discussion. In the interests of readability, endnotes have been kept to a minimum.

The particular concern shown by the author throughout the book for the needs of the industrial tutor should come as no surprise. John McIlroy is not only an Industrial Relations tutor at Manchester University's Extramural Department; he has for many years been an executive committee member of the Society of Industrial Tutors. It is with the Society's support that the book is published, and to the Society's special purpose in developing working class education that it is dedicated. The Society of Industrial Tutors has a distinguished history of publication in fields that are of importance for industrial tutors. They will have good reason to be proud of their latest production and to recommend it to all those who wish to understand what has been happening to labour relations in the last decade and what should be done about the revolution that has taken place.

Michael Barratt Brown
President, Society of Industrial Tutors
May 1991

Introduction

In the end, Thatcherism failed: and so in November 1990 its architect was done to political death by her own supporters. The cause of the demise was transparently economic — but perhaps employment legislation played a small role. Viewed discretely, its development has been much celebrated as an exercise in political mastery, certainly in comparison with the fumbling attempts of Harold Wilson in the 1960s and Ted Heath in the 1970s to get legislation restricting union activities on the statute book, into the courts and thence into the workplace. But in the final analysis employment legislation was held by the theorists of Thatcherism to be a key lever in the economic regeneration of Britain. Put simply but essentially, its aim was to increase productivity, profitability, competitiveness. Mrs Thatcher's legal project had its roots in economic restructuring; it was thus complicit in the wider failures of that restructuring.

Examined in narrow legal or political terms, the employment laws have been widely and with justification judged a success. They have restricted in practice union purposes and methods. The Dock Strike of 1989 provides an excellent example of this. And, of course, success here cannot be measured simply in terms of court cases. One recent if limited survey by *Labour Research* found that whilst legal action remained a rarity, in one in three workplaces examined employers had *threatened* to use the legislation and in one in five workplaces trade unionists had called off industrial action in response to such threats.

But there is neither unanimity nor detailed compelling evidence on the question of the influence the legislation has exercised on industrial relations generally and more specifically on trade union organisation and activity. To take a stark example, one recent econometric study by Freeman and Pelletier claims that the employment legislation was responsible for almost the entire decline in union density between 1980 and 1986. In the same journal another paper by Professor Disney argues its direct impact on union coverage was minimal (both in *British Journal of Industrial Relations*, June, 1990).

If we take union recognition in the 1980s then the legislation appears to have played a minimal role: the CBI reported no real change in the situation in 1986 compared with 1979 — a verdict supported by evidence from ACAS — although there are signs of a more recent growth in de-recognition. The influence of Conservative law on internal union government is even more questionable — at least in producing the results governments intended. There has been a *growth* not a decline in union political funds. There is no discernible trend towards the election of more moderate leaders as a result of compulsory balloting for union executives and executive officers.

On the other hand, the decline during the Thatcher decade in both the number of stoppages and the number of striker days is undeniable. In addition the government's *Workplace Industrial Relations Survey* notes a significant decline in the use of picketing. However, the drop in strike activity is part of an *international* decline. The drop in working days lost per thousand employees in the UK 1978-1988 was less than the decline in Australia, Canada, Ireland or the USA. And the UK maintained its position in the top half of the strike league table. Neither can the legislation explain conjunctural downturns and upturns, such as that in 1988-1989, in the incidence of strike activity. The view of ACAS is that economic rather than legal change has been the key factor. If legal initiatives have undoubtedly rendered striking more cumbersome, more expensive, more predictable — altogether a more difficult venture — the unions, in response, have undertaken a streamlining of organisation and a rationalisation of communications. A greater, if still inadequate, attention has been paid to strategy, to tactics and to logistics. In consequence, the immediate future may hold fewer strikes — although that will depend too on other factors. But they may pack a more powerful punch.

Even within the limited focus of industrial relations the impact of Conservative law has to be weighed in the currency of trade unions which are undoubtedly weaker in terms of coverage and in terms of social power and political influence than in the pre-Thatcher years, but which in terms of workplace organisation, wage levels, even the ability to mount offensive struggles over conditions — witness the 35 hour week strikes in 1990 — have demonstrated a supple resilience under fire. The legislation has more than paid its way in the big showpiece confrontations; in this case the big battles do not tell the whole story or necessarily win the war. In terms of industrial relations it may still be too early for definite judgements on success or failure; indeed it may — despite the best efforts of statisticians and econometricians — prove ultimately impossible to extricate and isolate the role of law, as distinct from economic, social and political pressures, in moulding industrial relations in the 1980s. This should occasion little surprise. Almost a century after the event, historians are still divided over the impact on wages and union activity of the Taff Vale judgement and the *1906 Trade Disputes Act.*

Evaluated from the broader vantage point of political economy, in a Britain in recession, many will question whether Mrs. Thatcher's legal project was really worth all the time, effort and conflict. The 'privileges' granted to the unions have, as Hayek, Joseph and Thatcher demanded, been revoked. Economic decline has not in consequence been reversed. The New Right proved poor prophets. As Mrs. Thatcher's reign came to an end, unit labour costs were increasing at more than 10%, the mark-up between union jobs and non-union jobs had scarcely changed since the seventies, and authoritative studies suggested that the differences in employment and productivity growth between union and non-union companies were insignificant. The role that de-regulation and the erosion of the floor of individual employment rights played in increasing industrial efficiency, as distinct from poverty, was widely questioned. For some, such as Employment Secretary Michael Howard, who announced in early 1991 that he was considering further moves on picketing and compulsory seven day notice periods before industrial action, the project of legal counter-revolution now seems to have more to do with symbolism and the manufacture of political problems for electoral advantage than with economic transformation. However, with all the surveys demonstrating that the unions are no longer perceived as an important political problem, the continuation of the legal offensive may, in the present economic context, be likened to fiddling while Rome burns.

The purpose of this book is to provide a primer and reference for those who have sought to keep up with developments since 1979 and who feel the end of the Thatcher era is an appropriate time to take stock. I have tried to document both the legal changes and their political origins, the objectives of the legislation, its impact on the unions, and the unions' response. Given the extensive terrain covered, treatment has at times had to be brief. The approach I have taken is historical. Parts of the earlier legislation are dealt with even though they have since been repealed or amended, so that the political unfolding of the law in relation to a changing balance of forces can be clearly grasped — and also the cynicism of government in cursorily discarding legislation on secondary action and the closed shop, legislation that they had spent acres of air and print justifying. I have also looked at proposals for legislation as, in the 1980s, they have been an intrinsic part of the process of industrial politics. And I have called in witness evidence from all the major disputes involving the legislation.

Whilst I have tried to put the Conservative case clearly, my own position is one of strong opposition to the legislation. I hope the following pages demonstrate that, to the extent it is effective, it is a force for authoritarianism, and for oppression in industry. Its scope is now quite breathtaking and requires some absorbing — the 1990 Act takes us clearly *beyond* Taff Vale. Small-minded, mean, vindictive, the new framework is all of this, particularly in what might be thought of as its minor aspects. The provision in the 1989 Act for deposits of up to £150 to be put up before applicants can bring a case before an industrial tribunal, and which can be confiscated as costs should they have the misfortune to draw a losing number in the legal lottery, typify a petty callousness which permeates the legislation. We may recall almost from another age that these tribunals were intended to be informal, accessible and cheap, whilst reflecting that in the mid-eighties the average basic wage of tribunal applicants was £113 a week.

Despite its protestations that it speaks in the name of the individual, the legislation formally weakens the rights of the individual — we need look no further than the shredding of employment protection. By undermining collectivism it undermines the practice of positive, effective individualism for the majority of workers who are unable, if acting in isolation, to realise their needs against the superior power of capital. By seeking to decisively weaken trade union power rather than to socialise it, the legislation seeks to weaken what is, in the final analysis and despite all its infirmities, a force for social health. It thus strengthens the state against civil society.

Speaking in the name of democracy, the employment laws, inasmuch as they are successful, undermine democracy, self activity and self realisation. The detailed, partisan and progressively more intrusive state regulation of the unions' internal government represents an erosion of social democracy — a curtailment of active citizenship. The legitimacy of democracy itself is sullied by the prohibition of majority voting in favour of entrenched 80% of the ballot requirements — which are themselves abolished when the results they produce are judged politically undesirable. And by legal protections for those who refuse to comply with the results of state proscribed ballots, whilst, in contrast, those who are deprived of their livelihood for abiding by the results and taking industrial action are denied the protection of the law.

If the unions are potentially undermined as an industrial welfare state and de-legitimised as social actors, one of the great failings in their response has been their inability to assert compellingly that this has been an offensive not just against one powerful interest in society but against society's interest in social freedom as a whole. Somehow the unions still often get left out of the general outrage expressed by decent people over the wounds inflicted by the Conservatives on our social institutions. Yet, to take one example, if the civil liberties implications of the *Public Order Act* need little underlining, the impact of legislation which constrains freedom of speech and movement by prohibiting peaceful picketing outside one's own workplace and solidarity action also requires addressing, not only by trade union activists but by all citizens.

None the less, whilst opposition should be encouraged and whilst workers may be successful in individual confrontations in favourable circumstances, the disablement and dismantling of this legislation will require a change of government. And here we enter upon a further controversy. The Labour Party leadership, conditioned by electoralism, wish to retain aspects of the Conservative legislation they opposed in the past. There is, from an electoral perspective, some sense in this; the voters have been conditioned by change wrought by the Conservatives, by a decade of Labour adaptation to Thatcherism, and by defeats for the left politically and in the unions. The history of the last decade and its impact on peoples' consciousness cannot be quickly and simply washed away by a different manifesto and a brief campaign. Labour is also aware that, if it wins, it will need a wages policy to plug the holes in its economic strategy. And that, whilst the TUC is if anything overwilling, there will be resistance to this — and to other policies — from the ranks. This is the second reason for wanting to retain some of the legislation.

Against this, it can be argued that such a stance could well provoke another conflict between a Labour government and the unions on the lines of 1978-1979. Elections, it can be asserted, are lost and won on economic matters, not on what the electorate will perceive as obscure arguments about secondary action. What is on offer generally from Labour is scarcely a recipe for trade union self denial and the sacrifice of important rights. If the unions accept what is on offer *now*, then despite the weaknesses of their position in comparison with 1979, they will end up rooked: they will get restrictive legislation *and* wage restraint. And that in the context of the serious limitations of Labour's programme in terms of economic strategy and egalitarianism, let alone social transformation, many on the left will see a need to reassert more radical purposes. We are far from seeing a major reversal in the fortunes of the left. Crucial problems remain which it would be perilous to ignore. But it is arguable that the left in the unions — and at leadership level — is still strong enough to reverse the present retreat on legislation which has given an almost blank cheque to Labour's leadership.

All in all, the unions will have to bargain and they should bargain hard. It seems to me that they should argue for a Charter of Positive Rights, discarding the piecemeal immunities approach of the past. A key lesson history teaches, which is reaffirmed by the experience detailed in this book, is that attempts by a defensive minded movement to retreat into its own protected social space, utilising techniques such as the immunities are, over time, doomed to failure. The Labour Movement must, in contrast, go forward to conquer the state and develop and universalise its best values. Of course, such an approach involves defining what unions and trade unionists cannot do as well as what they can do. But it enables the mystification of legal approaches to be decentred, and foregrounds explicit argument on the social and economic role and rights of the trade unions. Within such a framework the unions should bargain, amongst other things, for fully articulated rights to secondary action, peaceful picketing, freedom to finance political activities, and legal protection for the closed shop after a majority vote. They may well have to take on board the statutory enumeration of democratic criteria for their activities, but within a new framework this could well be acceptable.

Such a new positive framework could well be related to wider constitutional reform, but that is another story. In itself it raises the question of who would interpret the new rights. New Labour Court or no New Labour Court, Labour will not be immune from the intervention by the 'ordinary' judges through the appeal system. The urgent need for reform of the judiciary should require little justification in the light of the history of judgements not only on employment law but on social issues generally; the class composition of the judiciary; and its unrepresentative nature in terms of gender and ethnicity — in 1987, *Labour Research* found that of the top 465 judges, 17 were women and one was black. In the courts the Conservatives have always been in power. The reform of the legal profession tentatively set in train by the Conservatives should be boldly developed by a Labour government. All those put forward for appointment in the Higher Courts should be subject to detailed scrutiny and ratification by a Commons Committee. A system of rigorous training should be introduced. In selection, positive discrimination for under-represented groups should apply. Magistrates should be elected as part of the local government process. Statutes should include statements of social policy and explanatory rubric to guide the courts.

These are just some of the ingredients which could, if sifted and developed, constitute the bones of a policy for reform. What have the unions and their supporters got to lose? Only the tattered system of immunities, the shabby inheritance of a labour aristocracy steeped in Victorian values, a masonic, reactionary, anti-union judiciary, and centuries of judgements consistently inimical to basic union purposes. A reform policy would formally recognise what has always been the reality: employment law is a political battlefield. This approach would at least get more of the progressive troops onto the battlefield.

Such a stance could *open* a path to *progress*. But there are clearly no *panaceas*, and to realise this kind of bargaining position will certainly be an uphill task. In struggling to defend themselves, trade unionists can learn some lessons from the tenacious defence of their own interest mounted by the bar and the judges against the Lord Chancellor's reform proposals. And they can learn even more and take great inspiration from the struggle put up by ordinary working women and men against the Conservatives' employment laws chronicled in the pages which follow. To those men and women who have fought injustice on the picket lines and in the law courts this book is dedicated.

John McIlroy
May 1991

Abbreviations

ACAS	Advisory Conciliation and Arbitration Services
ACPO	Association of Chief Police Officers
ACTT	Association of Cinematograph, Television and Allied Technicians
AEU (formerly AUEW)	Amalgamated Engineering Union
APAC	Association of Patternmakers and Allied Craftsmen
APEX	Association of Professional, Executive, Clerical Staff (now part of GMB/APEX Partnership)
ASLEF	Associated Society of Locomotive Engineers and Firemen
ASTMS	Association of Scientific, Technical and Managerial Staff (now part of MSF)
BR	British Rail
CA	Court of Appeal
CAC	Central Arbitration Committee
CBI	Confederation of British Industry
COHSE	Confederation of Health Service Employees
CPSA	Civil and Public Services Association
DHA	District Health Authority
EA	Employment Act
EC	European Community
EEF	Engineering Employers' Federation
EETPU	Electrical, Electronic, Telecommunications and Plumbing Union
EP(C)A	Employment Protection (Consolidated) Act 1978
FOC	Father of the Chapel
GCHQ	General Communications Headquarters
GMB	General, Municipal, Boilermakers and Allied

(formerly GMBATU)	Trades Union (now part of GMB/APEX, Partnership)
HL	House of Lords
IEA	Institute of Economic Affairs
ILO	International Labour Organisation
IPCS	Institution of Professional Civil Servants (now Institute of Professional Managers and Specialists)
IPM	Institute of Personnel Management
IRC	Independent Review Committee (TUC)
IRLR	Industrial Relations Law Reports
ITWF	International Transport Workers' Federation
MB	Metropolitan Borough
MSC	Manpower Services Commission
NALGO	National and Local Government Officers' Association
NAS/UWT	National Association of Schoolmasters/Union of Women Teachers
NCB	National Coal Board (now British Coal)
NGA	National Graphical Association (now part of Graphical, Paper and Media Union)
NSMM	National Society of Metal Mechanics
NSSM	National Society of Sheet Metal Workers
NUJ	National Union of Journalists
NUM	National Union of Miners
NUPE	National Union of Public Employees
NUR	National Union of Railwayworkers (now part of Rail, Maritime and Transport Union)
NUS	National Union of Seafarers (now part of Rail, Maritime and Transport Union)
NUT	National Union of Teachers
OECD	Organisation for Economic Co-operation and Development
P&O	Peninsular and Oriental
PHA	Pre-Hearing Assessment
POEU	Post Office Engineering Union (now National Communications Union)
SDP	Social Democratic Party

SOGAT	Society of Graphical and Allied Trades (now part of Graphical, Paper and Media Union)
TASS	Technical, Administrative and Supervisory Section (now part of MSF)
TC	Training Commission
TEC	Training and Enterprise Council
TSSA	Transport Salaried Staffs' Association
TGWU	Transport & General Workers' Union
TUC	Trades Union Congress
TULRA	Trade Union and Labour Relations Act (1974) (amended 1976)
UCATT	Union of Construction, Allied Trades and Technicians
UKAPE	United Kingdom Association of Professional Engineers
UMA	Union Membership Agreement

TABLE 1

The Law and The Unions before 1979

1721	*Journeymen Tailors of Cambridge Case*	Judges declared trade unionism a criminal conspiracy.
1797	Unlawful Oaths Act —	These acts made all collective agreements
1799	Combination Act —	enhancing wages or conditions criminal and
1800	Combination Act —	trade unionism illegal.
1813	Statute of Artificers (Repeal) Act	Abolished some of the powers of magistrates to fix wages in favour of freedom of contract, a process completed in 1824.
1823	Master and Servant Act	Updated earlier legislation making breach of contract a criminal offence for *the employee*.
1824	Combination of Workmen Act —	Repealed Combination Acts and granted unions limited legality. But they were still
1825	Combination Laws Repeal (Amendment) Act —	liable to criminal offences when engaging in strikes and picketing.
1859	Molestation of Workmen Act	Limited the criminal liabilities of the unions.
1867	*Hornby v Close*	Judges declared union rules to be unenforceable.
1871	Criminal Law Amendment Act —	Gave unions greater protection against the
1871	Trade Union Act —	criminal law and restraint of trade — granted them a limited civil status.
1872	*R v Bunn*	Restricted policy of acceptance of unions by declaring strikes common law conspiracies and still criminal offences.
1875	Conspiracy and Protection of Property Act	Reversed *Bunn*'s case and protected strikes against criminal conspiracy if 'in contemplation or furtherance of a trade dispute'.
1875	Repeal of Master and Servant Legislation	
1901	*Quinn v Leathem*	The judges developed *civil law* liability for conspiracy, opening unions to attacks, the 1875 Act had sought to minimise by excluding the

		criminal law.
1901	*Taff Vale*	Landmark decision which allowed the new civil law remedies to be pursued against unions as legal persons.
1906	Trade Disputes Act	Reversed *Taff Vale* and protected unions from civil law liabilities such as conspiracy and inducing breach of contract when acting 'in contemplation or furtherance of a trade dispute'.
1910	*Osborne* Judgement	House of Lords limited trade unions political activities on birth of Labour Party.
1913	Trade Union Act	Reversed *Osborne* decision and introduced system of balloting for Political Funds and right to 'opt-out'.
1924	*Reynolds v Shipping Federation*	The courts went some way to accepting trade unionism as a legitimate social activity and recognising boycotting and the closed shop.
1927	Trade Disputes and Trade Unions Act	In aftermath of General Strike it limited picketing and secondary action, stopped civil service unions affiliating to the TUC and changed 'opting-out' of the political levy to 'opting-in'.
1942	*Crofter Case*	Further acceptance by judges of trade union purposes.
1946	Trade Disputes and Trade Unions Act	Repealed the Act of 1927.
1964	*Rookes v Barnard* Case	House of Lords judgement which opened trade unionists to tort of intimidation.
1965	Trade Disputes Act	Protected trade unionists from *Rookes and Barnard*.
1965	Prices and Incomes Act	Criminal enforcement of income policy.
1969	*In Place of Strife*	Labour Government unsuccesfully seeks to legislate to control industrial action.
1970	Equal Pay Act	Attempted to end pay discrimination against women.
1971	Industrial Relations Act	Heath's Conservative Government legislates to restrict strikes and picketing — also provisions on ballots, union recognition, membership and individual rights.
1972	Counter Inflation Act	Criminal offence to breach incomes policy.
1974	Trade Union and Labour Relations Act	Repeals Industrial Relations Act. Legislates in firmer form the immunities in the 1906 Act.
1975	Employment Protection Act	Extends the floor of rights for individual workers and also deals with union recognition and rights for officials.
1975	Sex Discrimination Act	Legislated against discrimination at work.
1976	Trade Union and Labour Relations (Amendment) Act	Strengthens the position on dismissal and union membership.
1976	Race Relations Act	Legislated against discrimination at work.
1978	Employment Protection (Consolidation) Act	Consolidating much of the legislation of 1974-79 Labour Governments.
1979	Mrs Thatcher's Legal Revolution	

Figure 1: The UK Legal System

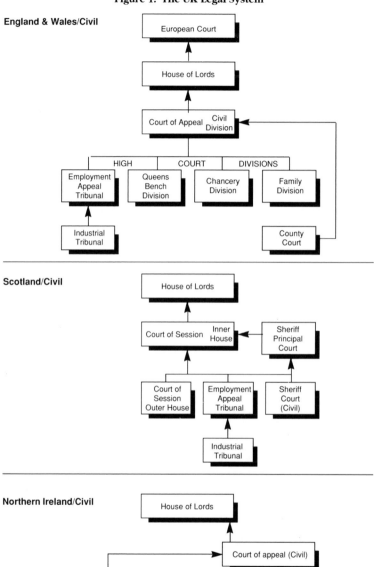

CHAPTER 1

Before the Flood

Laws grind the poor and rich men rule the law — *Oliver Goldsmith*

Since 1979 Britain's trade unions have been hit by wave after wave of trade union legislation. Not a year has passed without new proposals being aired, new bills being introduced into Parliament, new Acts receiving the Royal Assent. The trade union problem has scarcely been declared to have been solved by Conservative politicians before a new Green Paper proposing further measures to deal with it is up and running. After the great Acts of 1980, 1982 and 1984 had apparently, at least in Conservative eyes, dealt with the important abuses once and for all we have had further important statutes in 1988, 1989 and 1990 dealing with new problems — as well as a host of ancillary measures and still more promised. Britain has moved from a system of industrial relations whose legal framework was minimal to one where law progressively reaches into every nook and cranny of relations between employers and trade unions. To see why this has happened we need to look backwards at the history of industrial relations in this country.

BEFORE THATCHER

In the 1950s a prominent legal analyst wrote of UK industrial relations:

> There is perhaps no major country in the world in which the law has played a less significant role in the shaping of these relations than in Great Britain and in which today the law and the legal profession have less to do with labour relations ... British industrial relations have, in the main, developed by way of industrial autonomy. This notion of autonomy is fundamental ... it means that employers and employees have formulated their own codes of conduct and devised their own machinery for enforcing them.[1]

In Britain during the 1950s there were no laws on trade union recognition, or time off for shop stewards, or unfair dismissal, or redundancy. The legislation on strikes and picketing was drafted with the objective of *keeping the law out of industrial relations* and giving trade unionists a great degree of freedom to withdraw their labour. Employers and unions, it was held, should regulate industrial affairs through collective bargaining within only a minimal legal framework. The social security system, legislation on health, safety and welfare, Acts of Parliament dealing with wages councils and extension to unorganised employees of terms and conditions set by collective bargaining constituted a safety net, whilst collective bargaining was lubricated by measures such as the *Conciliation Act 1896* and the *Industrial Courts Act 1919*. Otherwise industrial autonomy held sway. Terms and conditions of employment and the procedure for their agreement were jointly regulated by employers and trade unions not by Parliament and the courts.

This system which was termed *voluntarism* or *collective laissez-faire* was seen as representing the maturity and sophistication of British industrial relations and as a guarantor of industrial peace. It was the product of more than a century of development in the regulation of industrial relations. The emerging British capitalists had sought to break down the earlier system of paternal state regulation of the primitive pre-capitalist pattern of terms and conditions of employment. They argued in favour of *laissez-faire*, *freedom of contract* and *state abstention*. The unrestrained pursuit by individuals of their economic interests would provide the most effective mechanism for the generation and allocation of productive resources and social wealth. Instead of wages being fixed by the local state, employers and workers should be left free to determine and fully develop their own economic relationships by voluntarily coming to legally binding agreements. The belief in individualism left no room for collectivism and trade unionism. As Baron Bramwell put it in an 1860s case on picketing:

> Everybody knows that the total aggregate happiness of mankind is increased by every man being left to the unbiased, unfettered determination of his own will and judgement as to how he will employ his industry and other means of getting on in the world ...[2]

Freedom of contract, the legal dimension of *laissez-faire*, was adjudicated by the courts. In the interests of individual freedom the developing judge-made law outlawed trade unions as "in restraint of trade" and as "criminal conspiracies". Strikes and picketing constituted "intimidation" and "inducement to breach of contract".

Despite their adherence to state abstention, the ruling class had no hesitation in turning, in times of particular unrest, to legislation to facilitate the efforts of the judges through the Common Law to proscribe trade unionism. The *Combination Acts* of 1799 and 1800 criminalised trade unionism whilst the *Master and Servant Acts* skewed the 'negotiation' of the contract of employment, already in essence, because of the imbalance of bargaining power between employer and employee, "a command under the guise of an agreement",[3] still further in favour of the employer.

The situation where judges could comment, "the jurisdiction of this court is to protect property"[4] and where the law buttressed the employers' power and consigned trade unionism to an underground, criminal existence was only gradually modified. This occurred through working class pressure, not only for legalisation of trade union organisation and activities, but for the extension of the franchise in 1867 and 1884. But the reaction of the rulers to this pressure was also important. The ruling class already possessed a tradition of incorporating new social forces. The legalisation of trade unionism was facilitated by the fact that for most of the 19th century the movement only embraced a small and often responsible stratum of respectable craft workers. They were a *small stratum* attached to the Liberal Party rather than a class wide movement with its own political party. The sectional union leaders were prepared to accept a gradual and piecemeal improvement and this was underpinned by Britain's economic success and its domination of world markets.

The legal acceptance of trade unionism, crucially in 1871, 1875 and 1906, did not take the form of a bill of rights, or a developed legal code, or a transformation of the judiciary. The armistice the cautious conservative union leaders sought involved no direct assault on the legal framework. Instead the trade unions sought *exemption* from the Common Law — not its replacement by a system of *positive rights* to organise, bargain and strike. If the social, political and economic role of trade unions is fully accepted then it can be seen that the consequent system of *immunities* by which unions were granted protection from Common Law doctrines of restraint of trade, conspiracy and inducement to breach of contract were not 'privileges' which 'placed trade unions above the law'. The system of immunities simply constituted the *method* by which unions were given basic rights to exist, organise and bargain. The results no more 'placed trade unions above the general law' than the removal of wage fixing by magistrates in favour of freedom of contract in the period of the industrial revolution placed capitalists 'above the general law'.

When in 1980 Lord Diplock talked of unions being given "a power to inflict by means which are contrary to the general law untold harm to industrial enterprises"[5] he was universalising for his own purposes an historically specific and class biased conception of "the general law". If the general law he spoke of had been left, unimpeded by legislative intervention, to regulate trade union activities then all industrial action, to take one example, would have been unlawful. For under the Common Law, as Lord Justice Lindley said as late as the 1890s, "you cannot make a strike effective without doing more than is lawful"[6].

Nonetheless, the broad form the legalisation of trade unions took facilitated this kind of attack on their 'privileges'. And *the specific form* the immunities took, exempting unions from legal liabilities only when certain requirements laid down in detailed legal formulae were met (see p.58) as well as the fact that the selection, training and class composition of the judiciary went unreformed, opened trade union immunities to periodic piercing by a judiciary whose class bias endured. In important cases, such as the *Crofter* case of 1942, the judges came to grudgingly accept the rationale for trade union activities and the protections crystallised in the immunities. But the immunities armistice had simply moth-balled areas of the Common Law. It had not wiped out the Common Law liabilities. It had not transformed the conservative ideology of the judges who often looked at the legislation as an artificial graft onto the real law. And their responses shifted with the disintegration of industrial peace and the sharpening of industrial struggle. In the 1960s in cases such as *Rookes v Barnard* the courts sought to limit the immunities and by the time of the 'Winter of Discontent' they were openly advocating their curtailment on the grounds that their existence was "intrinsically repugnant to anyone who has spent his life in the practice of law or the administration of justice".[7]

The incursions of judicial law-making, therefore, *always* constituted one important limitation on the British system of voluntarism. So too did the introduction by the state in war-time of quite far-reaching legislation. And so too did the introduction particularly from the 1960s of legal control over wages as part of prices and incomes policy. Moreover, it is questionable whether the maintenance of voluntarism in the 1920s and 1930s was as much the consequence of the maturity and sophistication of British industrial relations as the waning of trade union power in the face of unemployment and state confrontation. If you look at the table on p.xxi you will see that Mrs Thatcher's attempt to restrict union activities by law is nothing new. The struggle against legal intervention is not something unique to the 1980s: it has marked the entire history of trade unionism.

However, it is possible to regard voluntarism, in the sense of the abstention of law from industrial relations, taken together with Keynesian methods of economic management, a committment to the maintenance of full employment and support for the welfare state, as part of the post-war settlement which moulded British politics until the 1980s.

The Disintegration of Voluntarism

The disintegration of voluntarism which has seen the UK under Mrs Thatcher move from one of the most loosely to one of the most tightly legally regulated systems of industrial relations in advanced democracies has its roots in changes within the economy, changes within the trade unions and the failure of alternative methods of solving the problems of British capitalism. In comparison with Germany and the USA, the UK economy had been in decline since the early years of the century, suffering from antiquated plant and technology, low investment, export of capital, inefficient management, high arms spending and the vulnerability of the pound. Its recovery in the post-war period was based upon the world boom which under US leadership and underpinned by Marshall Aid and the Bretton Woods Agreement, tying all currencies to the dollar, was fuelled by war-time economic revitalisation; technological innovation; cheap labour available on a large scale; open markets; and the decisive weakening of trade unions in the USA, Japan and Germany. Keynesian methods of intervention with the state managing effective demand — expanding it in a slump, dampening it in an upturn — became the new and successful conventional wisdom. In the UK trade union leadership still related to the limited ambitions engendered by the inter-war years, and the growth of membership was sluggish: there was no great advance in union density, which continued at around 42% of the labour force from the late forties to the mid-sixties.

However, the guarantee of full employment gradually gave trade unionists greater confidence and its reality granted them greater power. Pressures to maintain full employment and expand the welfare state produced increases in taxation and public borrowing. Increased taxation, in turn, produced pressures for increased wages, increased prices and decreased competitive edge. As Japan and Germany recovered, their revitalised economies outstripped the ailing UK model. Between 1950 and 1972 Germany's annual growth rate was 6% and Japan's almost 10% whilst the UK limped along at 3%. In the early 1950s the UK's share of world markets was around 20%. But by the end of the 1960s it had fallen to 10%, whilst Germany had increased its share from 13% to 21% and Japan from 5% to 14%. As a prominent economic historian commented: "There is no record of any other power falling behind at such a startling speed".[8]

Awareness of decline led to attempts from the mid-1960s to introduce prices and incomes policies. Free collective bargaining was the heart of voluntarism. Wages were the heart of free collective bargaining. For voluntarism the writing was on the wall. The attempts of the 1964 and 1966 Wilson Governments to regulate prices and incomes in order to limit the increase in wages and labour costs and relate increases more directly to productivity faltered on the decentralised nature of UK trade unionism and collective bargaining. The 1960s saw the state intervene to a greater degree in industry to compensate for the problems stimulated by its original intervention to guarantee full employment and welfare rights. The war had seen a revival of shop steward organisation and the 1950s and 1960s its qualitative extension into new areas and new industries and the growth of workplace and sectional bargaining. The power that full employment gave shop stewards who bargained over pay and conditions, independent of national union leaderships and untrammelled by legal controls, was related to the fact that large monopolies were to a degree able to insulate pricing, investment and employment policies from central government strategies.

The failure of state intervention centred on the incomes policies of the 1960s led to a greater emphasis on reforming the industrial relations and trade union structures which facilitated their evasion. These structures and their impact on incomes policies were seen as inhibiting a lowering of unit labour costs — the relation of earnings to productivity — which were higher in the UK than in competing countries. The *Donovan Report* in 1968 was the last shot in the locker of real voluntarism. The Report argued that the wage drift, fuelled by the power to take unofficial industrial action, which disrupted incomes policies agreed or accepted by the national union leaders and the restrictive practices which inhibited productivity growth could be limited if collective bargaining and union structures were reformed to integrate shop stewards into new procedures at the workplace and a further constitutional role within the union. Employees should be given enhanced legal rights to increase security and motivation but restrictive legislation should be avoided unless management and unions demonstrated they could not put their own house in order.

This strategy for restoring management and union control over shop stewards and labour costs was rejected by the Wilson Government in favour of legislation to control strikes. The 1969 proposals, *In Place of Strife*, were defeated by a coalition of the TUC and Labour MPs aided and abetted by unofficially organised strikes against the measures; Wilson's economic and industrial failure contributed to his defeat at the polls in 1970.

His successor Ted Heath was determined to make at least a partial breach in the post-war settlement. He advocated a greater role for the market and went for a restrictive legal policy to restrain and restructure trade union power to deal with the problems of stagflation, high unit labour costs, low growth and constantly rising prices. The defeat of his *Industrial Relations Act* by the unions and his subsequent turn to incomes policy left the unions apparently victorious — but the UK's economic decline deeper than ever. By the mid-1970s economic difficulties were accelerating and awareness of the position had intensified. The UK's growth rate was 45% of the OECD average by 1975, compared with 70% in 1964. In that year our share of world trade in manufactured goods was 14%. Yet by 1975 it had crashed to 8.5%. State intervention in the processes of wage determination had stimulated an increase in union density which accelerated past the 50% in the decade from 1968: produced a strike wave unknown since the early 1920s; revived the political strike; led to the further extension of shop steward organisation; enhanced its legitimacy through its victories over incomes policy; and stoked still further the fires of inflation. Politicians of all parties were agreed that the trade unions must be reformed if relative economic decline was not to become absolute and that free collective bargaining was incompatible with full employment and price stability.

The Social Contract of the 1974-79 Wilson and Callaghan Governments represented, in all its aspirations, a qualitative deepening of the 'progressive management-incorporationist' approach of the *Donovan Report*. In return for the maintenance of full employment, welfare state expenditure, greater state intervention and action on prices, the trade union leaders would control incomes growth. The policy of legal abstention was put in question by the provisions of the *Trade Union and Labour Relations Acts*, the *Employment Protection Act* and the *Health and Safety At Work Act* which sought to both placate the unions and stimulate employers and unions to introduce many of the procedural and institutional reforms recommended by the *Donovan Report* — rather than relying on the voluntarist tradition of prodding and exhortation. By 1978 there was more Labour legislation in Britain than ever before, dealing not only with 'individual' issues, such as unfair dismissal and redundancy, but also with union recognition, the closed shop and shop steward facilities. Labour had carried out a quiet revolution in legal abstention and this, combined with incomes policy, heralded the wake of voluntarism.

It produced however a legal settlement which infuriated the judiciary who themselves stated that it "tended to stick in judicial gorges".[9] And it stimulated a judicial offensive of a kind not seen since before the First World War. The ambit of the new individual floor of rights was severely restricted by the courts and the immunities savaged by the Court of Appeal. In reversing some of these judgements on the grounds that the Court of Appeal had displayed over zealous legal ingenuity and misinterpreted the legislation the House of Lords declared: "Surely the time has come for it to be altered".[10]

All this however did little to solve the 'union problem'. Under the 1974-79 Labour Governments unemployment increased from half a million to 1.3 million, there were cuts in the welfare state and real living standards fell between 1974 and 1977. By 1978 the Social Contract had failed to overcome the UK's economic ailments and had become largely a policy of wage restraint aimed at lowering unit labour costs. The defeat of this policy in the 1978-79 'Winter of Discontent' represented the exhaustion of the Social Contract approach.

By 1979 there was a crisis of purpose and policy in the Labour Movement, intimately related to the political impasse and the serious position of the UK economy. The right wing and centrist leadership had placed its eggs in the incorporationist basket. Temporarily at least they had little to say, apart from blaming the unions for their difficulties. Their policies had failed. But the left too had to confront major problems. If the right wing had overestimated the power and efficacy of the bureaucratic state and the trade union leadership, the left had overestimated the potential for socialism in the ranks of the Labour Movement. The left had inscribed free collective bargaining on their banner, not only because it guaranteed a protected area of self-activity for workers, but because out of the struggles of collective bargaining and industrial action would come a growth of class consciousness and political radicalisation. This they felt would lead to the election of left Labour Governments — and push them even further left.

Yet the strike waves of 1968-74 and 1978-79 belied this argument. The rank and file, as represented by the shop stewards, had attained their greatest sense of a movement in the stoppages over *In Place of Strife*, the Industrial Relations Bill and the imprisonment of the dockers in Pentonville in 1972. But this militancy had provided in 1974 the smallest percentage vote Labour had received since the war. Labour's share of the vote in 1979, 36.9%, compared with 37.1% in February 1974, was even worse. Despite all the talk of the radicalising impact of strikes and state intervention politicising wage struggles, the major radicalisation and politicisation appeared to have been *in a rightwards direction*. Mrs Thatcher's victory was assured in 1979 by the desertion from Labour of key groups of skilled workers, the firmest advocates of free collective bargaining. Labour's policies acted to disillusion workers but they did not in response move left. If we look beyond Labour, the growth of the Far Left groups from 1968 was more than made up for by the collapse of Communist Party membership and by 1979 these groups lacked the working class composition and industrial influence the Communist Party had possessed in the 1940s and 1950s.

Moreover whilst trade union membership and density had soared, this had been, fundamentally, a response to changes in the wages-prices relationship and sometimes the product of the growth of closed shop agreements. The growth in trade union membership was often the product of narrowly calculative decisions or bureaucratic imposition rather than an understanding of working class solidarity and this problem was strengthened by the nature of the growth — largely in the white collar sector. This lack of attachment to union ideology and identification with union policy could be seen by the high percentages of members critical of trade unions, stating in opinion polls that 'unions were too powerful' and 'a bad thing' even as membership and militancy over wages and conditions increased.

By 1979, then, successive attempts to solve the UK's economic problems had failed and in doing so had made the problems worse. The use of legislation to control trade unionism was by now nothing new. Restrictive legislation had been attempted by Labour in 1969 and by the Conservatives in 1972 — as well as incorporationist legislation between 1974-78. The failure of these initiatives and the disarray in the Labour Movement provided a new opening for the hard right. A new and very different Conservative Government believed that it was not the policy of legal restriction of Wilson and Heath that was at fault — it was the way it had been integrated with wider policies of state intervention to maintain full employment, welfarism and subsidies to industry that had strengthened its trade union opponents and caused its failure. Moreover that policy had not been backed up by the full force of the state when the chips were down, as in 1972 with the Pentonville Dockers.

To repeat: there was nothing particularly novel about the broad approach of Mrs Thatcher's policy of legal restriction of unions. But compared, for example, with its 1970-74 predecessor the new government *strategically integrated* economic policy and legal restriction of the unions so that the unions' strength would be sapped, not increased, by economic policy at the very moment they were faced with a legal offensive. The new government's approach could be summed up as 'free market — strong state'. Crucially the 'new Conservatives' were prepared to renege on the post-war consensus committment to full employment to undermine union power and then use the full coercive power of the state to fatally weaken the unions once and for all.

Thatcherite Economics and Employment Law

The incoming Conservative Government in 1979 believed that the market was the most perfect way of allocating goods and determining prices and wages. The role of the state should be extremely limited, leaving largely to employers and workers the determination of economic decisions. The state's main economic role was to manage the money supply — the notes and coins in circulation as well as money in short term deposits, in transit, in deposit accounts and public sector deposits — what is called M3. For monetarists like Mrs Thatcher, Sir Keith Joseph and Norman Tebbit, governments in the 1960s and 1970s had made a major contribution to Britain's economic decline by policies of increased government spending and state intervention financed by printing money. This meant that there was too much money in circulation chasing too few goods and services. This speed up of M3 led to prices going up, wages going up and Britain's products becoming uncompetitive on the world market.

Increased state intervention had led to demands for still further state intervention and increased taxation to pay for it. This provoked, in turn, further wage demands by workers to compensate and further price increases to compensate for slimmer profit margins. This is where trade unions and Employment Law came into the picture as far as the Conservatives were concerned. Because of the monopoly power unions possessed they were able to press the workers' demands for more money and the employers found it easier to pay than to resist. Unions had not gained this monopoly power because of any law of nature but because of state intervention which had given them immunities. The unions had been able to pressurise and bribe governments so that strikes and picketing, which the courts had decided were unlawful, were rendered lawful through legislation. Thus armed the unions had also been able to force the state to provide their members with a still wider range of legal rights, which further artificially boosted the price of labour.

In order to restore economic health there was a need, so the monetarists insisted, for the new Conservative Government to *control the growth of the money supply* through higher interest rates. This makes credit more difficult to obtain and more expensive. Companies have to cut-back and, as fewer goods can be bought on credit, sales fall, bankruptcies occur, factories are closed and unemployment increases. The less competitive companies are in danger of going bust and have little alternative but to attack wages, and reorganise work practices to stimulate efficiency. This, in turn, impels them to resist unions, a process aided by the growth of unemployment which brings a new realism to workers' aspirations.

As unemployment grows and employers toughen up so wages and, in consequence, prices will fall. As inflation drops credit will become cheaper. The economy, monetarists believe, will now be able to grow and vigorous, high productivity firms, freed from the 'nanny state' and the blackmail of trade unions will be able to compete more effectively with Japan, Germany and the USA. Wages will now increase but they will reflect real increases in productivity and profit. Controlling the money supply also necessitates slashing state spending, cutting state employment, removing state subsidies to private industry and restoring state enterprise to the private sector. This will further contribute to the end of feather-bedding, and the removal of artificial protections against the rigours of the reviving market. But the state must directly facilitate this process of economic regeneration through market regeneration, spearheaded by control of the money supply and by a key supplementary policy of reducing trade union power.

Once the state had intervened to set the new rules then it should leave the regulation of industrial relations to employers, individuals and residual trade unions. The state's influence on industrial relations would then be 'weak'. Where it would be 'strong' would be where the rules of the game were not observed. The police and, if required, the army would intervene resolutely to deal with the disorders of mass picketing. The courts would intervene firmly to confiscate the assets of unions which defied the rule of law.

LEGISLATION TO REDUCE UNION POWER

For the Conservatives there was a close fit between the Common Law on employment, the market and economic prosperity. There was a need therefore to return to Victorian values and restore the market against trade unionism by cutting back on the protections the state had granted the unions and giving greater play to the Common Law.

Taken together with other policies, Mrs Thatcher believed, this legislative policy would reduce trade union power and diminish the harm it inflicted on the economy. Simultaneously there was a need to reduce the floor of rights that the state had given employees which interfered with employers' freedom to hire and fire and deploy labour as required. This burden on employers had been worsened by the policies of the 1974-79 Labour Government. But it stemmed initially not from Callaghan and Wilson but from Gladstone and Disraeli whose governments introducing legislation in 1871 and 1875, had started the rot. How could the market work, Mrs Thatcher asked, if an employer's ability to sack employees when business fell away was restrained by laws on industrial action, redundancy and unfair dismissal? How could employers operate in relation to the laws of supply and demand when Parliament introduced a procedure to force the recognition of trade unions — when in 1978 the government trembled on the brink of legislating the proposals in the *Bullock Report* which would have placed trade unionists in the very cockpit of decision-making by giving them seats on the board? How could employers appeal over the heads of left-wing union leaders to ordinary decent workers when those workers could, through the closed shop, lose their jobs? And how could the market operate to reduce wages to real productivity levels when inflated unemployment benefits operated to inhibit dismissed workers from competing with those already in employment by offering to work for reduced wage rates?

The Conservative attack on trade unions was based not only on *economics* but also on *politics*. It was impossible to run a capitalist economy effectively when one of the two great parties was in thrall to organisations whose leaders saw it as in their interest to thwart increased productivity and profitability and who were insulated from control by their more 'reasonable' members. Because, uniquely amongst western social democratic parties, the Labour Party was organisationally dominated by the votes of trade unions, any Labour Government would be the servant of the trade union leaders. Policies essential to the national interest would not be pressed. Policies in the interests of trade union leaders would be. During the 1970s internal union democracy and the relationship of the unions to the Labour Party took their place on the right's agenda of reform.

Now on the brink of the 1980s the real enemy of society for the new Conservatives was trade unionism: "the real exploiters in our present society are not egotistic capitalists or entrepreneurs and in fact not separate individuals but organisations which derive their power from the moral support of collective action and group loyalty".[11] Trade unionism — or legally inflated undemocratic trade unionism — was a particular barrier to specific initiatives the Conservatives wished to encourage to reinvigorate enterpreneurialism and enterprise culture. As Lord Keith remarked: "For someone trying to create a small business the increasing mass of new legislation especially the Employment Protection Act adds further strain".[12]

An important intellectual influence on the government, F.A. Hayek, went further stating:

> These legalised powers of the unions have become the biggest obstacle to raising the living standards of the working class as a whole. They are the chief cause of the unnecessarily big differences between the best-and worst-paid workers. They are the prime source of unemployment. They are the main reason for the decline of the British economy in general.[13]

He concluded that "There can be no salvation for Britain unless the special privileges granted to the trade unions three-quarters of a century ago are revoked".[14] Some of those around the think-tanks of the right, such as the Institute of Economic Affairs, went further still and called for "... the enactment of the British Combination Acts of 1799 and 1800 ... adapted to the 1970s"[15] arguing that "modern unionism in its typical form is a challenge to the authority of the state and in particular an affront to the rule of law".[16]

The judges saw the unions as engines of social disorder as well as economic calamity. Law Lord Salmon of Sandwich expressed the flavour of the times in the courts and the moral panic among the judges about union activities. Speaking in the political House of Lords in the debate on the *1975 Trade Union and Labour Relations (Amendment) Bill,* on proto-legislation he would later have to 'interpret' from the bench — this in a country which supposedly possesses a division of powers between judiciary and legislature — he stated:

> We cannot shut our eyes to the fact that there are groups very small numerically but extremely cohesive and tenacious who have infiltrated the unions with the intention of seizing power if they can. Their avowed purpose is to wreck the Social Contract and the democratic system under which we live. Their ethos derives from foreign lands where individual liberty is dead and where the courts and trade unions are mere tools of the Executive, to do its will.[17]

There was also attention to the idea that militant union leaders forced moderate members to go along with their policies. Jim Prior asserted that low participation in union meetings and elections was reflected in unrepresentative leaders and the problem — despite Conservative members no Conservative sat on the executive of any of the 13 biggest unions — could only be cured by legislation enforcing ballots.[18] Prior's future successor as Employment Secretary saw the unions as illegitimately abusing and paralysing the political process:

> What would we say if the red-capped colonels of the Army used their military power for political ends? What if they insisted on conscription as part of their price for allowing a government to stay in office? Would it be 'Army-bashing' to criticise

that? Yet today the cloth-capped colonels of the TUC use their industrial power for political ends. They insist on the conscription of the closed shop as part of their price for allowing a government to stay in office.[19]

Tebbit's views were shared by top civil servants who claimed "In the last ten years three successive Prime Ministers have been prevented by the industrial and political power of the unions from pursuing policies they declared essential to the national interest".[20] The legal offensive on the unions was a *state* offensive. It involved politicians, civil servants and judges — and the mobilisation of public opinion. There was general agreement among key state personnel that something must be done. The ideological godfather of the emergent Thatcherism, Sir Keith Joseph, returned to the legal diagnosis and the legal prescription for Britain's trade union problem.

> Our unions have been uniquely privileged for several decades ... The predictable result has been the growing use of strikes and the strike threat. In a trade dispute most things seem permitted for the union side: breaking contracts, inducing others to break contracts, picketing of non-involved companies, secondary boycotts. A trade dispute can be between workers and workers, it can concern matters of discipline, membership facilities; it may even relate to matters overseas. As we would expect this militants' charter has bred militants and driven moderates underground. Indeed we are now seeing militants increasingly taking over control from union officials ... The national good can be secured only by changing the framework, the rules of the game and then ensuring that everyone plays fairly by them. That is what Margaret Thatcher has called for.[21]

Margaret Thatcher had been calling for a revolutionary transformation of the unions since 1974 the year which saw the birth of the new Conservatism. "It was only in April 1974 that I was converted to Conservatism", Sir Keith Joseph later wrote, "I had thought that I was a Conservative but I now see I was not really one at all".[22] Margaret Thatcher proved a willing pupil for Sir Keith and the group gathered around the Centre for Policy Studies. The daughter of a small businessman and the wife of a capitalist she was raised and developed in an anti-union atmosphere. Looking back at her earlier political life her most recent biographer states "Hatred of union power has been a consistent theme".[23] This approach was strengthened by the experience of Ted Heath's government 1970-74, the failure of its *Industrial Relations Act*, its U-turn to reflation and incomes policy and its eventual humiliation at the hands of the miners. In the face of Heath's final failures — the two lost 1974 elections — the Joseph-Thatcher new Conservatism burgeoned and in 1975 Margaret Thatcher defeated Heath to become leader of the Party. Thatcherism defined itself largely in terms of Heath's failure: "The U-turn took on the status of a demon and its perpetrator was still regarded many years later as the devil incarnate: the man who had surrendered his belief to short term expediency".[24] And the unions were seen as playing the crucial part in that failure. For the Thatcherites the 'union question' was not simply a matter of cold political calculation, it was a burning personal pre-occupation.

MONETARISM AND FREEDOM

Two final points need to be made. Firstly, the fact that the government came to power with its leadership armed with a monetarist analysis does not mean that the Thatcher Governments since 1979 have acted consistently and coherently on this analysis — or that they have encountered success when they have sought to do so. Between 1979 and the 1983 election M3 rose significantly faster than government targets allowed for. After that date M3 progressively played a smaller and smaller role in government policy-making. The Thatcher Government have attempted to pursue the objectives of the approach outlined above — but the emphasis has increasingly been on lowering labour costs through government exhortation combined with action in the public sector.

Secondly, the fact that we have located the government's programme of employment legislation in its economic thinking should not lead us to underestimate the role political philosophy played in its motivations. The Conservatives were serious when they stated that they wished to legislate on the closed shop, not simply because it represented a threat to the market by artificially restricting the supply of labour, but also because it represented a threat to the freedom of the individual and the right to choose. And they were genuine when they stated that they felt impelled to legislate on picketing, not simply because as a practice it boosted the monopoly power of the unions, but because it constituted an interference with the right to work. The point is that the Conservatives' philosophy was integrated with their economics. If individuals exercised their rights not to join trade unions or to cross picket lines this would play a small but useful part in eroding union power and strengthening the ability of the employer to operate on market principles.

But the progress of the legislation illuminated important contradictions between the Conservatives' rhetoric of freedom and the needs of market economics. For example, it soon became clear that Conservative thinking implied an end result of their own choosing to the exercise of individual freedom. Union members were not given rights to ballot on the closed shop or election of executive members because the government wanted to give them an open-ended freedom to choose but because they believed members would vote *against* a closed shop and *against* militant candidates. When ordinary members used their freedom to make choices other than those the government had prescribed for them further measures had to be taken to steer them back in the right direction! The tension between the government's *authoritarianism* and its *populism*, its stated desire to give power to the people, exercised an increasing influence on its legislative programme.

KEY THEMES IN 1980s EMPLOYMENT LAW

Cutting the Unions Down to Size

In Germany, Japan or the USA — the main economic competitors of the UK in the eyes of Mrs Thatcher — a smaller proportion of the labour force in the 1970s was unionised as compared with the UK. Union density was around 50% in Britain compared with under 30% in Germany and under 20% in the USA. This was part of the anti-entrepreneurial culture of collectivism that Mrs Thatcher wished to erode. Changes in employment legislation dealing with union recognition and the closed shop would enable members to leave trade unions. They would be denied political purchase and their leaders would no longer be consulted by the Cabinet or 'beer and sandwiched' by the Prime Minister. Legislation on strikes and picketing would mean that unions would find it harder to deliver. Members would in consequence find membership less attractive. Wider policies such as privatisation would also undermine union power by depriving them of the fertile feeding ground of a complacent monopoly employer. Management would be freer to operate according to the dictates of the market rather than the whims of shop stewards and union leaders. This would be particularly important given the changing pattern of industry. If the blitz on manufacturing industry of the early 1980s had the beneficial side-effect of decimating many of the strongholds of trade unionism, it was vital that the poisonous weed of the old trade unionism should not take root in the new hi-tech industries. A key purpose of legislation was the restriction of trade unionism in the industries of the year 2000.

Changing the Nature of the Beast

Union leaders faced with a loss of membership, decreasing

industrial power and waning political influence might be expected to reconsider their role in industry and society. Legislation would encourage this by giving new rights to ordinary moderate members to exercise greater control over policy and selection of leaders. Here the emphasis was on postal ballots. Again in countries such as Germany, Japan and the USA the unions were less identified with one particular political party. Millions of British trade unionists voted Conservative yet their organisations were affiliated to the Labour Party. A swing to the left in the unions could lead to a swing to the left in the Labour Party and endanger the achievements of Conservative administrations — if not capitalism itself. There was also a need to establish a greater sense of identification on the part of trade unionists with their employers. If trade unionism in competing economies was *less political* it was also *more enterprise based*. The immunities protected union action beyond the workplace and beyond the enterprise. They reflected the idea of trade unionism as more than an employer based wages agency, trade unionism as a broad working class *movement*. Legislation on secondary action, picketing and solidarity strikes could help in conjunction with wider policies to produce a greater *identification with the employer*, so that aspects of the enterprise trade unionism of Japan with its benefits, in terms of flexibility, might be meshed with aspects of the market rationality exhibited by US unions in accepting the primacy of profit and institutionalising "give-backs" — cuts in real wages — when times were hard for the employers.

Undermining Collectivism

If many of the Conservative measures smacked of the creation of a business trade unionism, where trade unionists would accept, in a more coherent fashion than they had in post-war Britain, the logic of enterprise competition in a market economy and retreat from political involvement, others seemed to strike more fundamentally at the very logic of collective action. A stable business unionism would thrive on strong union leaders responsive to Thatcherite economics and an inactive rank and file who would "leave it to the professionals" to negotiate wages and conditions controlling them by periodic referenda. The power of the troublesome shop stewards would be diminished and the new, limited, enterprise unionism could be a useful adjunct to management. However, such a transformed trade unionism would still require collective action and, here, there seems to be some contradiction between different aspects of the Conservative legislation programme. The re-enactment of the *Taff Vale* case in 1982 and its extension in 1990 to make unions responsible for unofficial strikers show a tension between the desire for a strong centralised trade unionism and a decentralised, enterprise trade unionism where different groups go their own way.

Similarly, even business unionism requires industrial action, yet the right of the employer to dismiss strikers even after a compulsory ballot and the requirements of the 1988 Act allowing members to ignore the results of ballots for industrial action, undermine leadership and touch the nerve of collective action itself. Even in highly legally regulated systems of industrial relations, such as the USA, the unions, having cleared a number of hurdles, are not finally denied the means of mobilisation; in fact strikers are given clear protection. In order to control their members, even in the interests of management, unions need collective sanctions and collective action. Similarly the wave after wave of measures on the closed shop or ballots on elections have, to a degree, *disorganised* trade unions — both in terms of organising collective action and also expensive, time-consuming *administrative adaptation*. At times in the Conservative legislation there have been problems over who should be controlling whom: leaders controlling the led, or alternatively the rank and file controlling their leaders. There have also been tensions between a desire to decisively weaken and transform trade unionism and a desire to see the back of it altogether and encourage a 'no-union' approach.

Undermining Collective Bargaining

The Conservative ideal has become individual wage bargaining as part of a rehabilitation of the individual contract of employment over and against the collective agreement. The twentieth century in Britain has been marked by the triumphant march of collective regulation of terms and conditions of employment through negotiations between unions and employers. The individual contract of employment became a fiction as, impressed by the imbalance of power which made one to one determination of terms between employer and individual employee *dictation* of terms by the former to the latter, the majority of workers opted for collective negotiation. The lawyers and the courts continued to view industrial relations through the prism of the individual contract and Conservative legislative policies were aimed at rendering the fiction reality by rehabilitating one to one negotiations. This return to the individual contract of employment has been clearly related to the attempt to encourage a greater *flexibility of labour*. The removal of legal protection for workers on short term contracts and contracts for limited hours can be seen as facilitating moves towards greater *casualisation and intensification of labour* relating the enterprise more intimately to the market, developing the split between 'core' and 'periphery' — both in the enterprise and the wider workforce — and domesticating core employees whilst opening the majority to the up-turns and down-turns of immediate market and wider economy.

Weakening trade unions would of itself weaken collective bargaining but the Thatcher Governments also looked to undermine specific props to collective bargaining such as the Fair Wages Resolution, and Wages Councils. This approach culminated in the 1987 abolition of the teachers' collective bargaining machinery. It has also produced an increase in union derecognition in the second half of the 1980s and a determination by the government to resist EEC initiatives which might stimulate a strengthening or extension of collective bargaining.

De-regulating the Economy

As we have seen, whilst most workers regarded the law on dismissal, redundancy or discrimination as providing them with essential employment protection rights, the new Conservatives viewed the floor of rights as a 'burden on business', an incitement to low productivity and 'the world owes me a living' attitudes. These matters would, in an ideal world, be settled by the individual contract of employment not Parliamentary intervention. The Conservatives were therefore determined to whittle away the floor of rights but also took a *total* approach: the object of employment law reform was to transform the economy and it was no good just looking at *employees*. The reform of trade unions and collective bargaining to regenerate the UK's ailing economy also entailed the reform of the social security system. For example, an assessment of what benefits Joe or Jill Public could get when out of work, Mrs Thatcher firmly believed, influenced the attitude Joe or Jill would take to losing their job, or going on strike, or choosing another job when unemployed. And these attitudes and the action they bred would in their turn influence union power and the rate of inflation. Joe or Jill, happy on income related unemployment pay, would be little help in building the new Britain. Joe or Jill suffering a real change in their quality of life as a result of unemployment and haunting the factory gates looking for work was another matter entirely. Here, too, the state had to intervene.

HOW TO MAKE IT STICK

The supporters of Mrs Thatcher in the government did not believe that they could move quickly and completely to a free market economy and a residual state. Abolishing the National Health Service and unemployment benefit might be desirable. But in the real world they could not form part of a practical political programme in the forseeable future. Thatcherism wished to achieve a *significant readjustment* between market and state but under the rhetoric there was little intention to return to the 1850s. Even Thatcherism's more limited objectives were given a long time scale for achievement. This was realistic for, in 1979, Thatcherism did not even control the Cabinet.

The Thatcher wing of the party had won the leadership in 1975 but they were still opposed by the traditional, paternalist, 'one nation' wing of the party who like Ted Heath after 1972 wanted to discipline the unions to a limited degree so that they would make better collaborators and partners. The difficulties the Thatcherites faced could be seen from the fact that the 1977 policy statement *The Right Approach to the Economy* contained a very mild section on trade union reform. Divisions within the Party in opposition were often bitter ones with Norman Tebbit characterising Jim Prior's attitude to the unions as smacking of the "the morality of Pétain and Laval".[25]

Mrs Thatcher wanted to go further. She wanted to run the economy without co-operation with the trade union leaders. But even Mrs Thatcher did not, as a matter of practical politics, want to destroy trade unionism but to weaken it decisively and remould it. She did not want to abolish unfair dimissal but to drill important holes in it. With regard to the reform of employment legislation, therefore the government adopted a gradual step-by-step approach.

This 'salami tactic' was, to some extent, conditioned by the fact that the employers, still less the union members Mrs Thatcher wished to mobilise, were not convinced, active Thatcherites. In fact, throughout the decade employers' organisations have sometimes opposed, or greeted in lukewarm fashion, government initiatives. And employers on the ground showed an early reluctance to use new legislation or to clamour for more of the same. The division between government and employers has been an enduring problem for the Conservatives' wider industrial relations and economic policy.

The main obstacle facing Mrs Thatcher was, of course, not the divisions within the Conservative Party or what was seen as the supine nature of sections of the employers but the trade unions themselves. In 1979 they possessed 12 million members and had just given the country another taste of the malign power they possessed by unleashing the 'Winter of Discontent'. They had seen off Harold Wilson's attempt to clip their wings by legislation with *In Place of Strife* in 1969 and they had drawn the teeth of Ted Heath's monumental *Industrial Relations Act* in 1972 before humiliating Ted completely two years later. Mrs Thatcher was determined to ensure that her fate would be very different. She determined on a policy of forward planning and commissioned a series of studies on the problems that her government might face from the unions.

- *The Carrington Report* commissioned in 1975 sought to learn the lessons of Heath's fall from power in 1973-74. It analysed the power strategically placed groups of workers could deploy in a technologically advanced society particularly power workers and miners. The power of the state confronted with strong unions prepared to use the strike weapon had historically diminished. There was a need to look for alternatives to simply trying to face down the unions in a full employment economy.

- *The Ridley Report* leaked by *The Economist* in 1978 went on to plan how to deal with some of the problems raised by Carrington. It suggested paying above average wage increases to workers in key industries, fighting the less powerful groups — car workers and steel workers — first, recruiting strike-breakers, building up the strength and flexibility of the police force, planning carefully before any challenge was accepted in mining or electricity supply and legislating to control picketing and cut-off the money supply to strikers.

- *Stepping Stones* was a secret paper produced at Mrs Thatcher's request in 1977 by Sir John Hoskyns who later became the Prime Minister's political adviser and was then at the Centre For Political Studies fostered by Sir Keith Joseph. *Stepping Stones* advocated a propaganda offensive to make trade unionism dirty words with the electorate. A future Tory government should sever all links with the union leaders undermining their legitimacy and respectability. In Hoskyns's words: "We concluded that reform of trade union law was one of the necessary strategic objects and the union power would be *the* central election issue".[26]

All of this was important. But the term 'step-by-step' approach should not be taken to mean that because of the forward planning the government had undertaken in terms of legal changes and strike-breaking there was, somewhere, a complete, perfect master plan the provisions of which were gradually but remorselessly introduced. There were, for example, real differences over the content and limiting of legislation between Mrs Thatcher and her first Employment Secretary Jim Prior from the more traditional wing of the party. Both wanted restrictions on strikes, picketing and the closed shop and modifications to the floor of individual rights. There were differences as to *how far* these restrictions should go and *when* — differences rooted in different philosophies. Mrs Thatcher wanted weaker trade unions both in terms of their external ability to influence economics and politics and their internal ability to control their members. She wanted less union members, more workplace autonomy, more identification with the enterprise and less political involvement. Prior wanted to reduce union power to a degree but he still believed in relatively strong unions which once restored to their rightful place could play a role as junior partners to government.

Prior commented in 1979

> I do not subscribe to the view that we need weaker trade unions. On the contrary a strong and responsible trade union movement has a major part to play in our economic recovery ... We need unions which are strong enough to pursue consistent policies on behalf of their members. We also need unions strong enough to control those of their members who act irresponsibly in defiance of their union leaders and union policies.[27]

Both Thatcher and Prior were aware of the need to avoid the experience of Ted Heath's *1971 Industrial Relations Act* where one mammoth statute contributed to an explosive and successful union response. But whilst neither wanted to put all their eggs in one basket, Mrs Thatcher wanted to put more eggs in the first basket than Jim Prior did! It was, thus, partly caution engendered by the disastrous Conservative experience of the 1970s, which led to the step-by-step approach of 1979-83. Jim Prior wanted "to make changes which will be workable, changes which will stand the test of time and change, which will bring much needed stability"[28] and Norman Tebbit said "I was determined not to enact unenforceable legislation — the memory of the collapse of the 1972 (sic) Industrial Relations Act was very much in my mind".[29] But conflicts and compromises in the Cabinet as to the content, form and timetable of the legislation also stimulated the step-by-step approach.

The view that each piece of legislation was carefully tested before its successor was introduced can also be overstated. There was some pause between the 1980 and the 1982 Act and some cases on which to judge the impact of the 1980 measures. But the 1982 Act followed very speedily because the Thatcherites believed that its provisions should have been part of the 1980 Act and they had been thwarted in including them through constraints in the Cabinet. After 1983, as Mrs Thatcher and her supporters gained ascendancy in the Cabinet, these constraints all but disappeared. There was an armoury of weapons the government would like to see deployed. But as the decade advanced particular measures were often introduced not as part of some sequential strategy conceived prior to 1979 but as *ad hoc* responses to problems which occurred or opportunities which arose.

In relating to difficulties the government acted with tactical dexterity — witness its retreat before the miners in 1981 and its continuing caution over the use of law in 1984. However, as the government discovered it could get away with more and more and as employers began to use the courts, more and more legal initiatives were taken. However, the fact the government saw anti-union laws as very popular with its supporters and the wider electorate led to the programme of legislation being sustained, to a certain degree, for the purposes of wider political legitimation. New laws were brought in even when workers and employers were showing no desire to use the new rights the Conservatives had already given them.

Discussion Questions

1. "British trade unions in the 19th century should never have accepted the system of immunities. They should have gone for a system of positive rights to organise strikes and so on — like unions in other countries. The immunities form has weakened unions in the 20th century century". Discuss this statement.
2. "Recent attempts to use legislation to control trade unions are nothing new and are rooted in the facts of the UK's economic decline". What is the evidence for this?
3. How far did the position on trade unions taken by the governments of Harold Wilson and Ted Heath differ from each other? How does Mrs Thatcher's approach differ from both of them?
4. Why did the *Industrial Relations Act* fail?
5. "The judges are and always have been the agents of the ruling class who act in the interests of the bosses in opposing trade unions". Is this statement a fair one? Do we need to reform the judiciary?
6. Make a report on the strengths and weaknesses of trade unions in the UK in 1979.

CHAPTER 2

Softly, Softly, Turn the Key

Whenever the legislature attempts to regulate the differences between
masters and their workmen, its counsellors are always the masters
— *Adam Smith*

BACKGROUND

The Conservative Party's manifesto for the 1979 General Election
set their proposed legal changes firmly in the context of the
employment legislation of the Wilson and Callaghan governments.
Labour, they claimed, had enacted "a militants' charter"

> by heaping privilege without reponsibility on the trade unions Labour have given
> a minority of extremists the power to abuse individual liberties and to thwart
> Britain's chances of success.

The consequences for Mrs Thatcher were clear ones. Labour had

> tilted the balance of power in bargaining throughout industry away from
> responsible management and towards unions and sometimes unofficial groups
> of workers acting in defiance of their official union leadership.[1]

Key themes in the Conservative critique were succinctly enunciated.
To weaken union power and restore equilibrium the manifesto
promised action on picketing, secondary action and the closed
shop. Public funds would also be provided for unions to hold postal
ballots which the Conservatives believed mobilised the silent
moderate majority against the militants.

Changes to the employment protection legislation were quickly
introduced as Labour's legislation had provided that details, such
as qualification periods for rights, did not require legislation but
could be amended by *orders in council*. Two sets of consultative
working papers setting out the government's thinking on the reform
of employment legislation were then published in July and
September 1979. Setting a precedent for speedy follow through
which it was to adhere to throughout the decade, the government
then published its first Employment Bill in December 1979. The Act
became fully operative on October 1st 1980 and was swiftly
followed by Codes of Practice on Picketing and the Closed Shop.

The proposals for legislation was welcomed by the C.B.I. but
they expressed some concern over the problems that the closed
shop legislation could entail and felt that the complex provisions

on secondary action were not required "... on the question of trade union immunities our members are strongly of the view that, at this stage, changes should be confined to secondary picketing".[2] The Engineering Employers Federation urged redrafting of these provisions on the grounds that they would create uncertainty and had been "almost universally and strongly criticised".[3] The Institute of Personnel Management felt that some of the provisions were irrelevant and others would do little to improve industrial relations.[4] The TUC felt

> The proposals are irrelevant to the basic issues of improving industrial relations and promoting improvements in productivity, real earnings and job security. Worse, they would make it more difficult to achieve progress on these issues because they would introduce highly contentious laws into industrial relations.[5]

The Government paid little attention to these responses and their legislative programme largely went ahead as planned. The measures introduced by the Government in 1979 and 1980 covered a wide range of issues. We now look at each one in turn.

TRADE UNION ORGANISATION

In most countries comparable with the UK, legislation gives trade unions the right to organise. As long ago as 1949-50 the United Kingdom ratified the International Labour Organisation's Convention 87 on Freedom of Association and the Right to Organise and Convention 98 on the Application of the Right to Organise and to Bargain Collectively. These declarations required that workers should be given the right to establish and join unions of their choice, enjoy protection against acts of discrimination by anti-union employers and have available machinery to facilitate recognition by the employer for the purposes of collective bargaining. However, it was not until 1968 that the Royal Commission on Trade Unions advocated legislation in this area and not until 1971 that Ted Heath's Conservative Government enacted provisions on union organisation and recognition as part of the *Industrial Relations Act.*

Union Recognition
(Employment Act 1980 s.19(b))
In 1975 s.11-16 of the *Employment Protection Act* introduced by Harold Wilson's Labour administration sought to replace the cumbersome machinery of the *Industrial Relations Act* with a simpler procedure. An independent trade union could now refer a claim for recognition to the Advisory Conciliation and Arbitration

Service (ACAS). ACAS would then try to conciliate the parties and achieve a voluntary settlement to the dispute. If that proved impossible then ACAS had to establish the views of the workers involved on the question of recognition, look at the pros and cons of the problem and publish a report on its investigation. ACAS in its report could recommend that the employers recognise the union or, it could recommend that the union establish a stronger base.

An ACAS recommendation of recognition was not directly enforceable in the courts. But if the employer refused to abide by the ACAS decision and bargain with the union, the union could place a claim for improved terms and conditions before the Central Arbitration Committee. This body could then make an award on terms and conditions of employment which then became part of the contract of employment of each worker covered by the claim.

This procedure was tortuous and made for delays. An employer could spin out the process and in the end, at best, the unions got compulsory arbitration awards *not recognition*. In a series of cases the Court of Appeal intervened to protect the right of individual employers and non-unionists against ACAS, deciding that ACAS was going beyond its powers (in the *UKAPE* case) and that its report was void (in the *Grunwick* case).

Overall the record of ACAS in dealing with this issue was not as bad as was often made out. Over the period the recognition provisions remained on the statute book, ACAS dealt with 2,292 references. More than three-quarters were settled by voluntary means and two-fifths of these cases produced some form of recognition. However, in only a minority of the cases that went through the full procedure did the unions attain recognition. In total, 2,292 cases were dealt with by ACAS and some form of recognition was achieved in 981 or 43% of these involving 77,500 workers.

However, by mid-1979 the Chair of ACAS felt the need to inform the government that ACAS was unable to "satisfactorily operate the statutory recognition procedures as they stand". Key Court of Appeal decisions were overruled by the House of Lords in 1980. But by then it was too late. In September 1979, the new Conservative Government published a consultative paper *Trade Union Recognition* which suggested that in the face of the difficulties in operating the legislation it might be best if the law withdrew, leaving ACAS to deal voluntarily with recognition problems. Despite powerful arguments against this (notably by the Social Science Research Council's Industrial Relations Research Unit at the University of Warwick) *the 1980 Act repealed the s11-16 provisions on recognition*, in pursuit of weakening trade unions and reducing their membership. Recent research shows that the number of recognition cases referred to ACAS in its voluntary role has declined and so has the proportion resulting in recognition of the union.

The Closed Shop
(s. 7 EA 1980 amending s.23, 58 EPCA 1978)

The *Donovan Report* in 1968 confirmed earlier research which showed that around 3.75 million workers, 40% of union members, were in employment which required membership of a trade union and .75 million were covered by *pre-entry* closed shop arrangements where they were required to hold a union card prior to appointment. The *1971 Industrial Relations Act* introduced for the first time legislation dealing with unfair dismissal, membership or non-membership of a trade union and the closed shop. When the 1974 Labour Government repealed that legislation they remoulded and developed the provisions on dismissal and the closed shop. The law enacted in the *Trade Union and Labour Relations Act* 1974 and the *Trade Union and Labour Relations (Amendment) Act* 1976 was consolidated in the *Employment Protection (Consolidation) Act* 1978.

Essentially Labour's legislation provided that if an employer could demonstrate the existence of a *union membership agreement,* an arrangement or formal agreement which, in practice, required all workers covered by it to be members of a specified union, then the employer would be protected against action for unfair dismissal in an industrial tribunal if he sacked those who refused to join the union. Workers would only win an unfair dismissal case if they could show that their objection to trade unionism was based on *religious grounds.*

The law, therefore, did not *directly* support the closed shop. But by abstaining, by refusing to penalise its possible consequences, this legislation indirectly stimulated its extension in a period of relative union strength. Research carried out at the London School of Economics found that there had been a growth of formal closed shop agreements on the u.m.a. model during the 1970s and the practice had spread from manual to white collar employment. By 1979 5.2 million workers were covered by closed shops and around 830,000 workers were covered by pre-entry closed shops.[6]

The Conservative Government's objection to the closed shop was often articulated in terms of its violation of the freedom of the individual to decide whether or not to join a collective organisation. But the closed shop was also seen as a base and guarantor of union power, an engine for membership growth and a *sine qua non* for the discipline without which collective action would be impossible. It was also perceived as a restrictive practice interfering with management's prerogative to freely utilise labour and a barrier to enhanced work reorganisation, efficiency and increased productivity.

Criticism of the closed shop had been mounting throughout the second half of the 1970s and focused on the legislation which was fiercely contested by the Conservatives and bitterly opposed in the media. The TUC's *Guide on Trade Union Organisation and the Closed Shop*, published in February 1979 as part of the "Concordat" intended to shore up the waning Callaghan Government, could be viewed as a concession to this offensive. It talked about the need to be flexible about closed shops, look at the necessity for exemptions and attempt to achieve 100% trade unionism by voluntary means. In July 1979, the Conservatives' Manifesto commitment to action was followed up by a consultative working paper with suggestions for legislation which found fulfilment in the 1980 Act.

The Act made four important changes:

1. Workers sacked or victimised for non-membership of a union under the terms of closed shop agreements *which existed before the Act took effect on 15th August 1980* would succeed in cases before industrial tribunals if they could demonstrate that they had been required to join a union *but had never actually been a member.*

2. Workers sacked or victimised for non-membership of a union under the terms of a closed shop agreement which came into being *before or after* 15th August 1980 would now be protected against dismissal if they could show that they had been dismissed or victimised because they objected *on genuine grounds of conscience or other deeply held personal conviction* to membership of a trade union. In other words the "religious grounds" loophole was extended to embrace the wider *grounds of conscience.*

3. Workers sacked or victimised for non-membership of a union under the terms of closed shop agreements *taking effect on or after 15th August 1980* would win their case at an industrial tribunal unless their employer could show that
   — a *secret ballot* had been held amongst all those to be covered by the agreement or arrangement;
   — in the ballot *80% of those entitled to vote* voted for the closed shop;

— even if the employer could show the required majority in a secret ballot, those *in employment on the date of the ballot* would win a case as long as they had *never been union members.* The ballot did not bind existing workers, only new employees taken on after its completion — and they could try to bring themselves within the *genuine grounds of conscience loophole.*

4. Under the previous legislation a worker dismissed or victimised for non-membership in a closed shop situation could only take legal action against the *employer* who had sacked or victimised him or her. The union shop steward or members who may have exercised pressure on the employer to dismiss or victimise the non-unionist were specifically exempted from any legal comeback. However, the 1980 Act gave a right to *employers* to join the *union or individual trade unionists* as a party to the tribunal proceedings. This right applied if the employer was *induced* to sack the non-unionist *by the pressure of a strike, other industrial action or threats of industrial action.* If the union or shop steward *were* joined to the proceedings and the dismissed employee won the case then *part of the compensation for the dismissal could be awarded against the union or steward.*

The Code of Practice on Closed Shop Agreements and Arrangements
(Employment Act 1980 s.3)

The 1980 legislation gave the Secretary of State for Employment the power to issue Codes of Practice. These would contain practical guidance for employers and trade unionists on the implementation of the law. They could also be used by the courts and tribunals in interpreting the meaning and spirit of the law. What they said could also have an impact on the attitudes of workers, employers and lawyers and influence public opinion. Codes of Practice could be regarded as "legislation by the backdoor". They provided a useful mechanism by which the government could attempt to influence industrial relations practice and judicial law-making in a direction which would take matters beyond the specific wording of the statutes — without going through the process of legislation. For a Code to take effect the Minister simply had to lay it before Parliament. Before 1980 Codes of Practice had been drafted and published by ACAS. Although the Employment Secretary still had to consult ACAS, this power was now taken by government, partly because ACAS was concerned at the partisan nature of what was being planned.

The *Code of Practice on Closed Shop Agreements and Arrangements* came into effect on December 17 1980. It stated that employers should expect a union to demonstrate "a very high level of membership before agreeing to consider the introduction of a closed shop". But a high level of union membership, in itself, could not be taken as evidence of support for a closed shop when it came to holding a ballot. The Code stated that "80% is very much a minimum" and "this does not prevent an employer from deciding that there should be a higher percentage in favour before he agrees to such a radical change". Employers and unions should agree on the terms of a closed shop agreement, the definition of the electorate, the conduct of the ballot and the framing of the ballot paper. They should consider the use of independent scrutineers. Agreements should clearly define exemptions and allow for full rights of appeal.

The Code again went beyond the legislation by urging that there should be periodic reviews of closed shop arrangements. If 80% of those covered did not vote for the maintenance of the closed shop in such a review the arrangement should be terminated. Whilst the 1980 Act left pre-entry closed shops untouched, the Code stated baldly that they were unacceptable: "No new agreements of this type should be contemplated and where they currently exist the need for their continuation should be carefully reviewed". The Code again went far beyond the law by recommending that no disciplinary action should be taken by a union against members who refused to participate in industrial action where such action would break the law; or was not agreed by secret ballot; or was in breach of a procedure agreement; or would violate a code of professional ethics; or constitute a risk to public health and safety. The closed shop in the printing and publishing industries came in for special attention: it should be eschewed, according to the government, in these areas because of the threat it represented to the freedom of the press.

The Member and The Union
(Employment Act 1980 s.4, 5)

Before the arrival of Mrs Thatcher in Downing Street the legal rights individual members had against their unions depended largely on the union rule book. The courts treated union rules as a *contract* made between all the members. If the union broke the contract by, for example, taking disciplinary action against a member without following the procedures and requirements laid down in the rules then that member could successfully sue the union in the courts.

Moreover, the judges did not simply leave the scope and detail of the rules to union members. The courts insisted that the rules met the requirements of *natural justice*. Members charged under the rules must be given notice of the charges against them, have a fair hearing and be given the opportunity to defend themselves before an impartial body. Union rules also had to be in accord with the requirements *of public policy*. If, for example, they stated that black people were to be excluded from membership they would be struck down by the courts. Whilst the *Trade Union and Labour Relations Act* 1974 S.7 had given members who gave notice and complied with other reasonable conditions the right to resign, *applicants for membership* had no rights as they were not parties to the contract.

In the working paper on the closed shop, the government suggested the introduction of a new statutory right for workers *excluded or expelled from a trade union*. The legislation which eventually emerged was more limited. Workers who worked in a job *where a closed shop applied* or who were seeking a job in an area where a *closed shop applied* had the right

— not to have an application for union membership *unreasonably* refused

— not to be *unreasonably* expelled from the union.

These provisions represented a major development in the legal regulation of a union's internal affairs. Even if the union had followed its rules to the letter in taking action against a worker and those rules met the requirements of *natural justice* and *public policy* the judges could still find the rules *unreasonable*. The Act specifically stated that the judges should be guided by their own notions of reasonableness which might be very different from those of trade unionists. They should be guided by

> equity and the substantial merits of the case and in particular a union shall not be regarded as having acted reasonably only because it acted in accordance with the requirements of its rules or unreasonably only because it has acted in contravention of them. S4 (5).

Workers who felt that they had a grievance against a union could now bring a case to an industrial tribunal within six months of the date of expulsion or refusal. They could do this without exhausting internal appeals procedures laid down in the rule book. If the tribunal found that the union had acted unreasonably in refusing membership or in expelling a member it could issue a *declaration* to that effect. If the union accepted the declaration and admitted the worker or cancelled the expulsion the worker involved could still apply for *compensation* which would be assessed as in an unfair dismissal case. If the union refused to comply with the declaration the worker could take his or her case to the Employment Appeal Tribunal which would award compensation at a higher rate.

These provisions were aimed at weakening union discipline. The Conservatives saw union discipline as a weapon wielded by militant union leaders against the 'reasonable' rank and file, a means by which the leaders could coerce reluctant members into industrial action by threatening them with expulsion and consequently the loss of their livelihood if they did not do what the union bosses wanted. The law was seen as giving the members the chance to stand up to their leaders. By so doing they could limit their powers and reduce the number of strikes.

The unions, however, were able to argue convincingly that there was no serious evidence that the previous legal position was abused by the unions. To the degree that the prior law could be criticised it was on the grounds that the judges' interpretation of union rules had been restrictive not liberal. The rights of individuals were more than satisfactorily protected by the common law contract remedy. The diminution of union autonomy these clauses represented limited union democracy and thus democracy in the wider society. There was a danger that the courts would utilise the statements of the *Code of Practice on the Closed Shop* — no discipline where a strike was called in breach of procedure or without a secret ballot — to seriously impair unions' powers to discipline recalcitrant members and, thus, their powers to take effective industrial action. Without powers of discipline the unions ability to successfully mount collective action would be weakened.

Trade Union Ballots
(Employment Act 1980 s.1, 2; S.I. 1980 No.1252)

> There is wide public support for more extensive use of secret ballots within the union movement — Government Working Paper, July 1979.

Throughout the 1970s secret postal ballots as a means of taking decisions in the unions were increasingly prescribed as an antidote to militancy and industrial action. The Labour Government's *In Place of Strife* had, of course, provided for compulsory strike ballots and this proposal was taken up by the Conservatives and embodied in the *Industrial Relations Act*. Politicians of both major parties saw postal ballots as a force for moderation as against the militancy stoked up in mass meetings. This focus shifted to embrace proposals that postal ballots should be used in internal union elections. This would produce more reasonable and moderate leadership, as freed of the intimidation and hysteria of mass meetings the rank and file would vote responsibly in the privacy of their homes. The 1979 TUC statement, *The Economy, The Government and Trade Union Responsibilities* gave further ground to the campaign for secret postal ballots. The General Council stated that unions should incorporate a statement of principles covering strike ballots in their rules.

In accordance with the Conservatives' cautious approach, the July 1979, *Working Paper on Public Funds For Union Ballots* contained limited proposals eventually enacted in the 1980 legislation.

The Act allowed unions to apply for *state finance for postal ballots* held for the purposes of

— calling and terminating industrial action
— electing full time and principal lay officers of the union
— amending the rules of the union
— amalgamating with other unions under the provisions of the *Trade Union (Amalgamation) Act 1964*
— other union purposes specified from time to time by the Secretary of State for Employment.

Unions wishing to avail themselves of these provisions had to apply to the Certification Officer who had to approve the conduct of the ballot, ensure it was secret and postal and pay out reasonable expenses occurred according to the requirements laid down in detailed regulations.

An amendment to the 1980 Bill, introduced by Labour peers in the Lords, provided that in a situation where the union was recognised and more than 20 workers were employed by the employer, unions could demand *facilities for a workplace ballot* on any of the issues listed above. The ballot had to be *secret* but otherwise its conduct was not governed by the principles applying to ballots for which state finance was requested. If the employer failed to comply *so far as is reasonably practicable* with a union's request for facilities on the premises and/or failed to provide workers with *a convenient opportunity for voting* the union could apply to an industrial tribunal for a declaration and compensation.

These provisions were clearly part of the Conservative project of remoulding the internal operations of unions and mobilising an allegedly passive and cautious membership against the militants to produce greater moderation and fewer strikes. They were perceived by the unions as, once more, compromising their autonomy. As the TUC put it

It is clear that public funds cannot be handed over to unions without the acceptance by unions of some degree of public accountability.[7]

COLLECTIVE BARGAINING

(Employment Act 1980 s.19 (c))

All the changes in the 1980 legislation could affect collective bargaining to one degree or another. But the government were determined to deal, in particular, with the terms and conditions of employment provisions contained in schedule 11 of the *Employment Protection Act* 1975. Schedule 11 enabled a union to claim that an employer was observing terms and conditions of employment less favourable than those applied to comparable workers under collective agreements. Unions could also put in claims that employers should observe the 'going rate' for an industry in a particular area where there was no collective agreement but they could establish a 'general level' of terms and conditions of employment. Claims were reported to ACAS. If they were not settled voluntarily the case would be heard by the Central Arbitration Committee. If the Committee found for the union the CAC made an award which was incorporated into the contracts of employment of all those covered by it. Between 1977, when it became operative, and the summer of 1980, 1,939 references were made to the CAC. In the final complete year of operation 1979, awards were made in favour of 68,000 workers but claims involving 72,000 workers were rejected.

The Conservatives wished to weaken the influence of 'the going rate' and comparability arguments in negotiations generally. They wished to relate pay more directly to company performance and profitability. They, therefore, opposed Schedule 11. They argued that it had been used as a means of getting round the Labour Government's wages policy and its operation was inflationary. It distorted collective bargaining structures, failed to take account of the ability to pay of individual employers and had often been used to better the position of the already highly paid rather than helping the low paid.

Against this the unions cited the evidence of the Industrial Relations Research Unit at Warwick University that since 1977 the vast majority of successful claims had benefited workers on below average earnings. They quoted another study which reported that only 27% of managers complained of any industrial relations problems in the wake of a CAC award, 38% reported no effect and

35% stated that the award had contributed to an improvement in industrial relations. And they cited the view of the CAC itself that

> the suggestions that the Committee's awards add a twist to the inflationary spiral attributes to the CAC an importance in the national bargaining round which it does not have.[8]

Despite this, *Schedule 11 was removed from the statute book*. And for good measure the government also repealed the *Road Haulage Act 1938* which enabled workers in that industry to complain to ACAS and then the CAC that their terms and conditions were unfair in comparison with collective agreements or wage councils.

EMPLOYMENT PROTECTION

Central to Mrs Thatcher's policy of deregulating business and setting entrepreneurs free was an attack on the statutory floor of rights previous governments had established for individual employees. The philosophy behind this had been two-fold. First, was the argument from principle that employers should have to implement a basic minimum of civilised working practices and procedures if they wanted to run a business. And many also felt that the adoption by employers of good industrial relations practices would purchase the consent of the workforce, enhance management legitimacy and ultimately boost productivity.

Mrs Thatcher believed that the cost of this kind of social welfarism, just like the cost of working with the unions, was too great. Employment Protection rights led to featherbedding and provided a platform for unions to demand further rights to the detriment of efficiency and profitability. Decisions on benefits in employment and termination of employment were, like wages, best left to the market. An unprotected or weakly protected worker would have the goad of insecurity and the stimulus of fear — the best motivators to effective work performance. The feckless, unwilling or weak would, quite rightly, have their services dispensed with.

In 1979-80 the Conservatives mounted a range of arguments against the Employment Protection rights developed by the 1974-79 Labour Government. In July 1979, Employment Minister Patrick Mayhew told the Commons "... there is overwhelming evidence that the present provisions frustrate and unreasonably curtail the creation of jobs".[9] His colleague the Earl of Gowrie argued "... this legislation in its present form diverts management attention from the central task of running a business".[10] The Working Paper on Employment Protection asserted that such laws "bear over-harshly on employers, discouraging recruitment especially in small businesses". The erosion of employment protection legislation was intimately related to the government's wider economic policy.

Such reasoning attracted two lines of response. Firstly, it was pointed out that the UK's employment protection legislation compared unfavourably with that in many other countries. In the Scandinavian countries workers were protected against unfair dismissal from the first day of employment — there was no qualifying period. In countries such as Italy and West Germany, unlike Britain, the courts could enforce reinstatment. The median compensation award in unfair dismissal cases in Britain in 1979 was under £400. The anti-discrimination legislation had fallen into disrepute because of its cumbersome procedures and weak sanctions.

Secondly, research failed to bear out the government's assertions. A survey by Daniel and Stilgoe for the Policy Studies Institute stated

> There was no general indication that employment protection legislation was inhibiting management from taking on new labour where they otherwise would have done so.[11]

Only 58% of managers said that this legislation had affected them at all, only 17% said it had had "a great deal of effect". A second study for the Department of Employment by Clifton and Tatton-Brown found that only 2% of managers mentioned employment legislation amongst their main difficulties in running the business and the subject came fourteenth out of a list of 21 problems.[12]

The position was the same in relation to other areas such as maternity rights. Whilst the government could blandly assert in its Working Paper on Employment Protection that "the maternity pay and reinstatement provisions have not worked satisfactorily in practice", *Industrial Relations Review and Report* could state in February 1980

> According to over 80% of respondents (i.e. managers) to IR — RR Maternity Leave Survey the provisions have in fact been working well. This is one of the major findings of our survey covering one million workers.[13]

Nonetheless, the government ignored this evidence. They did not make a bonfire of controls, but they began to cumulatively peck away at the framework of protection riddling it with holes.

Unfair Dismissal
Qualifying Period
(Unfair Dismissal (Variation of Qualifying Period) Order 1979 S.I. 959)
The Government by an order in council taking effect on October

1st 1979 *extended the qualifying period for unfair dismissal claims from 26 weeks to 52 weeks.* In 1979 24% of applicants had service of between 26 weeks and 52 weeks and in future such workers would be excluded from protection.

Small Businesses

(Employment Act 1980 s.6, s.87)

Workers employed by *a company with less than 21 employees now had to work not for 26 weeks or 52 weeks to qualify for unfair dismissal rights but for 2 years.* Moreover, in any case, the tribunal now had to take into account the *"size and administrative resources of the employers undertaking"* when deciding whether the employer had behaved reasonably or unreasonably in dismissing the worker. This was again intended to benefit small firms, encourage disregard of effective procedures in this sector and penalise workers who worked in small employment units.

Fixed Term Contracts

(Employment Act 1980 s.8)

The *Employment Protection (Consolidation Act)* 1978 stated that employees could agree in writing to waive their rights to unfair dismissal where they were employed under a contract for a fixed term of two years or more. The new legislation extended this waiver provision to workers employed *on fixed term contracts of one year or more* and thus encouraged the growth of short term contracts containing clauses by which workers were deprived of their shrinking rights.

Compensation

(Employment Act 1980 s.9)

In 1980 compensation for unfair dismissal was assessed under three heads: a *basic award,* calculated in the same way as redundancy pay and intended to compensate all applicants for the *fact* of dismissal. The basic award could not be less than two weeks pay. An *additional award* granted if a recommendation of reinstatement or re-engagement was made but not complied with. And a *compensatory award* intended to reimburse the successful applicant for actual loss suffered.

The 1980 Act now *removed the minimum basic award* so that successful applicants could end up with nothing under this head. In 1978 more than 70% of basic awards had been for the two weeks pay minimum. In future such applicants would receive a *nil* award.

Redundancy Consultation

(Employment Protection (Handling of Redundancies) Variation
order 1979 S.I. 958)

The *Employment Protection Act 1975* required employers to consult
recognised unions before proposing to make any worker
redundant. Consultation, it stated, should be *at the earliest
opportunity* but it then prescribed detailed period depending on the
extent of possible redundancy. The Conservatives now changed
these provisions so that

— if 100 or more workers were to be sacked at one establishment
   over a period of up to 90 days the employer should consult with
   the union *at least 90 days before the first dismissal*
— if between 10 and 100 workers were to be sacked at one
   establishment over a period of 30 days the employer should
   consult the union(s) at least 30 days (not as previously at least
   60 days) before the first dismissal.

Guarantee Payments

(Employment Act 1980 s.14)

Under the terms of the *Employment Protection (Consolidation) Act
1978* employers had to pay a minimum guarantee payment — to
workers not provided with work for a full day in which they would
normally be required to work. The employer, however, only had
to make such payments for a period of up to 5 days in any fixed
calendar quarter period. As the quarters ran from 1st February, 1st
May, 1st August and 1st November some employers found
themselves paying for 5 days in January and 5 days in February.
The new legislation now restricted entitlement to a maximum of 5
days in *any three month period.*

Maternity Rights

(Employment Act 1980 s.11, 12, 13)

The major changes introduced here were four fold

Writing

Under the 1980 Act *all* notices had to be *in writing.* For example,
women taking maternity leave now had to inform their employer *in
writing* 21 days before they wanted to leave, stating the date of
expected week of confinement and intention to return to work after
the birth.

New Notice Requirements

In exercising their rights to return up to 29 weeks after the week
of confinement, women now had to meet two additional
requirements. Firstly, seven weeks after the birth your employer can

write asking if you still intend to exercise the right to return. If you don't answer in writing *within 14 days*, saying you still want to come back, you could lose your rights unless, as with the initial 21 days requirement, you can demonstrate that it was not *reasonably practicable* for you to reply in time.

Secondly, you must give your employer *21 days notice of the day you are going to come back* — although you can *postpone your return up to four weeks* on production of a medical certificate and your employer can also postpone your return for the same period.

Right to Return

The *Employment Protection (Consolidation) Act* gave a right to return to "the job in which you were employed under the original contract of employment and on terms and conditions not less favourable than those which would have been applicable" had leave not been taken. The 1980 Act widened the employers' loopholes. Employers could now argue that direct *reinstatment was not practicable because of redundancy*. A woman would only have a right to *suitable alternative employment* if there was *a vacancy available*. Employers could now also argue that reinstatement *was not reasonably practicable for reasons other than redundancy*. In this case, however, they *would* have to offer suitable alternative employment.

Ante-natal Care

All women whether or not they had the two years continuous employment required for statutory maternity leave were given a new right *to take time off with pay when pregnant for ante-natal care* — on production of a medical certificate or appointment card.

INDUSTRIAL TRIBUNAL PROCEDURE

(Industrial Tribunals (Rules of Procedure) Regulations 1980)

A number of changes were introduced by statutory instrument and took effect from 1st October 1980. The Government argued that they were justified by the fact that tribunal proceedings had become too technical and time consuming; that tribunals were being deluged with time wasting spurious cases; and that the existing rules on costs inadequately deterred litigation happy workers who consumed their employers valuable time and resources.

From their side the union argued, once more, that the Government's case lacked any supportive evidence. The real intention of the changes was not to make tribunals more efficient but to put a new series of hurdles in the path of those who sought to use them — thus ensuring that their protection against arbitrary acts of management was further minimised. The main changes were:-

Opening statement: The right to make such a statement was abolished.

Costs: The rules on costs were extended so that they could now be awarded against parties who brought or defended a case not only in a frivolous or vexatious fashion but where they acted "*otherwise unreasonably*".

Pre-hearing assessment: Either party could now request a pre-hearing to assess the strength of their opponents case. The pre-hearing considers whether the case is likely to succeed at the full hearing. Whatever the decision the parties can proceed to a full hearing but if the pre-hearing assessment found against a party that there was no reasonable prospect of success and that party loses then costs can be awarded against them.

Onus of proof: In unfair dismissal cases the onus of proof had been on the employer. If it was a 50-50 case the employer got the verdict. Now the onus of proof was neutralised. Whilst the employer still had to lead evidence, who got the verdict in the event of a draw was a matter for the discretion of the tribunal.

INDUSTRIAL ACTION

Picketing
(Employment Act 1980 s.16)

The Conservative Party's Manifesto for the 1979 election referred to widespread public concern over picketing, culminating in the "Winter of Discontent". It was particularly concerned about secondary picketing, its impact on employers not directly involved in disputes and on the general public. The Manifesto linked the growth of picketing with "the growth and greater formalisation of the closed shop since 1974" and deplored what it saw as an increase in intimidation and physical violence on picket lines. A July 1979 Working Paper reiterated the new government's determination to legislate. There was a need to change the law to ensure protection for:

> those not concerned in the dispute but who at present can suffer severely from secondary action so that a citizen's right to work and go about his lawful business free from intimidation or obstruction is guaranteed.[14]

INDUSTRIAL ACTION

If you go on strike then you are usually breaking your contract of employment. The courts have also found that a range of other industrial action, overtime bans, work to rules, mandatory chapel meetings, also involves employees in breaking their contracts of employment. An employer often has little to gain financially by suing employees for breach of contract, apart from the unhelpful impact this is likely to have on future industrial relations. However, there is a civil wrong developed by the courts termed *inducement to breach of contract*. If employers could show the courts that it was *the union* that instigated, influenced or supported the industrial action then they might be able to convince the courts that the union was inducing the workers to break their contracts of employment.

In many cases judges were willing to do this and grant a legal order, an *injunction* instructing the the union to call off the action. If the union did not do this, it would be *in contempt of court* and could be fined large sums of money or eventually have its assets *sequestrated*. The courts also developed other civil wrongs — conspiracy, intimidation, interference with contracts — which they used against union activities.

The position was made more difficult by the practice of the courts of issuing *interim injunctions*. An employer could within a matter of days secure a preliminary hearing of the case. The judge was only concerned as to whether on the face of it the employer had an arguable case, not whether it could be proved to the hilt, and whether looking at all the circumstances, the judge felt that it was more convenient to freeze the situation and restore the *status quo* by ordering the union to call off the industrial action until the full trial took place.

In the vast majority of cases the courts found for the employers, ignoring the problems this caused for unions and members who had to wait six months or a year before they could bring their bargaining power fully to bear on the employer. Of course, in most cases, the employers never returned to court for the full trial. The use of the interim injunction adequately met their purposes.

All of this meant, quite simply, that strikes and most forms of industrial action were unlawful. Trade unions therefore, pressed Parliament to *immunise* them from the impact of this judge-made law. If they were to carry out their functions of protecting their members then they needed *specific immunities* from, for example the civil wrong or tort of inducing breach of contract. Parliament decided unions would be protected where the industrial action is '**in contemplation or furtherance of a trade dispute**'. A *trade dispute* was defined quite widely as a dispute between employers and workers, or workers and workers, which was related to, or connected with one or more of a long list of industrial matters. The list covered such issues as terms and conditions of employment, engagement, or dismissal of employees, allocation of work, discipline procedures and so forth (see p.58).

If the industrial action fell within this definition of a trade dispute then it was protected — or at least the trade unions were over the first hurdle. If the action did not fall within this definition then the workers and their trade unions were in trouble. They then possessed no immunity and could be sued for committing one of the civil wrongs — most commonly inducement to breach of contract.

A major aim of the 1980 Act was to limit the immunities trade unionists possessed when taking industrial action.

In changing the law the government wanted to limit the scale and scope of picketing. Its detailed regulation would be left to the police and the criminal law. But by tightening the civil law the government hoped to both firm up the police and encourage employers to take action. A remodelled picketing practice stemming from a reformed law would *limit action to the workplace directly involved* and restrict the success of industrial action.

For these reasons the changes were bitterly opposed by the unions. It was argued that they would diminish solidarity and make disputes harder to win. In some disputes where the workplace strike was solid, work was transferred elsewhere by the employer and workers needed to picket the new source. In many disputes where there was a total shutdown there was little point in workers picketing their own workplace — but there was a need for secondary action to extend the dispute to other factories of the employer or customers or suppliers. Conservative allegations of intimidation and violence were exaggerated. Such behaviour had been condemned by the TUC in their 1979 Codes. If such abuse did occur then the law should deal with it — the criminal law remedies were numerous — not seek to outlaw *all* picketing beyond the workplace in dispute. A ban on secondary picketing also had important consequences for civil liberties and freedom of speech.

The pre-existing civil legislation on picketing was contained in s 15 of the *Trade Union and Labour Relations Act*. This stated that pickets would be protected from legal action where they were acting *in contemplation or furtherance of a trade dispute* (see p.58). If the pickets could show that their action fell within the definition of a trade dispute then they were protected if they were simply attending *at or near a place of work* in order to peacefully communicate information or to peacefully persuade workers not to work.

The scope of this protection had been severely limited by a series of criminal law decisions in the courts in the 1960s and 1970s. The 1980 Act now directly attacked it.

— Workers were now to be protected not when they were attending at or near *a place of work* but only when they were attending at or near *their own place of work*. This change attempted to limit pickets to the site on which they worked. Even if they were involved in company bargaining and involved in an official national strike they would lose the immunity past legislation gave them against civil law wrongs, such as conspiracy or inducement to breach of contract, if they successfully picketed other offices or factories of their own employer — or even the head office. Picketing the premises of suppliers or customers would also now be unlawful.

— *Mobile workers* such as lorry drivers had their workplace defined as any premises of their employer from *which they worked or from which their work was administered.* This provision again severely limited secondary action.

— Workers who worked at a place of work *whose location made picketing impracticable* such as oil rig workers were again entitled to picket the centre from which their work was administered.

— *Union officials* were protected if they were picketing at *or near the workplace of a member who they were accompanying and who they represented.*

— *Dismissed workers* were protected if they were picketing *their last place of work* if they were still *unemployed* and if their employment had been *terminated in connection with a trade dispute.*

Code of Practice on Picketing

In similar fashion to the Closed Shop Code this document, effective on 17th December 1980, sought to improve upon the law. The government hoped that the "extras" it contained would be read into the law by the judges but if not its principles could be embodied in legislation later on. Even more than in the Closed Shop Code, statements of the existing law were mixed in with new suggestions in confusing fashion.

The documents' main points were

— pickets and their organisers should ensure that, in general, the number of pickets does not exceed *six* at any entrance to a workplace, frequently a smaller number will be appropriate.

— picket organisers should control pickets, liaise with the police and ensure workers from other workplaces were not on the picket line.

— "Everyone has the right to decide for himself whether he will cross a picket line".

— Disciplinary action should not be taken by a union against a member who crosses a picket line which was not authorised or, which was not at the member's place of work.

— Pickets should not seek to halt essential supplies and services — a very widely defined category including "goods and services necessary to the maintenance of plant and machinery".

Secondary Action
(Employment Act 1980 s.17)

Having dealt with picketing, the government wanted to deal with the *secondary boycott*, the situation where workers taking industrial action requested workers employed by other employers — customers, suppliers, contractors, or transport workers — not to handle their product for the duration of the dispute. This was, once again, aimed at limiting the ambit of industrial action — if not quite to the workplace, nearer to the workplace. But the government proceeded cautiously leaving flesh to be put on the skeleton of the law by judicial interpretation.

Most forms of secondary action had been protected by the *Trade Union and Labour Relations Act* though the judges had discovered several loopholes in the 1970s. The 1980 Act now defined secondary action in the following terms. Action was *secondary action* where

1. Workers, stewards or union officers *induced* a group of workers *to break their contracts with their employer* who was *not himself a party to the dispute.* Alternatively workers, stewards or union officers *interfered with the performance the contracts of employment* or, *induced* somebody else to interfere with it, or *threatened* inducement or interference.

2. As a consequence of inducement to break or interference with *contracts of employment*, a party to a *commercial contract* has been induced to break it, or its performance has been interfered with, or threats to do this have been made.

If, for example, workers on strike ask drivers not to remove finished goods from their plant and the drivers agree — breaking their contract by refusing their employer's orders — and, as a result, their employer is in breach of his commercial contract with the struck employer then, on the face of it, there will be secondary action within the act.

But *such secondary action will not be automatically unlawful.* Rather, it will be protected where

— the *purpose* or the *principal purpose* of the secondary action is to directly *prevent or disrupt* the supply during a *trade dispute* of goods or services between an *employer party to the dispute* and the *employer under the contract of employment to which the secondary action relates* and

— the secondary action is *likely to achieve that purpose.*

These complex provisions meant that pure secondary action — solidarity strikes where there was no contractual relationship between those involved in the primary strike and those seeking to help them — was not protected. Engineering workers taking

Figure 2: SECONDARY ACTION AND THE TORT OF INDUCEMENT TO BREACH OF CONTRACT

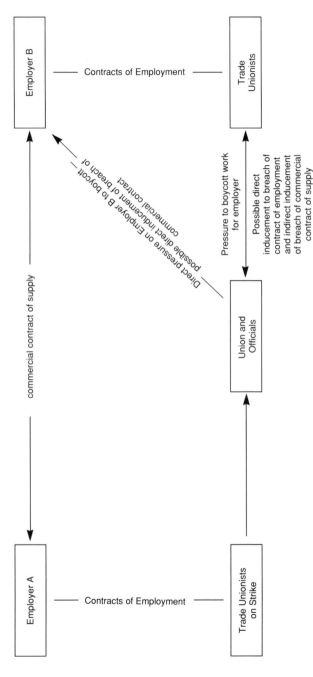

The 1974 Trade Union and Labour Relations Act sought to protect trade unionists against these liabilities where they took action in contemplation or furtherance of a trade dispute.

Figure 3: SECONDARY ACTION UNDER THE 1980 ACT

Only action in black square protected where 'in contemplation or futherance of a trade dispute' and subject to tests of 'purpose' and 'likelihood of achievement'.

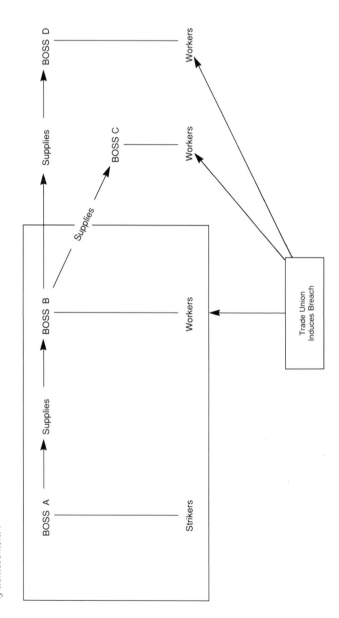

industrial action to support dismissed workers in another company, print workers taking action to support nurses, electrical workers taking action over GCHQ — none of these would come within the definition of secondary action and would therefore go unprotected.

Only secondary action where there was a *contractual relationship* between primary and secondary employers would, on the face of it, be lawful *subject to* surviving the tests of *purpose* and *likelihood of success.* And these tests were extremely open ones designed to cater for the fertile imagination of the judges.

For example, the year before the Act was passed the Court of Appeal had issued an injunction against the NUJ on the grounds that the *principal purpose* of members in Fleet Street boycotting Press Association copy was not *to prevent or disrupt the supply of goods* but only to demonstrate solidarity. The action was, moreover, according to the strike strategists on the bench, not reasonably capable of furthering the NUJ's dispute with the national newspaper.

Whilst the purpose of these provisions was clear, their complexity made them difficult to understand and there were loopholes. For example, they did not appear to cover the position where workers on strike *went directly to a secondary employer* and got *him not his workers* to break a commercial contract with the employer of the workers on strike.

Acts to Compel Union Membership (*Employment Act 1980 s.18*)

In the mid-1970s SLADE (which has now amalgamated with the National Graphical Association) recruited members in art studios and advertising agencies by informing employers that unless their workforce joined the union SLADE members in the printing industry would refuse to handle their work. This was an example of a union 'following the job' and responding to changes in technology and the organisation of industry. Similar methods were used by other unions. But, because of the importance closed shops in the printing industry had assumed for the Conservatives, this particular example attracted their attention.

In order to stimulate public opinion the new government commissioned an inquiry by a Q.C. Andrew Leggatt. The criticism of the unions in the Leggatt Report then laid the ground for proposals for legislation in a consultative paper, which portrayed SLADE as a gangster organisation extracting "protection money" from employers and mounting "a systematic campaign of recruitment in this industry without regard to the wishes of those it was seeking to recruit".

The 1980 Act aimed at making this kind of approach unlawful. Workers, it said, would lose the immunities and the protections that legislation such as the *Trade Union and Labour Relations Act* had given them against actions such as *conspiracy* or *inducement to breach of contract* if they attempted to use threats or interference to compel workers to become members of a particular union.

S.18 stated that if trade unionists interfered or threatened to interfere with employment contracts or with commercial contracts through interference with employment contracts with the *objective of compelling workers to become members of a particular union or unions* they would be open to legal action for injunctions and damages.

By threatening to instruct their members in print not to handle work from advertising agencies SLADE was threatening interference with the contracts of employment between the print workers and their employer. By doing this they were also indirectly interfering with the commercial contract between the printer and the advertising agency. This was done for the purpose of recruiting the advertising agency workers into a particular union. In future it *would be outlawed.*

Social Security
(Social Security Act 1980; Social Security (No.2) Act 1980)

In a further attempt to undermine industrial action legislation knocked £12 a week (later updated) off the social entitlement of dependents of strikers even though the majority of unions paid out less than this in dispute benefit. Those taking industrial action were also affected by other cuts in social security such as the de-indexation of benefits.

Discussion Questions

1. Was the legislation introduced by the Labour Governments 1974-79 'a militants' charter' as the Conservatives believed?
2. Why did Mrs Thatcher win the 1979 General Election? Did she have a mandate for her legislation on employment and unions programme?
3. What are the arguments for and against the closed shop? Was the legal position on the closed shop prior to 1980 satisfactory?
4. How useful was the *Employment Protection Act's* procedure on union recognition? Was it worth defending?
5. "The changes introduced in 1979-80 on unfair dismissal, maternity and other 'individual' employment rights, as well as the changes in industrial tribunal procedure represented some of the most important and overlooked of Mrs Thatcher's measures". Do you agree?

CHAPTER 3

The Second Cut is the Deepest

World history would indeed be very easy to make if the struggle were taken
up only on condition that the prospects were unmistakeably favourable —
Karl Marx

THE UNIONS' RESPONSE

The essence of the unions' argument against the 1980 measures
was straightforward. There was no need for legislative action. If
there *were* abuses in relation to the closed shop, union discipline,
picketing and secondary action they were too small scale to justify
legislation. They should be sorted out by voluntary means — at the
most by agreement between the TUC and the government. Legal
measures as well as the cuts in employment protection rights could
sour industrial relations, provoke conflict and arrest constructive
measures to improve industrial relations. Basically the TUC's
position was that the government was introducing conflict into an
industrial relations situation which was on the whole satisfactory
— any minor problems could be sorted out through negotiation not
legislation.

When it was clear that legislation was inevitable the practical
response was conditioned by the fact that the unions were
ideologically and organisationally unprepared for Thatcherism and
its legal offensive. This was particularly true of the TUC. As Len
Murray said in 1982 "we underestimated the extent to which the
ground had been prepared for the attack".[1] Reflecting later on he
commented

> We didn't believe a lot of what she was saying ... we just didn't believe it. Our
> major error was that we didn't believe that she was committed to a very radical
> reorganisation in the industrial relations field.[2]

The TUC initially comforted themselves with the belief that the
1980 Act and the related measures represented *the totality* of Mrs
Thatcher's serious legal plans. They did not understand Thatcherism
and they hoped and prayed that Thatcher would do a U-turn as
unemployment and industrial problems multiplied — just as her
predecessor Heath had done.

Whatever their position the bitty, piecemeal nature of the
legislation, despite its wide sweep when examined as a whole,

made co-ordinated opposition difficult. As the TUC pointed out, it lacked the "once and for all", monolithic nature of Ted Heath's massive *Industrial Relations Act*. There was no similar set of institutions focused on the National Industrial Relations Court. There was no central requirement in the 1980 legislation — such as the requirement to register under the 1971 legislation — opposition to which could establish a unifying focus for the unions. Moreover, there was the demoralising influence of the years 1974-79 with growing unemployment, wage cuts and wage controls and then the blitz on manufacturing industry from 1979. This placed the rank and file who had broken through the *Industrial Relations Act* over the imprisonment of the Pentonville Dockers in a weaker position. The TUC's response was, therefore, muted and limited.

● The TUC General Council met Jim Prior on November 29th 1979, January 10th and March 4th 1980. They stated their opposition to the proposed legislation and Len Murray urged on the Employment Secretary a voluntary approach: many of the problems the government was concerned about could be overcome by *using the TUC*, not by legislating. The TUC would, for example, be prepared to strengthen the *Codes of Practice on Picketing and the Closed Shop* issued under the Labour Government: "The TUC's willingness to discuss how employers, unions and government could improve industrial relations without legislation was reaffirmed".[3] This offer was rejected by the government which had no intention of maintaining the corporatist style relationship with the TUC which obtained under Labour.

● The Bill was published in December 1979 and in January 1980 a Conference of Principal Officers of Unions — rather than the more serious Conference of Executives — was convened by the TUC to discuss the legislation. It was followed, between February and April, by a series of half day conferences organised by the TUC Regional Councils. The TUC organised a public demonstration on March 9th 1980 with a march from Hyde Park to Trafalgar Square.

● In April 1980 the General Council informed affiliates that they should not apply for the public funds available for ballots as this could "lead the way for the Government to take steps to make ballots mandatory as was done under the previous government's Industrial Relations Act".[4]

● The TUC issued a number of pamphlets, *Beat The Act* and *Bargain To Beat The Act* which placed the emphasis of opposition on *collective bargaining* to restore the erosion of rights the legislation represented. The number of Campaign Workshops organised by the TUC Education Service between December and the autumn Congress was surprisingly low. The TUC did not even produce a video of the March 9th demonstration as "the costs were prohibitive".[5] There was no intention of mounting a campaign to stop the Bill reaching the statute book nor did affiliates attempt to mount industrial action as the engineers had over Ted Heath's Bill. In the build-up to the TUC's *Day of Action* on May 14th there was no call for strike action and the response to the initiative was patchy. The TUC's view that "the Day of Action had caught the attention of the British people, drawing sharply to their notice the crisis developing in the economy"[6] was an over optimistic one. The other major protest the *Union Day*, in June 1980, was presented largely in terms of lunchtime demonstrations and had only a small impact.

● The statement of opposition adopted by the September Congress was — apart from the prohibitions on funds for ballots — rhetorical. Congress called on the General Council "to maintain a sustained and vigorous campaign of non-co-operation with the Government including if necessary industrial action"[7] — but there were no specific proposals for non-co-operation such as a ban on talks or withdrawal from the NEDC, industrial tribunals or other bodies. Congress again stressed collective bargaining as an antidote to the law, despite the deteriorating climate as unemployment soared, and called on the next Labour Government to repeal the Tory measures.

● In accordance with this approach as the 1980 Act began to be used against trade unionists in early 1980, the TUC left decisions on response to individual affiliates.

BACKGROUND TO THE 1982 ACT

The 1980 Act had hardly settled on the statute book before the campaign for 'the other half' was underway. In November 1980 the Conservative Party Centre for Policy Studies produced a paper *Liberties and Liabilities: The Case For Trade Union Reform* which argued that the 1980 measures were simply a beginning — there was a need to press on, particularly to curtail further the ambit of legitimate industrial action. A poll organised by the right wing Institute of Directors showed its members 8-1 in favour of new legislation in the 1981-82 Parliamentary Session. More than 100

Conservative backbenchers signed a Commons motion calling on Jim Prior to take tougher action on the Closed Shop.

Prior had managed to convince the Cabinet not to go too far too fast. The price he had agreed to pay was the publication of proposals for a second round of legislation. In January 1981, he introduced a 110 page Green Paper *Trade Union Immunities*. This document outlined the Conservative case for further trade union reform, arguing that, "trade unions have too few obligations and too much power" and that the unions' present power resulted in economically disruptive strikes and underpinned

> The persistence of restrictive practices, of outdated working methods and of overmanning ... (which) have contributed just as powerfully, if more insidiously, to our economic problems. Such practices and the attitudes they embody have stood in the way of the achievement of high productivity, high output and high real wages.[8]

The Green Paper examined the full range of possible changes in employment law, including a move away from a system of immunities in favour of positive rights and proposals for making collective agreements enforceable, although it was clear that the Government were not treating these and many of the other ideas floated very seriously. Detailed consideration *was* given to the possibility of a return to the legal position after the 1901 *Taff Vale Case* in which unions had been made financially responsible for the unlawful acts of their officials. The great advantage in this, it was felt, was that it would place unions in the same position as companies and individuals and stimulate them to exercise greater control over their officials and members. On the other hand, there would be a need to carefully define the extent of the unions' responsibility and guard against the danger of internal dissension and unofficial breakaways. Proposals to use the law to make *all* closed shop agreements void were also examined. However, it was felt that this could lead to further difficulties as it would be necessary to then penalise employers or unions seeking to enforce these agreements. Such a change might also simply produce a reversion to informal custom and practice and strengthen employer collusion in the maintenance of 100% trade unionism.

The Green Paper contained no precise proposals but it enabled groups like the CBI to discuss and formulate what they wanted. The CBI had now come round to the Government's point of view and in the words of Director-General Sir Terence Beckett they "wanted tougher union laws". The EEF were more cautious and the IPM pronounced themselves "opposed to any further legislation".[9] The TUC insisted that the Green Paper's basic assumption was incorrect:

as the economy went into recession the unions were not *too strong*. They were *weaker* than in the previous two decades. The TUC opposed any change in the definition of a trade dispute, secondary action and the closed shop. They were particularly exercised at the idea of trade union funds being put at risk. They argued that proposals to make the union responsible for the wrongs of its officers and representatives was to misunderstand the democratic basis of trade union organisation where power lay at the bottom of the pyramid not at the top. The closed shop was supported by many managers as well as the workforce. Abuses were few and did not require the legal sledgehammer to deal with them.[10]

Mrs Thatcher, in turn, expressed impatience with Jim Prior and talked directly to employers about what she thought they should want. She personally met Joanna Harris, sacked from her job by a local authority in the West Midlands because she would not join NALGO. The judgement of the European Court of Justice in *Young, James and Webster v United Kingdom* ([1983] Industrial Relations Law Reports 35), which involved three railway workers sacked under the British Rail closed shop agreement was published in the summer of 1981 and provided further opportunities to develop public opinion.

The first cases under the 1980 legislation were also beginning to come on stream. They were few in number. For example, by the end of 1981 only 16 cases had been brought under s.4 and a smaller number under s.7. However, as cases under the crucial industrial action provisions reached the courts — *Wilkes PCA Data Supplies v Bunn* in March 1981, *Chloride Automotive Batteries v Bunfield* April 1981, *Mersey Docks and Harbour Board v Verrinder*, August 1981, ([1982] Industrial Relations Law Reports 152), — it became clear that the trade union officials against whom injunctions were being granted were *obeying these injunctions*. There was no rank and file revolt, no backlash, no mass solidarity action. In practice the unions were rolling with the punches and accepting the legislation. From the vantage point of 10 Downing Street mass unemployment and internal differences were seen as having taken the wind out of their sails.

For Mrs Thatcher it was time to go again. In the summer of 1981 as the newspapers headlined, in reference to the Conservative Party and employer organisations, "Chorus to curb the unions" Jim Prior was removed as Employment Secretary and despatched to Belfast. He was replaced by Norman Tebbit and a second major round of legislation was announced in the Queen's Speech in November. What became the *Employment Act 1982* was intended to build upon the foundations of its predecessor and plug some of the gaps the 1980 Act had left unsealed. It covered a wide range of issues. We again look at each in turn.

UNION ORGANISATION

As union membership declined because of the increase in unemployment in 1980-81, the Government hoped that the closed shop provisions in the 1980 Act would facilitate a secondary haemorrhage and encourage workers in employment to leave their unions — further weakening union organisation. There was little evidence of this and critics of Jim Prior's policies began to argue that, whilst the 1980 Act had curbed the *extension* of trade unionism, it did little to weaken it where it was already well established. Moreover, the levels of compensation offered to whose who left the unions and suffered for it in areas of strong organisation were such as to deter anybody from standing up to be counted. Who was going to risk losing their job, where a union could ensure that this would happen, in return for an average industrial tribunal award of under £500? The government agreed that there was a need for further action to weaken union organisation.

The Closed Shop
(Employment Act 1982 s.2, 7, sch.1)
Norman Tebbit now followed up Jim Prior's legislation on the closed shop.

Ballots for all Closed Shops
You will recall that the 1980 Act required that closed shop agreements or arrangements taking effect after 14th August 1980 needed approval by *an 80% vote in a secret ballot* before they could be used to protect an employer against an action in an industrial tribunal alleging that he had unfairly dismissed or victimised a non-unionist. The 1982 Act now applied this provision to closed shops *in existence before August 1980 i.e. to all closed shops.* This is a classic example of the step-by-step approach. The Act now provided that
— where a closed shop agreement or arrangement took effect *before* 15th August 1980 then, to protect an employer against legal action for dismissal or victimisation, it would have to be approved in a ballot. The ballots would have to be *held every 5 years.* In the ballot *80% of those to be covered* by the agreement or *85% of those actually voting* would have to agree to a closed shop.

— where a closed shop agreement took effect on or *after* 15th August 1980, then to protect an employer against legal action for dismissal or victimisation, it would have to be approved in a ballot in which *80% of those to be covered by the agreement* voted for the closed shop (1980 Act). But approval of the closed shop would have to be *renewed every 5 years* by a ballot in which either *80% of those eligible to vote* or, alternatively, *85% of those actually voting* agreed to the closed shop.

— These provisions of the 1982 Act would take effect on *1st November 1984.*

Existing Workers Not Covered

— As with the 1980 provisions employers would only be protected against legal action by employees on the grounds of their non-membership of a union *if the dismissed or victimised worker was not employed at the date of the ballot.*

Joining Trade Unions

— If pressure was brought to bear against employers to sack or victimise a non-unionist then, under the previous law, an *employer* could join the union or trade unionists to any legal case. The individual or union might have to bear a share of any compensation awarded. The 1982 Act now extended this right to join the union or an individual to the case to *the complainant* — the dismissed or victimised worker — who was more likely, in practice, to join unions or shop stewards to the proceedings than an employer. Between 1980 and 1982 there was no reported case of an *employer* using the mechanism.

Interim Relief

— *The Employment Protection (Consolidation) Act 1978* had enabled workers who claimed unfair dismissal on the grounds that they were being sacked because of their union membership or activities to avail themselves of a procedure for *interim relief.* They could present a complaint to a tribunal within seven days of the dismissal and the tribunal could grant an order continuing the workers employment until a full hearing took place. The new Act extended this right to workers *claiming dismissal for non-membership of a trade union.*

Higher Compensation

The level of compensation available to workers found by tribunals to have been dismissed for non-membership of a trade union was increased beyond the levels normally awarded in unfair dismissal cases. Having in 1980 abolished the minimum Basic Award of two weeks pay in unfair dismissal cases the government now stated that in cases involving non-membership of a union *the basic award should not be less than £2,000.* In addition to the Basic Award and the Compensatory Award, a new *Special Award* would be available to successful applicants in these cases

— Where applicants requested re-instatement or re-engagement, where the tribunal did not make an order for re-instatement or re-engagement, or where it did make such an order but was satisfied by the employers' argument that compliance was not practicable, the Special Award would be either 104 weeks pay or £10,000 — whichever was the bigger sum subject to a limit of £20,000.

— Where a tribunal made an order for re-instatement or re-engagement which was simply not complied with by an employer, then the Special Award would be increased to 156 weeks pay or £15,000, whichever was the greater sum. This calculation would not be subject to a maximum figure.

— These new levels of compensation were extended by the government, after the disparity was pointed out, to apply to cases where workers were dismissed for *membership of a trade union.*

— These compensation figures have been subsequently updated to take account of inflation.

Relief For Closed Shop Victims

The 1982 Act gave Norman Tebbit powers to compensate workers sacked for non-membership of a trade union between 1974 and 1980. This was *in spite of the fact that under the law of the land as it then existed, having passed democratically through Parliament, these individuals were fairly dismissed.* The government believed that the numbers involved were under 400, although, in practice, only half that figure applied for compensation. The government estimated the cost to the taxpayer of this retrospective legislation at £2.25 million.

Union Labour Only Contracts (*Employment Act 1982 s.12-14*)

In a further step to weaken trade union organisation and the spread of trade union membership

— The 1982 Act rendered void any term or condition in a contract for the supply of goods or services which required work under the contract to be performed by non-union labour or *by union labour.*

— The Act also outlawed terminating a contract because non-union labour was used. Also, keeping a contractor off an approved list for supplying goods or services or tendering, because that contractor employed non-trade unionists.

— Trade unions which used pressure against an employer to ensure that he continued to operate union labour only practices would not be protected by the immunities. They would also be liable if they induced workers to break their contracts of employment by refusing to work with non-trade unionists or handle goods supplied by them.

INDUSTRIAL ACTION

I use the word 'neuter' because I've been told I must not use the vernacular when describing what I'm doing to the unions.
Norman Tebbit

Mrs Thatcher and Norman Tebbit were dissatisfied with what they saw as Prior's "tinkering" with union rights to take industrial action. They wanted to do two things: take Prior's piecemeal changes several stages further. But, also, anchor past, present and future piecemeal changes within a framework which went to the heart of trade union activities. This framework was provided by the principle enunciated in the *Taff Vale Case* and shunned since 1906. This principle stated that unions were responsible for the unlawful acts of their agents — officers, stewards and sometimes members. Legal action could, therefore, be taken against a union as an organisation if such unlawful action occurred. And if injunctions were awarded against such action and it continued, then the union and its assets would be on the line and subject to sequestration if the union was found guilty of contempt of court.

Trade Disputes
(Employment Act 1982 s.18)

By limiting the scope of 'the golden formula' the definition of a trade dispute which protected trade unions, the government could make key types of industrial action unlawful. They were also concerned about one or two recent decisions of the courts which appeared to give the unions too much room for manoeuvre. For example, the judges had held that a strike over an issue which would have an *eventual* rather than an *immediate* impact on terms and conditions of employment fell within the definition of a trade dispute and could be protected *(Crazy Prices (N.I.) Ltd. v Hewitt* [1980] Industrial

MEANING OF TRADE DISPUTE

29(1)-

In this Act "trade dispute" means a dispute between employers and workers, or between workers and workers, which is connected with one or more of the following, that is to say -

(a) terms and conditions of employment, or the physical conditions in which any workers are required to work;

(b) engagement or non-engagement, or termination or suspension of employment or the duties of employment, of one or more workers;

(c) allocation of work or the duties of employment as between workers or groups of workers;

(d) matters of discipline;

(e) the membership or non-membership of a trade union on the part of a worker;

(f) facilities for officials of trade unions; and

(g) machinery for negotiation or consultation, and other procedures, relating to any of the foregoing matters, including the recognition by employers or employers' associations of the right of a trade union to represent workers in any such negotiation or consultation or in the carrying out of such procedures.

(2) A dispute between a Minister of the Crown and any workers shall, notwithstanding that he is not the employer of those workers, be treated for the purposes of this Act as a dispute between employer and those workers if the dispute relates-

(a) to matters which have been referred for consideration by a joint body on which, by virtue of any provision made by or under any enactment, that Minister is presented; or

(b) to matters which cannot be settled without that Minister exercising a power conferred on him by or under an enactment.

(3) There is a trade dispute for the purposes of this Act even though it relates to matters occurring outside Great Britain.

(4) A dispute to which a trade union or employers' association is a party shall be treated for the purposes of this Act as a dispute to which workers or, as the case may be, employers are parties.

(5) An act, threat or demand done or made by one person or organisation against another which, if resisted, would have led to a trade dispute with that other, shall, notwithstanding that because that other submits to the act or threat or accedes to the demand no dispute arises, be treated for the purposes of this Act as being done or made in contemplation of a trade dispute with that other.

Relations Law Reports 396). And that a dispute about *possible future* job loss where an employer decided to contract out services also fell within the definition (*Health Computing Ltd. v Meek* [1980] Industrial Relations Law Reports 437).

It was felt that there was a need to tighten up on the definition.

1. Workers And Their Employer

Before 1982, a trade dispute meant a dispute between *employers and workers.* The Act now changed this to *workers and their employer.* This would mean that in cases where trade unionists, in order to ensure basic terms and conditions were maintained, took industrial action against an employer *whose own employees —* perhaps non-trade unionists or a substitute workforce — *were not taking action* the dispute would not be protected. In 1982 this kind of case had already come up in relation to dockers taking action against shipowners who were not meeting the minimum conditions laid down by the International Transport Federation.

2. Workers And Workers

Before the 1982 Act, disputes which to some degree involved conflicts between different groups of workers — for example, over demarcation, or the introduction of new technology, fell within the definition of a trade dispute. Now the words *workers and workers* (see p.58) were simply deleted.

3. Wholly Or Mainly

Before the 1982 Act, the definition of a trade dispute stated that the dispute taking place must simply *be connected with* one or more of the matters listed on p.58. The 1982 Act deleted *connected with* and replaced those words with *relate wholly or mainly* to one or more of those matters.

This meant that where there were mixed elements in a dispute, where, for example, action was directed against government policies and could be said to have a political dimension but where the action was inspired ultimately by defence of job conditions it would be harder for the union to get the protection of the trade dispute formula. It was much easier to argue that a dispute was *connected with* the list of industrial matters in the definition than to argue that it was *wholly* — presumably 100% — or *mainly* — presumably 51% — related to these matters.

Disputes Outside the United Kingdom

Before the 1982 Act, the definition of a trade dispute stated "There is a trade dispute ... even though it relates to matters outside Great Britain" (see p.58). The 1982 Act made it unlawful for workers in Britain to take industrial action to support workers in dispute in other countries — unless the workers in Britain were *likely to be affected by the outcome* of the dispute taking place abroad in relation to one of the matters listed in the definition of a trade dispute.

If British workers employed by the same multinational as workers in other countries took solidarity action they could be subject to successful legal action unless they could convince the courts that they were likely to receive some *direct industrial benefit* if the dispute was won. International solidarity action was therefore likely to be judged unlawful in most cases.

Union Liability
(Employment Act 1982 s.15-17)

Industrial action was now more likely to be unlawful than in the past. The next step was to ensure that the union carried the can for it. If the union was to be financially penalised it was more likely to look to its assets and therefore police industrial action — and its officers and shop stewards — in a more conservative and cautious fashion.

Authorised Or Endorsed

The Act changed the law so that trade unions could be *sued in their own name* for any action which fell outside the definition of a trade dispute or specific immunities. The union would be liable whenever unlawful industrial action was *authorised or endorsed* by a *responsible person* namely

— the union executive
— anyone with power under the rulebook to authorise or endorse industrial action
— executive officers of the union such as the General Secretary or President
— any other employed official of the union
— any committee to which such an officer reports.

The industrial action would not be taken as *'authorised'* or *'endorsed'*

— if any of the above officers or committees were *prevented by the unions rules from authorising a dispute*

or

— *if the union executive or executive officers repudiated* the action of any of the above offices and bodies in authorising or endorsing the industrial action — so long as the executive or executive officers then *acted consistently with the repudiation.* The repudiation must be genuine not just a tactical means of avoiding legal penalties.

The exact scope of *authorise, endorse* and *repudiate* were left for determination by the courts in specific cases.

Damages

The Act also set limits on the damages which could be awarded against unions in any one legal action. The limits were

— £10,000 for unions with less than 5,000 members
— £15,000 for unions with between 5,000 and 25,000 members
— £125,000 for unions with between 25,000 and 100,000 members
— £250,000 for unions with more than 100,000 members.

Of course such damages would only be awarded at a full trial of the case. What was likely to trouble unions more were the unlimited fines that courts could levy and the *sequestration* of its assets that they could utilise for *contempt* if interim injunctions issued against the union were not complied with.

Sacking Strikers
(Employment Act 1982 s.9)

Under the common law employers could treat workers' action in going on strike as a repudiation of their contracts warranting dismissal. *The Employment Protection (Consolidation) Act* 1978, the product of a Labour Government, expressly stated that if an employer dismissed and refused to offer re-engagement to *all* those involved in a strike or other industrial action i.e. *if no selection took place*, then an industrial tribunal would have no jurisdiction to hear claims for unfair dismissal by any of the workers involved.

From the point of view of the employer problems occurred as to which was the unit of relevant workers from which selection could not take place. If some strikers returned to work and the employer then dismissed or refused to re-engage those still on strike at a later date had selection taken place? Was the unit from which selection cannot be made the group who walked out, or the group on strike at the time of the final dismissal decision? There was, moreover, no time limit on when selective re-engagement of an employee would give tribunals jurisdiction to hear complaints by other dismissed employees.

Time Limits

The Act changed the law to allow an employer to selectively re-engage sacked strikers provided that *more than three months has elapsed since the date of the worker's dismissal.* If an employer follows this procedure other strikers dismissed and not re-engaged will have no right to a tribunal hearing. Moreover, if an employer *does* selectively re-engage *within* three months, a worker who is not taken back must now bring a complaint to a tribunal within *six months* of the date of his or her dismissal.

Relevant Employees

The group of workers from which selection cannot take place is now defined as "those employees at the establishment who were taking part in the action at the complainant's date of dismissal". Moreover, because of the insertion, of the word 'establishment', where more than one workplace is involved in a strike or industrial action the relevant unit is the workers *at each workplace*, not *all* the workers taking action. So an employer could sack all workers at workplace 'A' but none at workplace 'B' without being guilty of selection. Therefore none of the sacked workers would be able to bring an unfair dismissal case.

These provisions thus strengthened the employers' hand in a strike situation and undermined workers' rights.

Worker Involvement
(*Employment Act s.1*)

Because of pressure from the EEC the Act included an obligation on employers to state in their company's annual report what steps had been taken in the previous 12 months to improve consultation and employee involvement.

Miscellaneous changes
(*Employment Act s.20*)

The Act also introduced a number of minor changes. Computation of qualifying periods for unfair dismissal, redundancy and for rights to minimum notice as well as computation of periods of continuous service were changed from weeks to months and years. There were very minor changes to the employers obligation to provide written particulars of employment under the *Employment Protection (Consolidation) Act* 1978.

FAIR WAGES RESOLUTION 1946

This measure required all government contractors and subcontractors to pay wages and observe terms and conditions of employment not less favourable than those established by collective bargaining in a particular trade or industry. It did not apply directly to nationalised industries or local authorities but was adopted by them. The Fair Wages Resolution was repealed by the government in 1983.

TRANSFER OF UNDERTAKINGS REGULATIONS 1981

These regulations were introduced by the government to comply with an EEC Directive. The regulations provide that where a business changes hands as a going concern there will be an automatic transfer of employment contracts, union recognition and collective agreements to the new owners. Duties are also imposed on the employer to give the unions information on transfer and to consult with them. The Regulations were far from watertight, reflecting the letter rather than the spirit of the EEC directives. They did not apply to many common takeover situations, such as a sale of shares or assets short of the whole company changing hands and there was a mechanism by which the new employer could repudiate contractual obligations.

EQUAL PAY (AMENDMENT) REGULATIONS 1983

The *Equal Pay Act* 1970 was challenged by the European Commission on the grounds that it only applied where a man and a woman did similar work. If the work was different women could claim equality only where a job evaluation study had been carried out — something a woman had no right to demand. In 1982 the European Court ruled that the UK legislation did not provide for equal pay for work of equal value as required by the Equal Pay Directive and the Treaty of Rome. As a result, these regulations, which came into effect on January 1984, allowed a woman to claim equal pay when she does work which is "in terms of the demands made on her (for instance under such headings as effort, skill and decision-making) of equal value to that of a man in the same employment". The regulations provided for an evaluation to be carried out by independent experts who drew up a report for the industrial tribunal which made the final decisions. Women found the regulations an improvement on the existing law and there was an upsurge in cases. However, applicants soon encountered legal difficulties with the courts and tribunals.

THE UNIONS' RESPONSE

Does this mean that one is inviting people to break the law?
Yes it does ...
Bill Keyes Chair of the TUC Employment Committee.

The TUC opposed the 1982 measures from an old style consensus position. Using the same language as in 1980 they condemned the proposals:

because they would introduce highly contentious laws into industrial relations — laws which could be exploited by unscrupulous employers and eccentric individuals seeking to disrupt established customary arrangements and to inflame feelings in already difficult disputes.[11]

If this was naive and failed to understand that for the government the collaboration and partnership in industrial relations of the 1960s and 1970s was a thing of the past — the government was jam-packed with "eccentric individuals seeking to disrupt customary arrangements" and the government wanted *all* employers, with or without scruples, to exploit the new laws — the TUC did argue forcefully that the legislation could undermine union organisation, destabilise the closed shop and "restrict severely the range of actions trade unionists can lawfully take to bring pressure to bear on employers in dispute. A wide range of traditional and hitherto accepted forms of union action will potentially be affected".[12]

The publication of Norman Tebbit's proposals for further legislation in a consultative document on 23rd November 1981, therefore, convinced the TUC of the need for a firmer and more co-ordinated approach. Tebbit's proposals, Len Murray stated, were "non-negotiable". The proposals on union funds struck at the heart of union activities and the consensus on their legal position in society. Nonetheless, the General Council's Employment Committee met Tebbit on 16th December although the aim was to impress upon him their "outright rejection of his proposals". At their December meeting the General Council agreed to step up their campaign and this resolve was strengthened when the Bill was published on 28th January 1982.[13]

However, there were differences as to the approach to be taken. The position of the TUC staff was, as usual, careful and cautious. In a paper produced for the Employment Committee in January, they emphasised that attempts by the TUC to co-ordinate action against the legislation would be very difficult. When it came to refusing to comply with injunctions, the paper claimed that events were likely to move very speedily leaving the TUC with little scope for co-ordination. Individual unions were unlikely to give the

General Council strong powers to co-ordinate action. A call for sympathy strikes in defence of a union challenging the law could, in any case, open the TUC itself to legal action. The paper again stressed the lack of any central institution compared with the *Industrial Relations Act* on which union hostility could be focused. When it came to decisions on refusing to comply with injunctions, or with closed shop ballots, the TUC itself stated that "ultimately the choice must be for the unions to make in the light of their own circumstances".[14]

The Wembley Principles

This conservative approach was not shared by union leaders representing a majority of trade unionists. It must be remembered that throughout 1981 the Government was facing serious economic difficulties and was behind in the opinion polls. In the Labour Party the left — if very temporarily — had the upper hand. There was still hope for a Thatcher U-turn. Nonetheless the position taken by the moderate General Secretary of the GMBATU David Basnett who called for strikes against the government and discipline against unions which co-operated with its legislation was particularly surprising. Whilst the AEU and the EETPU shared the doubts of Congress House, the militant position of David Basnett — and of the print unions who felt particularly endangered by the closed shop and recruitment provisions of the law — swung the balance towards the left on the General Council, such as the TGWU and NUM who favoured a hard co-ordinated approach led by the TUC.

A conference of Executives of TUC affiliated unions met at the Wembley Conference Centre on 5th April 1982. A platform of opposition to the legislation was agreed almost unanimously — only Equity and the National Union of Teachers opposed one or two points. The right wing led by Len Murray were able to stop initial proposals for withdrawal from the NEDC and similar bodies and limit the withdrawal from industrial tribunals. Otherwise the majority got what they wanted although key points in the principles were surrounded by more moderate small print.

At Wembley the air was red hot with militant declarations. A union leader well on the right of the movement, such as Bill Sirs, could say of the agreed statement "... my union will support it 100 per cent on the basis that it just does not go far enough".[15] Len Murray in urging adoption of the Wembley Principles stormed: "Employers have got to understand — they have got to be made to understand — that they could become casualties of this Act. We should not pretend to threaten what we cannot be sure to deliver".[16] The statesmanlike

The Wembley Principles

1 Campaign
Affiliated unions should affirm their commitment to conduct a campaign among their own members to highlight the dangers in the Employment Bill. They should also affirm their support for the TUC's campaign against the proposed legislation.

2 100 per cent trade union membership
Affiliated unions shall not hold or participate in secret ballots on union membership agreements under conditions laid down in the Employment Act 1980 and the Employment Bill 1982.

3 Public funds for union ballots
Affiliated unions shall observe Congress policy and not seek or accept public funds for union ballots under the Employment Act 1980 ballot funds scheme.

4 Closer working between unions
Affiliated unions should, when in dispute with an employer, consult closely with other unions whose support may be necessary to make industrial action effective or whose interests will be affected by the action. The further aim, wherever possible, should be to co-ordinate and concert negotiations and industrial action.

5 Support from the Movement
Where the General Council receive a request to assist a union faced by or experiencing legal action by an employer, and are satisfied that assistance from the Movement is justified, they are empowered
(i)   to co-ordinate action by other affiliated unions in support of the union in difficulties, including, if necessary, calling for industrial action against the employer concerned, or more widely;
(ii) to provide financial assistance to a union which experiences severe financial problems as a result of damaging actions.

6 The TUC Disputes Principles and Procedures
Affiliated unions shall continue to observe strictly the requirements of the TUC Disputes Principles and Procedures. The General Council will support affiliated unions which, having consulted the TUC, take steps in accordance with its advice to maintain TUC procedures, and will be prepared to assist unions where necessary to meet the costs of defending a legal action and consequent compensation awards which may arise in these circumstances.

7 Industrial Tribunals and the Employment Appeal Tribunal
No trade union member of an industrial tribunal or the Employment Appeal Tribunal should serve *on cases arising from the application of a union membership agreement or arrangement.*

8 Levy
The General Council shall be empowered to impose on all affiliated unions a levy of 10p per member in order to establish a Campaign and Defence Fund to meet financial commitments arising from the proposed legislation. The General Council shall be empowered to impose a further levy, or levies, if, in their view, this is necessary.

David Basnett urged that the Act must be stopped when used by widespread industrial action led and co-ordinated by the TUC

> I will not mince words. The General Council are recommending that we use our industrial strength. ... We either act swiftly and decisively to make sure that the new law cannot work or we risk emasculation ... Let none of us be in any doubt whatsoever of the seriousness of the step we are taking here today. We are empowering the General Council to co-ordinate the action of affiliated unions against employers seeking to use this law. That is a massive step for this movement to take and it is a historically unique step .. it means that the General Council will be prepared to recommend actions which may well make affiliated unions vulnerable to legal action and could indeed make the TUC itself vulnerable.[17]

As *The Guardian* noted: "If rhetoric and ringing endorsements by union delegates are any guide then the TUC and the Government are on collision course".[18] The principles looked to provide a firm platform for co-ordinated opposition. But the moderates had not completely gone over the top, nor had Congress House staff been completely outflanked. For example, the key point 5 was softened by the following statement

> That cannot mean ... that a union encountering legal difficulties should automatically receive support from the TUC. They would need to be satisfied that the union was justified in the action it was taking and would also expect the union to take full account of views they might express about the form and continuation of the action which had given rise to the legal case.[19]

The TUC was therefore far from committed to confrontation. On the contrary, the Wembley Principles gave it ample room for manoeuvre.

From Advance To Retreat

Despite the orgy of verbal militancy the second major Employment Bill wended its way through Parliament, receiving the Royal Assent on 28th October 1982. A number of further cases came to court under the 1980 Act. But they were few and they were handled carefully. For example, when Sean Geraghty, the EETPU's Fleet Street Branch Secretary, was found in contempt of an injunction restraining industrial action in support of the NHS pay claim, in August 1982, the judge imposed only a derisory fine of £350. It was backed up with the threat of a prison sentence of one week if it was not paid within two months. (*Express Newspapers plc and others v Mitchell and others* [1982] Industrial Relations Law Reports 465). The hesitancy concerning the law of employers facing strong trade unions and the hangover of 1970s attitudes was demonstrated when an anonymous donor, reckoned to be a Fleet Street proprietor, paid the fine.

Developments in the case law on industrial action centred on the definition of a trade dispute were also running against the unions.

Workers might, for example, ask a secondary employer not to instruct his employees to work on production for a struck office. If there was a refusal there would, arguably, be a dispute over the terms and conditions of the secondary workers so that secondary action would be protected. However, in a House of Lords case, three out of five Law Lords refused to accept this:

> A trade union cannot turn a dispute which in reality has no connection with terms and conditions of employment into a dispute connected with terms and conditions of employment by insisting that the employer inserts appropriate terms and conditions into the contracts of employment into which he enters. Lord Cross in *Universe Tankships of Monrovia v International Transport Workers Federation* [1983] 1 A.C 366.

This would appear to put in question all 'hot cargo' clauses in agreements stating that workers will not have to handle certain products. Even more extreme was a statement by Lord Diplock in the *Dimbleby* case (see p.73) where he claimed that a trade dispute could only be about *current* terms and conditions of employment — a view which would place the majority of disputes over pay and conditions outside the protection of the now very reduced 'Golden Formula'. It was clear that the judges not workers in struggle would decide when there was a trade dispute and the changes in the 1980 and 1982 Act greatly facilitated judicial control.

A more direct test of the new law came in October 1983, some 18 months after the Wembley Conference. But those 18 months had seen the Falklands War, the stabilisation of unemployment at well over 3 million, most importantly, a crushing Conservative victory in the 1983 General Election which gave the upper hand to the conservative forces in the TUC expounding the new realism and, in consequence, the election of the 'new realist' Kinnock-Hattersley leadership in the Labour Party.

In the *Mercury Communication* case (*Mercury Communications Ltd v Post Office Engineering Union* [1983] Industrial Relations Law Reports 485, 494) the Post Office Engineering Union was instructing its members not to connect Mercury, a new company, to the British Telecom network. This was part of its fight against privatisation which the union believed would lead to job loss amongst its members. The High Court refused to grant Mercury an injunction but the Court of Appeal, led by Sir John Donaldson whose family owned shares in Mercury's parent company, reversed the High Court's decision. The Court of Appeal based its judgement on the fact that the 1982 Act had changed the definition of a trade dispute. In order to bring themselves within its protection a union now had to show its dispute was *wholly* or *mainly* about terms and conditions of employment rather than just *connected* with them (see p.59). The

Appeal Court felt that defence of jobs was a minor ingredient in this dispute. The major factor was the campaign that the union was mounting against the government's privatisation policies. *That* was what the industrial action was *mainly* about the court held. The action was mainly *political* not *industrial*, motivated by political hostility to Thatcher not fear of job loss.

An injunction was, therefore, issued and the union held a special conference to decide whether or not to comply with it. Len Murray's advice in a letter to the executive was non-committal but he stated that it was not TUC policy to encourage unions to break the law. The union decided to accept the injunction.

The implications for the unions of the far reaching changes in legislation were now becoming very clear. In the case of *NWL v Woods* ([1979] Industrial Relations Law Reports 478) a ship, the *Nawala*, was sold by its owners who observed the conditions laid down by the International Transport Workers Federation to a Hong Kong Company which hired a new crew at rates below ITWF minima. When the ITWF got TGWU dockers to boycott the ship the owners won an injunction on the grounds that the dispute was about flags of convenience not conditions of employment: the dispute was a political not an industrial dispute. This was overturned on appeal and the House of Lords held the dispute fell within the Golden Formula as it was genuinely *connected* with terms and conditions of employment. Now under the *Mercury* crystallisation of the 1982 Act's provisions such a dispute would be unlawful because it did not involve a dispute between workers and their own employers, because it was about conditions outside the UK and because, in all probability, it was political not industrial. Given the increasing reach of government policies and their increasing impact on trade unionists the "wholly or mainly" test was a godsend to judges and employers — given the existence of a political element in so many disputes. The change meant that not only were restrictions on using industrial action for clearly political ends ruled out — in violation of basic human rights to withdraw labour — but the right to strike was compromised as in *Mercury*, where it was essentially industrial matters concerning job security which were at issue. In this sense public sector employees were being disadvantaged as against their private sector counterparts.

The law was working. But not for long. At the same time Shell, ignoring the 1982 Act, successfully took out injunctions against two TGWU shop stewards at Stanlow under the picketing provisions of the 1980 Act. When the orders were ignored they did not move against the union itself, nor did they initiate proceedings for contempt. In the following month the *Dimbleby* case broke and

SOGAT was fined £10,000 for contempt of court when it ignored injunctions in two cases involving newspaper distributors and BPCC. That same month a major test of the law began.

*   *   *

THE EDDIE SHAH STORY

Eddie Shah ran a small group which published five *Messenger* free newspapers in the Lancashire and Cheshire area. He had problems with the National Graphical Association and when he opened a new typesetting plant at Bury he tried to exclude the union. The dismissal of six NGA members at the *Stockport Messenger* led the union to mount pickets at Bury and more importantly at Shah's Warrington plant to which most of the work done by NGA members had been transferred. For the NGA, the closed shop, control of membership and control of technology in the growing freesheet sector of the industry were key issues. They, therefore, asked all other NGA members not to work on and all advertisers not to use the Messenger group's papers. This meant that for Eddie Shah his business was at stake.

In October 1983, Shah obtained injunctions against the print union and against the NUJ whose members had been asked not to handle copy. The two injunctions issued against the NGA under the 1980 and 1982 Acts ordered a halt to secondary picketing at Shah's Bury and Warrington plants and the withdrawal of NGA instructions to members to boycott Messenger newspapers which under s.14 of the 1982 Act constituted pressure to enforce 100% membership. The NGA ignored the orders and, on 17th November 1983, the High Court found the Association in contempt of court. A £50,000 fine was increased by a further £100,000 on 25th November as mass picketing of Shah's Warrington depot intensified and the judge also ordered the sequestration of the NGA's assets. In December the NGA was fined a further half a million pounds. An NGA strike in Fleet Street at the end of November produced further legal action by the Newspaper Proprietors Association.

Lessons

Certain key issues were already discernible in this dispute. The mass picketing at Warrington had been greeted by mass policing. The firmness and the strategic and technological sophistication of the police demonstrated that, supported by the government, they were determined to banish mass picketing from industrial disputes. At Warrington they succeeded in drawing its sting. Employers like

Eddie Shah facing acute financial pressures were prepared to go to law. In this they received encouragement from bodies like the Institute of Directors and Mrs Thatcher herself.

When the law *was* used it was clear in practice that it made it extremely difficult for unions to win disputes outside the struck workplace. The legislation protected employers transferring work and it protected their dismissal of striking workers at the primary workplace. It was pointless for the Stockport Six to picket their workplace — nothing was happening there! Yet they were banned by the 1980 Act from picketing the depot at Warrington to which their work had been transferred whilst boycotts of the Messenger Group by other workers was restrained by the 1982 Act. If the law was *accepted* the closed shop, union control of labour and union control of the work process were endangered. Moreover, if the police in a new political climate were demonstrating a new resolve, so were the judges. They were now prepared to move swiftly to sequestration and total sequestration — the first in British trade union history — at that, rather than simply sending in accountants to collect fines.

The Wembley Principles at Work

All the factors which had provoked the necessity for co-ordinated resistance and the Wembley Principles had now come to fruition. The Wembley Principles had been drafted on the clear basis that unions could not fight the law one by one. They would all hang individually if they did not hang together. The truth of this was now being proved in practice. The NGA, one of the unions with most to lose if the law bit and industrial relations began to be conducted according to the principles of the Conservative legislation, had been one of the strongest partisans of the Wembley declaration. They were now determined to use it.

The NGA approached the TUC for help under clause 5 of the Wembley Principles. That clause, however, as we have seen, only *empowered* the TUC to organise supportive action. It did not direct or mandate the TUC to support a union subject to legal action under the Employment legislation. The TUC had to be "satisfied that assistance from the Movement is justified". Len Murray and the TUC bureaucracy now used a variety of *ad hoc* arguments to justify not using their discretion to support the NGA — Eddie Shah was a small employer; other unions would not answer a call for supportive action; the time was not ripe.

There was, of course, some truth in these arguments. Shah could not be pressurized in the way a big conglomerate could be pressurized. He had more to lose and less to lose. He was the darling of Thatcherism. He might well hold out even if the whole printing industry was halted. It is, however, very difficult to believe that the TUC was acting strategically, weighing up the pros and cons of going over the top in this case or in another case, searching for the right moment, willing to operate Wembley against Robert Maxwell but not Eddie Shah.

In reality, the refusal to use the discretion Wembley had given them was for the TUC a matter of *principle*. They feared with some justification that if they supported the NGA the writ-happy Shah would sue them too! They were not, and, in any foreseeable circumstances never would be, prepared to take this risk. Len Murray convinced the General Council as the NGA's action spread to Fleet Street that the TUC should not call for supportive industrial action from other unions. When, in early December, the NGA called a 24 hour print strike and the Employment Committee reversed this position, the General Secretary publically disowned them. His position was later endorsed by the General Council but condemned — when it was too late — by the 1984 Congress.

The limitations of the Wembley Principles — already theoretically evident from a close scrutiny of the small print — were now exposed in practice. The TUC was not prepared to use the powers of clause 5, the heart without which the platform of opposition could never move into effective opposition. Everybody in the heady atmosphere of Wembley had assumed that where a union was attacked in the fashion the NGA was, then the General Council would automatically be "satisfied that assistance from the Movement is justified" because the orchestration of an effective response to attacks like Eddie Shah's was what clause 5 *was there for.* But when it came to the crunch the majority of the General Council turned turtle.

A Real Set-Back

It could be argued that there was justification for backing-down. Unemployment was well over 3 million. A strong Conservative Government had only six months previously been returned with a massive majority. The Labour Party leadership was firmly moderate. The roots of rank and file resistance had been sapped by developments since 1979, particularly the blitz of manufacturing industry. Right or wrong the government was winning the battle of ideas, the unions were unpopular and what would be tantamount to a call for a general strike in support of the NGA might not be

Union Liability For Officers and Stewards

In the case of *Express and Star Ltd v NGA* ([1985] Industrial Relations Law Reports 455; [1986] Industrial Relations Law Reports 322) an injunction had been issued against the NGA for instructing its members on the *Express and Star* to boycott work without holding a ballot under the 1984 Act. The union declared its intention to obey the injunction and comply with the law but attempts by NGA members to boycott the work continued. The High Court fined the union £15,000 for contempt despite its decision on compliance. There was evidence that a branch secretary and a national officer had sought to get members to carry on the boycott and to avoid liability for their actions the NGA would have had to *clearly and openly disavow and disown the acts of its officials and communicate the repudiation to the employer concerned.* The court decided that where contempt was involved, rather than an action for damages, the provisions of the *1982 Employment Act* would not decide whether the union was responsible for the actions of its officials. This would be decided by the common law principles of *vicarious liability* — the law which decides when employers are legally responsible for the actions of their employees. This case established that in situations where injunctions are accepted by the union but breached by shop stewards it would be very difficult for unions to get off the hook.

answered by trade unionists and would provoke an unpopular constitutional crisis if it did.

These arguments obviously have some validity. The major indictment of the TUC is twofold. Firstly, its policies from 1979 contributed to the position arrived at in December 1983. And secondly, it failed to ensure that these arguments were debated through and informed policy. Policy in relation to the legislation was informed by one view of the world, *action* in relation to the legislation was informed by a different view. The entire raison d'etre of TUC policy had been based on the unions acting together on a unified basis once one was attacked, on the basis "an injury to one is an injury to all". Now they were asserting in practice a different policy: "fend for yourself ... you made your bed ... now lie on it". Employers observing the situation could be more and more certain that unions taking on the law would be left isolated as far as the TUC was concerned. And that in the changed circumstances of the 1980s, spontaneous rank and file solidarity action was unlikely. The Wembley Principles were an empty facade and the unions could be picked off one by one. That was the signal sent out to government and employer. The NGA affair thus represented a turning point in the unions' response to the employment legislation. It now looked to government and employers as if the implementation of the existing legislation and the development of

Figure 4: THE JOURNALISTS' TALE

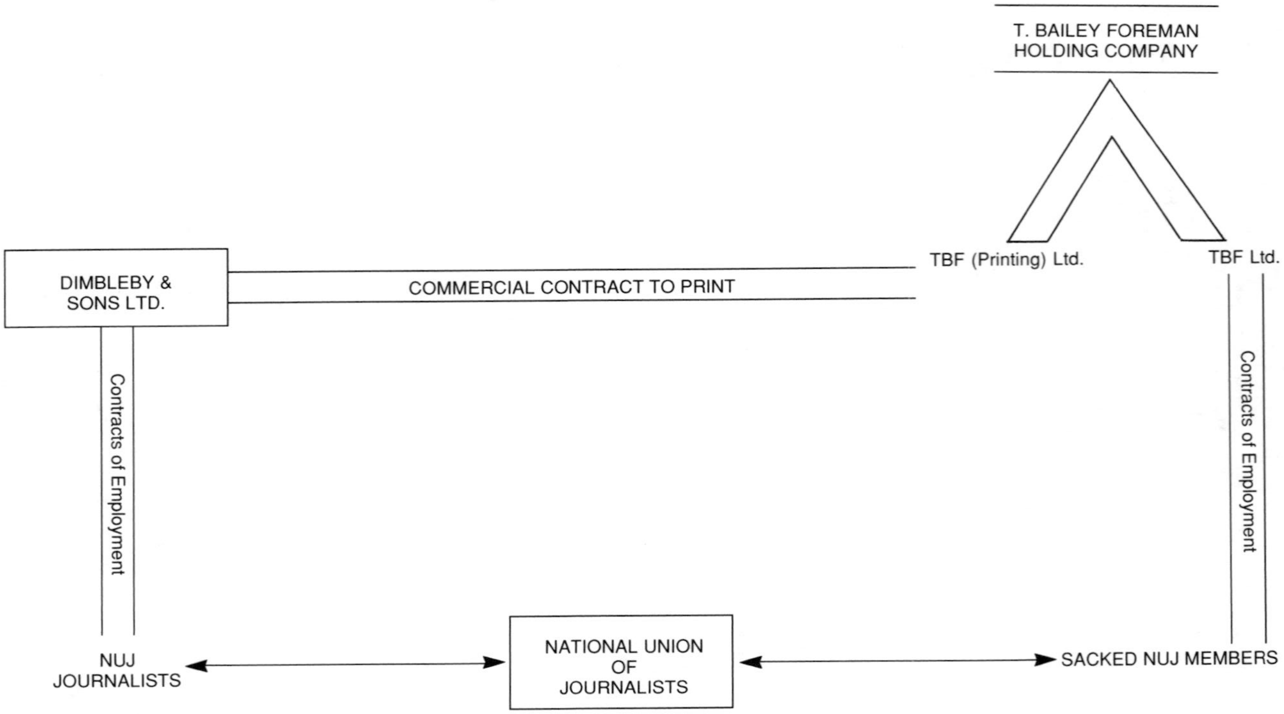

further rounds of legislation would be an easier job than they had imagined.

*   *   *

THE JOURNALISTS' TALE

T. Bailey Foreman Ltd. published the *Nottingham Evening Post.* Another company in the group T.B.F. (Printers) Ltd. printed the *Post.* At the end of the 1978-79 national strike of journalists working on provincial newspapers, T. Bailey Foreman went non-union and unlike other members of the Newspaper Society they refused to reinstate the NUJ members dismissed during the dispute. The NUJ, in turn, together with the print unions, announced a boycott of all work associated with the group.

In 1983 Dimbleby and Sons who published local papers in South London were locked in a dispute with the NGA over redundancies at their subsidiary Dimbleby Printers Ltd. David Dimbleby looked for alternative printers and eventually signed a contract with T.B.F. (Printers) Ltd. In October 1983, the NUJ, because of its dispute with T. Bailey Foreman instructed its members not to submit any copy that would be printed by T.B.F. (Printers) Ltd. The NUJ members were suspended and David Dimbleby then took legal action against their union.

In November 1982, the High Court issued an interim injunction restraining the union from inducing breaches of the contracts of employment between their members and Dimbleby and Sons and from thereby inducing breaches or interfering with the commercial contract between Dimbleby and Sons and T.B.F. (Printers) Ltd. The decision of the High Court was upheld by the Court of Appeal in December 1983 and the House of Lords in March 1984. (*Dimbleby & Sons Ltd v National Union of Journalists* [1984] Industrial Relations Law Reports 67, 161).

The courts held that the only *trade dispute* protected under the definition in s.13(i) of the *Trade Union and Labour Relations Act* was between the NUJ and T. Bailey Foreman Ltd. (see p.58). The NUJ boycott interfered with the commercial contract between Dimbleby and Sons and T.B.F. (Printers) Ltd. The NUJ boycott and interference with this contract was unlikely to be protected secondary action under s.17 of the *1980 Employment Act* (see p.44) because T.B.F. (Printers) Ltd. as distinct from T. Bailey Foreman were not parties to a dispute with the NUJ and there was no contract for the supply of goods or services between T. Bailey Foreman and Dimbleby and Sons — only between T.B.F. (Printers) Ltd. and Dimbleby and Sons.

The courts also refused to accept the NUJ's argument that by refusing to accept copy for T.B.F. (Printers) Ltd. its members were seeking to vary their terms of employment and Dimbleby's refusal to accept this constituted a separate trade dispute about the allocation of work and terms and conditions of employment between the NUJ members and Dimbleby and Sons. Trade unionists who for wider purposes put demands on their employer which were then turned down could not, the judges held, argue that they were in dispute over terms and conditions of employment. This was to manufacture a trade dispute where none in reality existed.

This case illustrated the opportunities open to employers to reorganise their operations and manipulate company structures to outlaw secondary action in industrial disputes. It also demonstrated that the judges were likely, as in the past, to extend the grasp of the legislation, rather than interpret it in relation to industrial realities. In real life the two T.B.F. companies had the same directors and the same shareholders. In real life they constituted one opponent to the NUJ. In real life the future of both companies was bound up with the dispute. T.B.F. (Printers) Ltd. was not some outsider, some innocent bystander in the dispute between the NUJ and T. Bailey Foreman. In real life the NUJ's dispute was with T.B.F. (Printers) Ltd. every bit as much as with T. Bailey Foreman. But the judges refused to 'lift the veil' and look at real life. Their insistence on looking only at the legal technicalities meant that in real life the law was 100% on the side of the employers in this dispute.

The Dimbleby affair also highlighted the reach of the new legislation. In March 1984 when the NUJ, banned by the law from using more direct means, asked its members at the BBC to boycott David Dimbleby's budget appearance, the BBC was granted an interim injunction on the grounds that it was unlikely that this could be shown at a full hearing to be lawful secondary action.

Discussion Questions

1. Draw up a report assessing the strengths and weaknesses of the TUC campaign against the *1980 Employment Act.*
2. "The 1980 and 1982 Acts brought a new and long needed element of democracy to the closed shop". Do you agree with this judgement?
3. What were the strengths and weaknesses of the Wembley Principles?
4. Why was the *Mercury* case important? Discuss the degree to which the new legislation on picketing and secondary action was successful in limiting the strategy of the unions in the *Messenger* and Dimbleby disputes.

CHAPTER 4

Bullets and Ballots

*No law is binding on the subject that assaults the person or violates the
conscience — Blackstone*

The face of the future seemed clearly etched in early 1984 when the
TUC put its money where its mouth was and, as a substitute for
co-ordinated action, presented the NGA with £420,000 from the
Wembley Campaign Fund to pay its legal expenses. Left isolated,
the NGA decided to purge its contempt and call off the dispute. But
the courts and Eddie Shah were not quite finished yet. In July 1984
the full case against the NGA came on in the High Court. The
Messenger Group were awarded £90,051 compensation for lost
production, £10,000 aggravated damages and £25,000 exemplary
damages against the NGA. (*Messenger Newspapers Group Ltd v
National Graphical Association* [1984] Industrial Relations Law
Reports 397)

It was clear that the NGA's experience would now deter most
unions from playing the head-on confrontation with the law scene
from the Wembley script. But it was also true that there was still
room for unions to tactically manoeuvre in specific situations. For
example, in April 1984, the British Printing and Communications
Corporation paid the £150,000 contempt fine imposed on NGA and
SOGAT under the legislation in order to avoid the dispute escalating
to embrace the whole company.

THE NEW REALISM

But in such disputes it was clear that little could be expected from
the TUC. For the 31-20 vote of the TUC General Council not to aid
the NGA was not simply bound up with attitudes to the legislation.
It represented the high point of the 'new realism' developed in the
aftermath of the 1983 General Election by Len Murray and the
Congress House staff, articulated by General Council members such
as Alistair Graham of the CPSA and supported by unions such as the
EETPU and the AEU. The advocates of 'new realism' related Labour's
crushing defeat to the posture of opposition to the government
adopted since 1979. Faced with membership loss and financial

problems, divested of political influence, the unions needed to emphasise their essential moderacy and responsibility, sue for peace with Thatcher and take some distance from the fluctuating fortunes of the Labour Party. The 'new realism' as expounded in the document *TUC Strategy* was essentially a plea for a return to the 1950s when the TUC had worked well with relatively non-interventionist Conservative governments. It was a calling card for the TUC's readmission into politics and society based upon an acceptance of the government's achievements 1979-83 and the consequent scaling down of union influence. A TUC which had rid itself of the meglomania of the 1970s, it was suggested, could still be useful to a right wing administration in regulating society.

National Security and GCHQ

From its establishment in 1947 employees at GCHQ were encouraged to join trade unions. In Mrs Thatcher's second term things changed. In January 1984 the Minister for the Civil Service, acting under powers given to him by Article 4 of the Civil Service Order in Council 1982, moved into action. He issued an instruction which changed the terms and conditions of employment of those working at GCHQ. From now on they would be prohibited from being members of a trade union and would only be entitled to belong to a staff association. This body required approval by the Director of GCHQ and its rules prohibited industrial action and affiliation to other union bodies.

At the same time the Minister issued certificates under s.138 (3) of EPCA 1978 and s.121 (4) of EPA 1975 withdrawing GCHQ staff's legal right to take a case to an industrial tribunal if unfairly dismissed. The trap was closed. GCHQ staff would be sacked if they refused the government's "union free" directive. And they would have no comeback if they were.

The issue was fought through the courts. But the GCHQ workers had little chance of victory as in English law there is no positive right to belong to a trade union. They argued on the broad grounds of *natural justice*: there had been no consultation with the unions before the decision was taken. The House of Lords agreed with the view that the unions had a right to be consulted before their members' terms and conditions were drastically revised. But, the Law Lords decided, this right was outweighed by the interest of the state in national security — and the government was the custodian of that interest. What the government saw as required *was* required by national security. The ban on union membership was, the Law Lords accepted, genuinely motivated by government fears over the national security issue and it was acting within its legal rights.

The European Commission of Human Rights decided that the case was inadmissible as the international convention allows governments to impose non-trade unionism on the army, police force and certain categories of state employee. In November 1988 250,000 workers took some form of action in support of the 18 remaining trade unionists at GCHQ another four of whom were threatened with the sack. Despite heroic tenacity on the part of many workers, by 1989 trade unionism had all but been uprooted in GCHQ.

This approach, this Priorism without Prior, which illustrated once again the TUC's failure to grasp the essentials of Thatcherism, was at least temporarily derailed by the GCHQ affair and the miners' strike. The government's decision to ban trade unionism at the GCHQ signals centre at Cheltenham was a further token of its determination to uproot the unions in key areas. The TUC's response in offering a no-strike deal failed to soften Mrs Thatcher's wrath. Len Murray found his policy in ruins as the General Council voted for a (temporary) withdrawal from the National Economic Development Council, a position he had bitterly and successfully fought against at the September Congress. Murray's subsequent resignation, in the Spring of 1984, meant that the signals to the government of December 1983 were in vain. The Conservatives were determined on a third round of legislation — no matter what stance the TUC took.

THE THIRD ROUND

The objective of the third round of employment legislation was clear: it was the unions' internal organisation that was next on the agenda for change. Having, as they saw it, set the immunities and the closed shop to rights, the government wished to develop the incursions into the union rulebook set in train in 1980. The watchword — and the Trojan horse — was *ballots*.

Conservative proposals for secret postal ballots before industrial action and internal union elections go back at least as far as the 1958 statement *A Giant's Strength*. They were developed in the 1968 policy statement *Fair Deal At Work*. And they were legislated for in the 1971 *Industrial Relations Act*. As we have noted, these proposals were part of a programme for remodelling trade unions. It was believed that they would mobilise the moderate majority who were not prepared to attend meetings to vote, restrain militant union chiefs, outflank the active shop steward layer and produce more moderate leadership and fewer strikes. The government stuck rigidly to this position, although the evidence to justify it was limited. For example, research by the Oxford Centre for Management Studies after reviewing arrangements in a wide variety of unions found:

> there is no evidence that secret postal ballots ... are more likely than any other system of selection to produce majorities for left or right-wing candidates.[1]

The government had already put out modest feelers with the provisions for public funds for ballots in the 1980 Act. But they had

had few takers. Although the AEU Executive and the EETPU had shown some interest they had been restrained by their own membership and the TUC. To keep the pressure up Norman Tebbit issued, in January 1983, a Green Paper *Democracy in Trade Unions.* In introducing the Paper, Tebbit outlined and justified his agenda for further reform with vigour

> There is widespread concern in the country about the way in which trade unions are run. Successive soundings of public opinion have clearly shown the strong feeling that trade unions ought to be democratic institutions responsive to the views and wishes of their members ... Many unions still fail to ballot their members on even the most major decisions ... if all trade unions were to take the views of their members through secret ballots before embarking on industrial action many unnecessary and damaging strikes could be avoided ... Another area of great concern is the political activities of trade unions often carried on with scant regard for the wishes of individual members ... this Green Paper is about restoring democracy in trade unions. Surely nobody can argue against that principle.[2]

The Green Paper itself criticised existing union arrangements as undemocratic and ineffective. Unions wielded great power over the economy yet "Time and again union leaders are seen to be out of touch with their rank and file and often appear to be neither representative of the majority of their members nor directly responsible to them".[3] Voting in the unions was bedevilled by low turnout and malpractice. Voting at meetings was criticised on the grounds of inconvenience, manipulation, intimidation of voters and low turnout. The Green Paper reviewed a range of alternative ways of legislating over pre-strike ballots and internal elections. That it was concerned not with improving democratic methods but with the *end result* that different methods produced was clear. Throughout the document statements such as, "where union leadership is weak triggered ballots might be used by militants to force the hand of more responsible leaders and to put at risk the functioning of established collective bargaining arrangements"[4] demonstrated a concern, not with ascertaining the wishes of the membership in relation to strikes, but with making even a genuine desire for industrial action more difficult to realise.

What *was* new was the chapter on the "Political Activities of Trade Unions" which, in contrast with previous Conservative statements, raised the possibility of legislation on ballots over the maintenance of union political funds and the obligation of members to opt-out of paying the political levy rather than to opt-in.

The Green Paper was intended as were its predecessors to develop and crystallize public opinion, help the Conservatives in the General Election and prepare the ground for future legal initiatives. Its key suggestions were boiled down and included in the Conservative Manifesto for the June election. On 12th July 1983, hot-on-the-heels of the election victory, a White Paper, *Proposals For Legislation on Democracy in Trade Unions* was published. On 26th October 1983, Norman Tebbit having given way to Tom King as Employment Secretary, the Trade Union Bill which was to become the Trade Union Act 1984 first saw the light of day.

THE 1984 TRADE UNION ACT

The Act dealt with three issues — ballots in union elections, ballots prior to industrial action and ballots on the maintenance of unions' political funds.

Union Elections
(Trade Union Act 1984 s.1-9)

The Act stated that

- All members of union executive committees who had a right to vote on the executive had to stand for election at least *every 5 years.*

- Executive officers of a trade union, such as the General Secretary or President, were only covered if, under the union rules, they possessed the right to vote at executive meetings.

- All union members must be entitled to vote unless they belong to certain defined groups such as new members or those in arrears. So the practice of lower level *committees* electing executive members rather than the members directly, as with the TGWU's trade groups, could not be continued.

- Members who can vote for specific seats on the executive could, however, be restricted by rule to members who work in particular trades or industries or, in particular sections of the union. So elections to the executive on a trade group basis as in the TGWU could be maintained.

- No member could be required to belong to a particular political party as a condition of standing for the executive or executive office. And no member could be unreasonably excluded from standing unless they belonged to a class of members all of whom were excluded from standing under the union's rules.

The Act then went on to prescribe in detail the method of voting. It stated

- members must be able to vote without incurring *any direct cost* to themselves

- voting papers must be sent *by post* to members' *home address* or to any other address requested. And members must be given an opportunity to *return their votes by post*.

However, the Act *did not insist on postal ballots*. Unions could instead organise *ballots at the workplace* or *even at the branch* so long as they were *secret* and involved *marking a ballot paper*. But they could only avail themselves of this option of voting at the workplace if they could demonstrate that there were no reasonable grounds for believing that all the requirements for postal ballots listed above could not be satisfied adequately by following this procedure at the workplace:

— Making ballot papers available to all members immediately before, immediately after, or during working hours — either at their workplace or at a more convenient place.

— Giving all members an opportunity to vote immediately before, immediately after, or during working hours, either at their workplace or, at a more convenient place.

The Act also required that

- unions should compile and maintain a *register of names and addresses of all members* and ensure that so far as reasonably practicable it is kept up to date.

- unions should take measures to ensure all votes are fairly and accurately counted.

Enforcement

If members felt a union was not complying with the law they could apply to the Certification Officer or to the High Court for a *declaration* that the union had failed to comply. The High Court could make an order requiring the union to re-run the election or take other steps to remedy the situation. Complaints had to be brought within *a year* of the declaration of the election result.

Ballots Prior To Industrial Action
(Trade Union Act 1984 s.10, 11)

The Act applied not only to strikes but to other industrial action such as an overtime ban or work to rule. It stated that the immunities which protect unions from the torts of inducing a breach of contract or interfering with a contract when they are taking industrial action, whittled down as they had been by the 1980 and 1982 Act, would only continue to apply where a union authorised or endorsed industrial action if the following procedure was followed

- There had to be a ballot of all those whom the union reasonably believes will be called on to take part in the strike or *other industrial action.*

- The ballot must be *secret,* involve *marking a paper* and be *conducted by post.* All the other conditions outlined above in relation to executive elections applied — but so too did the exception. The ballot could be conducted at the workplace if held immediately before, after, or during, working hours.

- The ballot must be held not more than *28 days* before the action begins or not more than *28 days* before the action is *authorised or endorsed* where the union support previously unofficial action. In other words if you held a ballot but delayed in taking action for more than *28 days* perhaps because you were negotiating or restrained by an injunction, you would then have to hold another ballot.

- The question on the ballot paper must invite a straight *'yes'* or *'no'* answer from those balloted about whether they are willing to participate in industrial action. It must explicitly state that going on strike or taking other industrial action will involve them in *a breach of their employment contracts.*

- Ensuing action will only be protected as far as the union is concerned if the members balloted vote *'yes'* by a *straight majority.* But there will then be no obligation on a union to support industrial action and *no legal protection for members taking action against dismissal* by their employer.

- The Act said nothing at all about the decision to *return to work* after industrial action which raised questions about the partiality of the government's concern for union democracy.

Enforcement

If the above procedure is not followed then the 1984 Act gave a right to *employers, customers and suppliers,* affected by consequent industrial action, *not members dissatisfied with the unions procedures,* to take action for an injunction and damages in the High Court.

Union Political Funds
(Trade Union Act 1984, s.12-19)

The existing law governing trade union Political Funds was well established and laid down in the *Trade Union Acts 1913, 1946.* Unions wishing to spend money on political objectives — defined in the 1913 Act as payments towards the expenses of candidates for Parliament or other public office, the holding of meetings and distribution of literature for such purposes, or the holding of political meetings or distribution of political literature of any kind — had to include *political objectives in their rulebooks*. Spending on political purposes had to come from a special *Political Fund* separate from the unions general funds. This fund had to be financed by a special *political levy* separated from the remainder of members subscriptions. This structure could only be established after a successful *secret ballot* of all members. Even if the majority voted for a political fund in such a ballot all members would still have the legal right to *contract out* of paying the political levy.

It should be stressed that in theory whether or not a union had a political fund had nothing to do with whether or not it supported the Labour Party. Affiliation to the Labour Party was a separate matter. A union could have a political fund but not be affiliated to the Party using its fund for a variety of other political purposes covered by the legislation. On the other hand, a union which did not have a political fund could not affiliate to the Labour Party. In 1984, 47 of the unions which had political funds were affiliated to the Labour Party.

The 1984 Act did not, as had been earlier suggested, change opting-out of paying the political levy to opting-in. In return for the government not pressing this, the TUC agreed that affiliated unions should

— Review existing arrangements to see if members faced any difficulties in opting-out.

— circulate information to members on their right to opt-out of paying the political levy.

The Act itself stated:

— In future ballots on political expenditure would not be "once and for all" affairs. Instead they must now be held once every *10 years*. Unions were given 12 months from March 1985 in which to hold the first ballot.

— The ballots must be *secret* and follow the criteria outlined above — postal or held immediately before, after, or during working hours. Additional criteria would be established by the Certification Officer, who had to approve procedures for conducting the ballots.

— The ballots were about the maintenance of political expenditure not about the related but separate issue of affiliation to the Labour Party. Only unions with political funds had to ballot and decision was by a simple majority of those voting.

— If such a majority was not achieved then *six months after the date of the ballot declaration all political expenditure had to cease*. If unions refused to comply with the law then political expenditure had to cease on the deadline for the first round of ballots which was 31st March 1986.

— The cut-off was not automatic. It was left to a member to take the union to court. The court could order a ballot to be held or alternatively they could simply order all political expenditure to cease from the date of the hearing.

— If the union ignored a court order it could be enforced by any member. A union continuing defiance could have its funds sequestrated.

— The pre-existing definition of "political objects" was extended by s.17 of the Act. The most important change stated that expenditure on any literature, document, film, sound recording, or advert which had as its main purpose persuading people to vote or not to vote for a particular party or candidate had to come from a union's political fund not its general fund. It was felt that in the context of the government's policy this could hit public sector unions as defence of their members terms and conditions of employment involved an element of political partisanship particularly around election time.

Strikes In Essential Services

The threat of legislation as a response to day-to-day developments in industrial relations was by 1983 becoming a characteristic of the government's employment policy. Confronted with the water-workers' strike in early 1983, Norman Tebbit announced to the Commons Select Committee on Employment that "the government might make strikes in essential services illegal if the workers broke their contract of employment".[5] The idea was seized upon and pushed by the Institute of Directors but the practical difficulties — how to define essential services, what to give the workers in return, what if there was defiance — deterred legislative action at least at this stage.

THE UNIONS' RESPONSE

The TUC totally opposed the Green Paper and the unions refused to make formal comments to the Department of Employment. On the publication of the Bill, Len Murray commented:

> Claims by Mr Tebbit that he is seeking to enhance democracy in unions are wholly unfounded. ... The government does not want to enhance freedom, it wants to curtail it. It wants to take away from union members the right to run their own affairs in the way they themselves choose and it wants to minimise the financial backing which some unions give to the Labour Party.[6]

The TUC's response was contained in a pamphlet *Hands Up For Democracy* which put the arguments against the legislation with more pep and vim than usual. They argued that the ability of unions to make their own arrangements for internal decision-making, subject to the basic legal safeguards that had always existed, was an important increment to democracy in society, extending and enriching it. Unions had adopted a wide variety of measures for ascertaining their members wishes but all were, to one degree or another, democratic. Every union member had the right and the ability to influence the policies of their union. Evidence of abuse was negligible. There was no 'one best way' for union democracy; workplace ballots had their advantages and worked well for some unions just as postal ballots did for others. The union's members should be given the freedom to choose. Unions had a right to a political voice. Links with the Labour Party were democratically determined and could be broken if the members so desired. The Conservatives' policies in this particular area were motivated by political partisanship.

The unions, the TUC argued, were a progressive force in society, espousing the cause of not only workers but the unemployed, the old, women and youth. Their arrangements for giving voice to the wishes of their members might bear improvement in certain aspects. But they contrasted starkly with the lack of democracy in companies, banks, pension funds and the media. There were no laws controlling company donations to the Conservative Party and no proposals for ballots of shareholders on this issue. The government had bitterly opposed attempts by the EEC to introduce more democratic arrangements into the operations of companies. And if they were looking for areas of reform what about the Conservative Party? Mrs Thatcher was only the second Party leader to be elected but only by MPs not the ordinary members. And she had not had to fight an election for the leadership in eight years.

The 1984 Act received the Royal Assent on 26th July. The Tories' third major piece of legislation produced no Congress of Executives and the howls of defiance were a little more muted. Instead, in August 1984, the TUC General Council issued a statement *1984 Trade Union Act. The Trade Union Response To The New Legislation.* Whilst the eviscerated Wembley Principles were reaffirmed as TUC policy, decisions as to whether or not to comply with the provisions on strike ballots, union leaders and political funds were formally left to affiliated unions. This, thus, represented a clear and perhaps historic stepback by the TUC from the position of co-ordination of opposition adopted in 1969, 1971 and 1982.

In one sense the element of co-ordination that remained saw the TUC giving support to acceptance of the legislation. They noted that unions were considering "how best to campaign effectively to retain their political funds in the review ballots made necessary by the Act". And whilst — for what it was worth — the document stated that unions which were the subject of injunctions for failure to hold strike ballots could ask the TUC for help, no such offer was made to unions who refused to comply with court orders on executive or political fund elections. The summer of 1984 saw the change from opposition to compliance firmed up, even if formal defiance was maintained in relation to certain aspects of the legislation.

But this was not true of all the unions. As the TUC retreated affiliates reacted differently. The provisions on strike ballots became operative at the end of September 1984. The first major confrontation swiftly occurred. In November 1984 the joint negotiating committee at Austin Rover called a strike on the breakdown of pay negotiations. No ballots had been held and the company were quickly awarded injunctions against all six of the unions involved. Austin Rover dropped the action against the EETPU when it agreed to hold a ballot. The AUEW apparently repudiated its members' action. The other unions also made adequate repudiation although TASS was found to be in contempt although not seriously enough to warrant a fine. (*Austin Rover Group Ltd v Amalgamated Union of Engineering Workers (TASS)* [1985] Industrial Relations Law Reports 162) The one union which firmly supported its members action, the TGWU, was fined £200,000 for breach of the injunction. Whilst the TGWU Executive reaffirmed its policy of "Business as usual", it was clear by early 1985 that more and more unions were participating in strike ballots, more and more unions were holding closed shop ballots — the law on this had also become operative in the autumn of 1984 — and more and more unions were planning to change their rules in order to comply with the 1984 Act.

*   *   *

THE MINERS' TALE

The Miners' strike which began in March 1984 demonstrated that, despite the set-backs of the *Messenger* dispute and the lack of support for individual unions from the TUC, unions were still prepared to defy the law. It graphically demonstrated in the willingness of the government to apply coercion more firmly and use the police more fully than any of its post-war predecessors the 'strong state' side of the Thatcherite 'free market-strong state' formula. The strike also, however, illustrated the continuing caution of the state and the big employers in relation to the use of the employment legislation. On the other hand, the NUM was a 'best case'. Even more than the NGA they were firm in their opposition to the law and determined to resist it. In the recent past they had demonstrated their ability to resist the law to contribute to the fall of the Heath Government and in 1982 to provoke a small U-turn from Mrs Thatcher. The fact that the NUM were, in the end, forced to bow before the coercion of the legal process confirmed the lessons of the *Messenger* dispute. Even the Praetorian Guards of the Labour Movement could not take on the law in a set-piece battle without going down to defeat.

However, the two specific features in this strike were the absence of a ballot and the deep divisions within the union which provided an entry-point for the law to exploit and develop. And the fact that the major legal influences on the dispute were the use of the police operating under the criminal law and the use by union members of long established common law rights, rather than the legislation of the 1980s — although that legislation did play a role in the dispute. The strike showed that contemporary legislation had to be related to a wider legal landscape every bit as antagonistic to the unions and highlighted the flexibility and extended repertoire of British employment law.

The Police And The Strike

The scale and the duration of the police operation in the strike was unprecedented in post-war industrial disputes, although the *Messenger* dispute had given a foretaste. By the second week of the strike 20,000 police drawn from 43 different forces were available to police the picket lines on the basis that the police must possess an overwhelmingly superiority of numbers. Mass picketing would be dwarfed by mass policing and if the number of pickets grew more police would be brought in with no expense spared. At Orgreave alone 3,300 police were deployed and at the end of the dispute the cost of police overtime throughout was put at £140 million. Centralisation was achieved through national direction of the operation by the Association of Chief Police Officers, co-ordinating operations from the National Reporting Centre established at Scotland Yard after the 1972 miners' strike. The transfer of police all over the country under the mutual-aid system and the highlighting of the lack of even minimal control local police authorities could exercise over their local force meant that the miners were confronted in reality by a national police force.

To numbers and national co-ordination must be added new aggressive tactics and the use of new technology and hardware developed in the context of the conflicts of the late 1970s and early 1980s, particularly the urban riots. A confidential ACPO manual, *Public Order: Tactical Options*, suggested that, for example, officers armed with truncheons should "run at the crowd in pairs to disperse and/or incapacitate them". It talked of "striking in a controlled manner with batons about the arms and legs or torso" as well as using horses to charge and "battle cries" to intimidate the crowds. The police used mass indiscriminate arrests, spotter planes, helicopters, tracker dogs and roadblocks. The strategy evolved was to stop pickets getting to the picket-lines, disperse pickets who did get through, refuse to allow any effective picketing by using the six pickets only rule and pursue active pickets back into their local communities which were subjected to saturation policing.

9,808 people were arrested during the strike in England and Wales and 1,483 arrested and charged in Scotland. In England and Wales only 80% of those arrested were charged and in Scotland the figure was 57%. The charges brought were minor ones. In England and Wales 98% of were charges of breach of the peace, obstructing the police, breach of bail conditions or vandalism and in Scotland the figure was 75%.

When the police control of the dispute was questioned it received firm backing from the courts. For example in *Moss and Others v McLachlan* ([1985] Industrial Relations Law Reports 76), the police set up a roadblock in Nottinghamshire between four or five miles from one pit and two miles from another. They refused to let miners through and arrested those who attempted to push their way through the police cordon. The court upheld the magistrates finding that they were acting within the law as they reasonably feared the development of a mass picket and a breach of the peace. The policy of roadblocks was thus sanctioned and so was the practice of using bail conditions to prohibit arrested miners from picketing at any pit other than their own on the grounds that the magistrates saw a real risk that an offence would be committed during secondary picketing even if they lacked substantial grounds *(R v The Mansfield Justices ex parte Sharkey* [1984] Industrial Relations Law Reports 496).

The view that picketing was inherently violent and unlawful was given further support in *Thomas v NUM (South Wales Area)* ([1985] Industrial Relations Law Reports 136), where Mr Justice Scott suggested that mass picketing in itself could amount to intimidatory conduct in breach of s.7 of the *Conspiracy and Protection of*

Property Act 1875 and constituted a new tort of unreasonable harassment.

The miners' strike illustrated that, as compared with the previous decades, the government would now insist on the use of mass aggressive policing to ensure effective picketing did not occur. The day-to-day running of the dispute was left to the police urged on by the government and backed by the law. The police were used and increasingly saw themselves, not as a buffer between the two parties to an industrial dispute, but as active protagonists whose purpose was to weaken the miners and speed the termination of the dispute. Following on the events at Warrington in the NGA dispute, the miners' strike underlined the effectiveness of mass policing and the inherent weaknesses of mass picketing on the part of an isolated union confronted by a determined state.

Employment Legislation and the Strike

The Employment Acts, advertised as the answer to the kind of problems employers faced in the miners strike, played a smaller role and were disregarded by the major employers, given the use of direct state coercion and the common law. The National Coal Board went to court in the first days of the strike in March 1984 and were awarded an injunction against the Yorkshire Area of the NUM to restrain the organisation of picketing in Nottingham. The injunction was disregarded and the NCB were granted leave to bring contempt of court proceedings. But with Nottingham working and mass policing developing the Board considered discretion to be the better part of valour. They failed to return to the courts to press their case fearing a large fine or sequestration of the areas' assets might, with matters so finely poised, play a role in uniting the divided union.

The NCB's position was emulated by other larger employers indirectly involved such as British Steel and the Central Electricity Generating Board. But small private firms were more immune from political considerations and issues of wider strategy. On 17th April 1984 two Welsh road haulage companies run by George and Richard Read were successful in the courts and in June another small firm, Wright Contractors of Llanelli, was granted an injunction against the South Wales Area. When the latter maintained its policy of non-acceptance of the law the Reads returned to court. The area was fined £50,000 and its assets were subsequently sequestrated (*Richard Read (Transport) Ltd v NUM (South Wales Area)* [1985] Industrial Relations Law Reports 67). The accountants sent in by the court foiled NUM attempts at transfer of funds and calls by the South

Wales area for wider solidarity action fell on stony ground. There were several other cases brought under the Employment legislation, such as that by British Benzol and Coal Distillation Co. Ltd. to restrain picketing of its coke-making plant in Bedwas and the action by H.J. Banks, a transport company, against the Durham Area NUM. But, on the whole, the strike failed to provide the testing ground for the new legislation that many had predicted. As the strike went on there was no need for the NCB to use the legislation: other legal means were slowly but surely bringing the union to heel.

The Common Law and the Strike

The common law has always treated a union's rule-book as a contract made between its members so that breach of the rules is legally actionable as breach of contract. The bulk of the litigation and the major thrust of the civil law offensive consisted of actions brought against areas and the national union by NUM members claiming breach of rule.

In a series of cases the courts declared that the strike was unlawful in Nottingham, Lancashire and North Wales. In cases brought against the Derbyshire and Yorkshire areas it was held that the call for a national strike was not lawful as there had been no national ballot under rule 43. As there had been no area ballot in Yorkshire and an unsuccessful ballot in Derbyshire the strike was unlawful as in breach of area rules and also because it was in reality part of a national strike (*Taylor v NUM (Derbyshire Area, No.1)* [1985] Industrial Relations Law Reports 440); (*Taylor v NUM (Yorkshire Area)* [1985] Industrial Relations Law Reports 445). The Yorkshire reasoning was rejected, in Scotland: the strike complied with rule 41 and the 19th April decision of the special delegate conference calling on all areas to join the strike did not transform the lawful local stoppage into a component of an unlawful national strike (*Fettes v NUM (Scottish Area)* — *The Scotsman* 25 September 1984).

Because the strike was unlawful at national level and in most areas, the union could not refer to the stoppage as official, issue instructions to the membership to strike and to respect picket lines or initiate disciplinary action against strike breakers. The major practical development flowing from these decisions was the sequestration of the funds of the national union in October 1984 for failure to pay fines imposed and failing to comply with injunctions ordering it not to refer to the strike as official. This was followed in November by the removal of the union trustees and the appointment by the court of the receiver.

Other cases of note in the first nine months of the strike involved orders restraining the NUM conference, in July 1984, from changing its rules and the declaration that the consequent rule changes were void (*Clarke v Chadburn (No.2)* [1984] Industrial Relations Law Reports 350); the ruling that NUM members had the right to inspect the books accompanied by an accountant and the injunction restraining expenditure from Derbyshire funds on the strike (*Taylor v NUM (Derbyshire Area) (No.2)* [1985] Industrial Relations Law Reports 65; (*Taylor v NUM (Derbyshire Area) (No.3)* [1985] Industrial Relations Law Reports 99); and the finding that union officials are, in principle, liable for payments made in breach of rules. But other cases went in favour of the union — the refusal to grant damages against the Derbyshire officials for spending money on the strike (*Taylor v NUM (Derbyshire Area) (No.3)* [1985] Industrial Relations Law Reports 99); the decision that the National Union of Seafarers had the right to make payments to the NUM to alleviate hardship (*Hopkins v NUS* [1985] Industrial Relations Law Reports 157); and the decision that, whilst "mass secondary picketing" was both criminal and tortuous, torts outside the immunities cannot be restrained at the suit of members and that it was not ultra vires for the NUM to take decisions which involved a risk that criminal offences or torts *might* be committed — as distinct from conduct which ensured they would be committed (*Thomas v NUM (South Wales Area)* [1985] Industrial Relations Law Reports 136).

The Union And The Law

From late 1984 a change occurred in the NUM stance on litigation. In the majority of cases until then, the defendants did not appear. However, in the Read case, the South Wales miners put in a statement at the contempt stage and in this case and the *Banks* and *British Benzol and Coal Distillation* cases, picketing against the companies ultimately ceased. Nonetheless, the position of the national union was that the legal interventions should be ignored. In October 1984, however, it was announced that the union would support an important social security appeal and a definite change occurred by December when the union appealed against the appointment of the receiver and offered to cooperate with the courts.

In February 1985, both Yorkshire and South Wales agreed to abide by High Court decisions on picketing and instructed their members to that effect. In March, South Wales purged its contempt and regained its assets and Durham attempted to have an order on discipline lifted. In July, the High Court refused a request by the national union, who had appointed new trustees, to have the sequestration and receivership orders lifted, despite assurances that future court orders would be obeyed. A further hearing in October led to a further postponement. But, on 14th November 1985, the NUM purged its contempt by a written apology and sequestration was ended on payment of costs of around £400,000 and agreement by the union to cooperate with the court-appointed receiver.

The national union had direct recourse to the courts in July, when Nottingham loyalists attempted to restrain the breakaway. The case was adjourned on agreement by the Notts Area not to secede or change area rules without a ballot. A month later Mr Justice Tudor Price refused an injunction ordering the Notts Area to cease breakaway moves, restore Henry Richardson to office and treat NUM loyalists no less favourable than others in the coming ballot. The transformation in attitudes to, and use of the courts was further emphasised in December when a South Derbyshire loyalist failed to convince the High Court to order a branch by branch breakdown of the narrow vote for breakaway in that area and the press could refer to the "delicious ironies" of the new approach to the capitalist courts.

Lessons

The scale on which the law was used in the strike — compare it with any other major post-war dispute including the two previous national miners' strikes — confirmed the growing "legalisation" of industrial conflict in Britain. It also highlighted the fact that employment legislation did not stand alone. The dispute illustrated the fluidity of the law and its interlocking nature, with criminal law integrated with civil law and employment legislation with common law, as well as its overall scope for development as an impediment to effective union activity. The Miners' strike confirmed the impotence of the TUC in organising supporting industrial action in major conflicts and the potency of the key coercive legal mechanism — sequestration. The use of the receiver had shown how this weapon could be developed to avoid any evasion.

If greater caution and greater acceptance of the law was the likeliest result on the union side, the Conservatives were impressed at the range of unusual remedies the courts had granted, such as the right for accountants to inspect the unions books and the use of injunctions to restrain expenditure. They hoped that the experience of the strike would not only strengthen the use of law by employers in industrial disputes but would encourage ordinary members to use the new legislation on union discipline, ballots and the closed shop.

Discussion Questions

1. "The TUC's refusal to co-ordinate industrial action to support the NGA in December 1983 was courageous, prudent and shrewd. The Tories had just won a massive electoral victory and the rank and file would not have answered any call for wider industrial action. Moreover, Len Murray was well within his rights to refuse help under the Wembley Principles". Comment on this verdict.
2. Is there any substance in the arguments put forward by Norman Tebbit that unions in the period before 1984 were undemocratic organisations?
3. What are the arguments for and against secret postal ballots for union elections and before industrial action? Should the state impose them on unions? How far did the 1984 Act go in this direction?
4. "The Miners were beaten in the Great Strike because of Arthur Scargill's stubbornness in refusing to call a national ballot". Do you agree?
5. Draw up a report on the use of law during the miners' strike 1984-5. What lessons should the Labour Movement draw from the involvement of the courts and the police in this dispute?

CHAPTER 5

Heroes and Villains

So one has to be a fox in order to recognise traps and a lion to frighten off
wolves — *Niccolo Machiavelli*

By 1985, with the end of the miners' strike and the third instalment
of the legislation on the statute book, it was possible to take some
stock of the half a decade of new legislation. It was now clear that
the new laws were being used to a greater extent than the *1971
Industrial Relations Act* had been. Research which probably
underestimated the position found 34 cases, largely applications for
interim injunctions, had been heard under the 1980 and 1982 Acts
between 1980 and the start of the miners' strike. Activity was initially
slow but it gathered momentum. There was one case in 1980, 11
in 1981 and 12 in 1982. The *Messenger* dispute and the miners' strike
then appear to have provoked a spurt in activity. *Labour Research*
reported that 70 cases had been heard by the summer of 1985.

Activity outside the area of industrial action was insignificant. For
example, only a handful of cases were brought under the closed
shop provisions of the legislation. However, as we have seen,
1984-85 saw an upsurge of ballots over the closed shop with the
unions winning in the great majority of cases. The limitations of the
legislation's impact were reported by the government sponsored
Survey of Workplace Industrial Relations in Britain which found a
decline between 1980 and 1984 in the number of closed shops and
the number of employees covered by such arrangements. But, the
research recorded, this decline was related to unemployment and
closures in manufacturing industry, rather than the impact of
employment legislation.[1]

Whilst the effect of the new laws could be seen very clearly in
the big set piece disputes, the question of its general impact on
day-to-day trade unionism was more difficult to assess. The number
of cases provides only a crude measure of the influence of the new
laws on industrial relations as it neglects the degree to which an
awareness of the legislation or fear that it could be used or the threat
that it would be used, led trade unions and employers to change
their behaviour. It is also difficult to divorce the legislation as an
influence for change from economic factors such as the level of
unemployment and the wages-prices relationship — as well as the

wider political climate. Given the step-by-step approach of the government perhaps it was still a little early to make a judgement. Certainly the degree of success or failure the unions experienced in the political fund ballots would be an important ingredient in any future judgement.

When it came to the incursions the new government had made into the floor of individual rights, judgements on impact were also difficult. But there was evidence that the system was not, whatever the causes, providing effective protection for individual workers. In 1984 28,000 complaints of unfair dismissal, to take the most numerically significant example, were dealt with. Of the 7,578 complaints which reached tribunals workers were successful in only 28.7% of cases. In only 78 cases were recommendations of reinstatement made and it was in an even smaller number of cases that workers actually returned to their jobs. The median awards of compensation increased. But, rising between 1980 and 1984 from £598 to £1,345, they remained derisory satisfaction for those who had demonstrated the unfairness of their deprivation of employment in a period when longer periods of unemployment were also on the increase. The principles in cases like *British Labour Pump Ltd v Byrne* [1979] Industrial Relations Law Reports 94, which asserted that, even if ACAS-recommended procedures had not been followed, dismissal could still be held to be fair had by mid-decade

> grown into triffid doctrines that can blind the tribunals by the reassuring reflection that they have considered all the factors and that things would not have been so different in the end even if the employer *had* followed all proper procedures.[2]

The verdict of the major authority on employment law was that in this area

> ...the control of management by 'civilised' standards in dismissal has both in substantive and procedural terms, largely given way to priority for managerial prerogative.[3]

The position with regard to discrimination legislation was even grimmer. In 1983 there were 265 applications to industrial tribunals under the *Sex Discrimination Act* and 310 applications under the *Race Relations Act.* These figures demonstrated a steep decline from the mid-1970s whilst Equal Pay claims had collapsed from 1,742 in 1976 to 35 in 1983. It was noted that:

> The number of claims under the RRA and SDA is minute when viewed in the context of evidence of widespread and continuing discrimination in employment and the relatively poor record of collective bargaining in combatting it.[4]

This was related once again to the inadequacy of the remedies. In 1983 46% of those winning sex discrimination and 62% of those winning race discrimination cases received compensation of less than £500.

THE DATA PROTECTION ACT 1984

This legislation which only came fully into effect in 1987 gave limited rights to individuals seeking access to information held about them *on computer.* All those storing information on computer have to register the fact with the Data Protection Registrar. This would cover unions storing the names and addresses of members. Individuals can then request from the "data user" information held about them personally on computer. This would enable workers to ask their employers for details held about them personally.

THE POLITICAL FUND BALLOTS: TRIUMPH IN ADVERSITY

The Green Paper *Democracy in Trade Unions* had criticised the *status quo* on political funds on a number of grounds. It claimed that the fact that the establishment and maintenance of political funds required only a once-and-for-all ballot was a giant limitation on democracy. Today's trade unionists, the Green Paper asserted, were often denied the right to choose and were bound by the way their grandparents had voted in quite different circumstances. The wide disparities between the levels of contracting-out in different unions suggested that in some cases contracting-out was made difficult for independently-minded members by union activists. Real choice, the paper argued, was often denied to members as the political levy was compounded with the union's general subscription and the total sum deducted at source. In some unions members were disqualified from holding certain posts if they were not Labour Party members.

Whilst it would appear that the inertia effect of having to contract-out boosted the number of political levy payers, the government could produce little or no evidence to back-up these criticisms of the existing system. Indeed there seemed to *be* little evidence: in the four years prior to the publication of the bill, a period when increasing attention was paid to the operation of political funds, only 77 complaints were received by the

Certification Officer. This point was emphasised by the trade unions in their response to the government's offensive. The lack of even-handedness between the law's treatment of employers whose freedom of expenditure on political matters contrasted starkly with the tight controls applying to the unions was also reiterated.

There was, however, another agenda behind the political fund provisions of the 1984 Act — an agenda about which the Green Paper was understandably coy. The underlying objectives were to, at one and the same time, strengthen business unionism and make the world safe for capitalism by divorcing the unions from Labour — in the process bankrupting the Party and weakening its election prospects at the expense of the safer, more moderate SDP/Liberal Alliance. The aim was, as Norman Tebbit put it, with characteristic bluntness

> ... to encourage a split in the TUC which could bring social-democrats and right-wing Labour people together with backing from the same trade unions. I hoped that if the ballots for Political Funds were accompanied by a real national debate led by the media it might precipitate a questioning of why the funds were wasted on the support of an unelectable, muddled, semi-Marxist party. The idea of creating an electable rival to the Conservative Party, I agreed, sounded crazy, but it could set the scene for a long-lasting consensus on Thatcherite terms with no risk of a regression into socialism. What is more it would ensure victories for us in 1987-88 and 1991-92 giving time for our reforms to become deeply established.[5]

In pursuing this strategy the government was heartened by the fact that only 39% of trade unionists voted Labour in 1983. There was in the eyes of the government a majority against political involvement — if it could be mobilised. There were, moreover, signs that some leading trade unionists were beginning to flirt with the SDP. And the opinion polls showed that in key unions such as the TGWU, NUPE, and the EETPU a majority would vote to end the unions' Political Funds. The government felt, moreover, that the form of the legislation — giving members themselves a right to vote rather than replacing contracting-out with contracting-in from on high — would increase their electoral popularity.

A Government Defeat

From the government's point of view the whole scheme backfired. The Political Fund ballots were carried out through 1985-86. And in not a single case was the vote in favour of ending the Political Fund. On the contrary, the majorities for its maintenance were overwhelming. In the TGWU, the vote was 511,014 (82%) in favour of retaining the fund with only 119,823 (18%) in favour of its abolition. In the GMB, the figure were 448,426 (89%) for and 54,637

(11%) against. In the EETPU, 140,913 (84%) were for the fund with only 26,830 (16%) opposed. Whilst in the AEU, 238,604 (84%) supported the *status quo*, as against 44,399 (16%) in favour of a change. Even in white collar unions, like APEX — over 70% — and ASTMS — over 50% — there were healthy majorities for the maintenance of the funds. Overall, 83% were in favour and 17% against in a 50% plus turnout.

This overwhelming rebuff for Mrs Thatcher seems to have been the product of government miscalculation, membership loyalty, understanding of the necessity for union political activities and careful imaginative campaigning by the unions themselves. The TUC itself, of course, is not affiliated to the Labour Party. Neither are important affiliates some of which, such as NALGO and the CPSA, did not have political funds. The campaign for a 'yes' vote was, therefore, co-ordinated by a special *ad hoc* Trade Union Co-ordinating Committee.

The committee decided to mount the ballots over the whole 12 month period thus robbing their opposition of the key focus for intervention that balloting on one day or a few days would have afforded. The time-table was carefully planned with the likely winners going first and the likely losers last. This enabled experience, confidence and momentum to be gradually built-up. As the committee's surveys confirmed commonsense intuition — members were more likely to support a blanket call for union involvement in politics rather than a plea to support Neil Kinnock — the Labour Party connection was played down. The key theme was 'yes to a voice in Parliament' not 'yes to the Labour Party'. The scale of the unions' response and the imaginative use of meetings and propaganda, allied to the fact that *one* clear-cut issue was involved which was, in itself, absolutely vital to the unions, meant that the campaign was superior to those mounted around the 1980 and 1982 Acts.

The unions' whitewash was perhaps their best news since 1979. It signalled the powerful residual loyalty of workers to the maintenance of union organisation, a feeling that the government was acting unfairly in the interests of the Conservative Party and an acceptance of the argument concerning the inequity of the legal imbalance between the freedoms of employers and the restraints on unions in the field of political expenditure. The unions' success enabled them, at least in this area, to go on the offensive. A year after the conclusion of the ballots seven unions without political funds in 1984 had successfully balloted to establish them and further ballots were in the pipeline.

Financing The Conservative Party

In 1986 *Labour Research* reported that 294 companies gave nearly £3 million in donations to the Conservative Party — yet only 13 of them, 4%, balloted their shareholders. This was a big increase on the figure in 1984-85 when only 6 companies held ballots. Only one company Aidcom International balloted not its shareholders but its employees.

The following year — election year — donations from big business to the Conservative Party soared to £5 million. Only one company Singleton Holdings — a bingo hall operator — made a small donation of £1,000 to the Labour Party. The figures undoubtedly underestimate the total funds channelled to the Conservative Party by industrialists. Thousands more are channelled through buffer organisations like British United Industrialists, an organisation which "champions the cause of free enterprise". The figures *Labour Research* dug out of company accounts only represent the tip of the iceberg. In 1989 *Sunday Times* journalists collected material which demonstrated that for 40 years Conservative Central Office staff had operated a secret network of companies which laundered money from companies to the Conservative Party coffers. The *Sunday Times* refused to publish the story which was eventually broken by *The Independent.*

In the 1980s there have been several private members bills seeking to impose controls over company political expenditure requiring for example a ballot of shareholders and publication of detailed figures. They have been opposed by the Conservative Party and the government's reaction has been that if shareholders don't like what is happening they can sell their shares. They seem reluctant to apply the same reasoning to trade unions and do not argue that there is no need for legal controls over political expenditure there either *i.e.* if members don't like what their union is doing they can leave the union.

In early 1989 the government was defeated in the House of Lords and the Companies Bill successfully amended to give shareholders the right to veto company donations to political parties. But the clause was removed in the Commons. There is thus a double standard operating: one rule for the Conservatives and big business, a quite different one for Labour and the unions.

STATE FUNDS FOR UNION BALLOTS: OPPOSITION DISINTEGRATES

Even in their hour of success new problems were piling up for the unions and their opposition to Mrs Thatcher's employment legislation. Once again problems stemmed from the divisions *within* the movement. Was it any accident that the unions' biggest success had come when they declared a truce on internal differences and closed ranks in defence of the political funds? As we have seen the TUC informed affiliates in the Spring of 1980 that they should not apply for state funding to allay the cost of union ballots. This position was strengthened by point 3 in the Wembley declaration which stated "Affiliated unions shall observe Congress Policy and not seek or accept public funds for union ballots under the Employment Act 1980 ballot funds scheme".

The money on offer tempted some unions more than others. Unions like the EETPU or the AEU whose rules provided for postal ballots over a range of issues were more discomforted by the TUC prohibition than a union like the TGWU which operated a system of branch and workplace ballots. In early 1981, heavily hit as the union was by loss of membership and a depressing financial position, the executive of the AEU moved towards breaking the TUC embargo. But they were overruled by the National Committee (the union's governing body). Whilst by 1983, 19 unions had applied to the Certification Officer for public funds for ballots, none of these were affiliated to the TUC. However, the enactment of the 1982 legislation on the closed shop and the 1984 Act's provisions on ballots meant that in future *all* unions would be involved in forms of balloting which could well be more expensive than those adopted in the past. Moreover, the argument that if the unions were to accept the form of democracy dictated by the state then they might as well get the state to pay the bill was now increasingly heard.

Whilst the Wembley Principles also prohibited union involvement in ballots over the closed shop, the 'take-effect' date of the provisions of the 1982 Act in the autumn of 1984 saw a small but growing move towards union participation. ACAS reported that 97 closed shop ballots had been held under the Act's provisions between November 1984 and September 1985. Moreover, those who were luke-warm about the TUC boycott had their views strengthened by the fact that in more than 70% of these cases the unions achieved the very high majority required to win the ballot. The doubters were able to show some evidence for the view that unions could use the balloting provisions of the Tory legislation successfully *for their own purposes*.

Norman Tebbit had already sought to exploit differences within the TUC over the "funds for ballots" issue. If the TUC, he argued, was so determined to keep its hands clean by refusing public money for internal union purposes over the ballots issue, why was it so keen to keep on receiving public money for the internal union purpose of training union representatives? If, he stated, the TUC was determined to be inconsistent, the government might have to restore it to the path of principle by ceasing to give the TUC £1.5 million of taxpayers' money annually for trade union education. To keep the heat on the unions and exploit the differences between them, the government also announced, in late 1984, that all claims for state aid for ballots held between 1980 and 1984 had to be in by February 1985 — otherwise there would be no entitlement. The government kept pressing these issues for they saw the ballot issue as a popular one with voters who were likely to see union resistance as incomprehensible and reactionary.

A Defeat for the TUC

The first union to break under the pressure was the AEU. If they did not get their claims into the Certification Officer by the cut-off date they would lose a small fortune in back-pay for ballots already held. The executive decided to ballot the membership and won a majority vote for breaking the TUC boycott. The TUC sought to pressurise the AEU back into line and in February 1985 announced a review of the position on the legislation.

The consequent evaluation, *Trade Union Law: Developing TUC Policy* argued that there was no need to change the existing policy elaborated at Wembley and developed in relation to the 1984 Act — although it did document the degree to which the Wembley decisions were being ignored. In particular, the statement argued, accepting the position of the AEU — now joined by the electricians — on state funding of ballots would give the government an important foot in the door of internal union organisation. Whilst the strings presently attached to the provision of funds were few, they could be strengthened once the unions had taken the financial bait. The document represented another compromise based on internal union politics. It was motivated by the view that a limited, quiet or adroit disregard for Wembley in practice was tolerable. But to accept *formal revision* of the TUC principles over the ballots issue could lead to a final formal discarding of the other Wembley Principles in the glare of publicity and a humiliating loss of face by the TUC.

However, the ballot problem would not go away. The two major dissidents refused to accept the document's verdict. The Wembley Principles, they argued, were in practice as dead as a dodo. The TUC had done nothing over the NGA, or over the miners' difficulties. They were doing nothing over participation in closed shop ballots by affiliated unions, a clear breach of point 2 of the Wembley Principles. Yet they were making a terrific song and dance over one small aspect of the legislation which, in reality, held tremendous financial advantages for trade unions.

The strings attached to state funding of union education in terms of limitations on the subject matter of union training courses for shop stewards which could be paid for out of the state subsidy were, the AEU and EETPU argued, every bit as great, if not greater, than those attached to the funds for ballots scheme. Unions, such as the TGWU, which had less to gain and to lose than the AEU and EETPU were using the language of principle to cloak vested interest and handicap their competitors in the struggle for membership and influence. There was a need to close the gap between the practice on the ground — increasing acceptance of the legislation — and the practice on the platform of political posturing.

In June 1985 the General Council voted to investigate the AEU when it received its first tranche of money under the government scheme. At the September Congress a split was averted by a TUC back-down. Action which could lead to the expulsion of the AEU was to be suspended whilst the union held a second ballot. This would give a detailed statement of the TUC position as well as that of the executive on the ballot paper. The EETPU also held a ballot on this issue and in both unions there were majorities for accepting the state funds.

The TUC's final back-down came in February 1986 when a Conference of Principal Officers discussed the problem. In its aftermath, the General Council — in a further blow to the Wembley Principles — agreed that future decisions on whether or not to accept state funds should be left *to the discretion of individual affiliates*, although the TUC would inform unions that it still had grave fears about the long term impact of acceptance of such funds on the independence of trade unions. This decision also had longer term implications in that it gave the impression that unions opposing TUC policy could change it simply by defying it.

THE PUBLIC ORDER ACT 1986

The unions' success over the political fund ballots did not blunt the government's appetite for further legislation. It was, they felt, a small miscalculation, a small reverse to be measured against their heartening victories in the miners' strike and the disintegration of the TUC's policy of opposition to the legislation. The best way to overcome this set back was to pile on the punishment. In particular, the Conservatives wished to *formalise* and *legitimise* some of the powers that the police had arrogated to themselves during the mining strike. A 1985 White Paper, *Review Of Public Order Law* cited the picketing at Warrington and during the miners' strike as a major threat to public order requiring legislative attention. It was followed the following year by important legislation.

The 1986 Act provided the police with new powers to *impose conditions on the location, duration and size of certain public assemblies and demonstrations* — which would include *mass pickets*. The assemblies covered were defined as gatherings of *20 or more people.* The police could impose conditions where they believed such a public assembly could lead to

— *serious public disorder* or *serious damage to property*
— or *serious disruption to the life of the community*
— or where the purpose of the organisers is the *intimidation* of others with a view to compelling them not to do an act they have a right to do or to do an act they have right to do.

Ignoring police conditions constituted a specific criminal offence whilst *intimidation* was an arrestable offence with increased penalties of 6 months imprisonment or a fine of £2,000. And a new criminal offence of *disorderly behaviour likely to cause alarm, distress or harassment to another person* was introduced.

Social Security and Unemployment Benefit

The concept of public benevolence provided by the state is one I find difficult to comprehend.

Lord Bridge in *Westwood v Secretary of State for Employment* [1985] ICR 220

As part of its policy of increasing flexibility and reducing wages the government took a step-by-step approach to cutting unemployment benefit and social security payments. The idea was that this would make unemployment less attractive and make the unemployed readier to take work at lower wages. If state benefits to the unemployed were lowered wages too could be lowered in relative terms. The unemployed would have a greater incentive to take low paid jobs and the low paid would be frightened of losing their jobs and therefore have a greater incentive to work harder, be more obedient and more satisfied with poor terms and conditions. The government has thus

— abolished the earnings related supplement for unemployment and sickness benefits *(Social Security (No.2) Act 1980)*
— taxed for the first time basic levels of benefit *(Finance (No.1) Act 1981)*
— changed the method of uprating benefits so that now they rise annually only with the average of price increases not as in the past with the average price *or wages* increase whichever was the higher *(Social Security (No.2) Act 1980)*
— increased the period of disqualification for "voluntary" unemployment — where you leave your job or are sacked for "misconduct" from 6 to 13 and then to 26 weeks *(Social Security Act 1986)*
— uncoupled pensions from earnings so that they are protected only against price inflation and changed the rules governing the state occupational pensions scheme SERPs which lowered the level of real benefit and tightened up on qualification. Henceforth pension would be calculated only on the basis of 20% not 25% of average earnings over the period now to be calculated not on the twenty best years but over the whole lifetime earnings *(Social Security Act 1986)*.

Despite Douglas Hurd's statement that "pickets whose real purpose is to peacefully dissuade or communicate information will not be touched by the measure", the act built upon the case law in the miners' strike — particularly *Thomas v NUM (South Wales Area)* [1985] Industrial Relations Law Reports 136, where the judge had argued that insulting language could constitute intimidation. It was likely to make life more difficult for pickets.

BUILDING BUSINESSES NOT BARRIERS, 1986

In case there was any doubt about its resolve to keep on legislating the government published in May 1986 a further White Paper, *Building Businesses Not Barriers*. This contained a mini-programme for future enactment to further reduce what was termed "the legal burden on employers". The White Paper suggested future legislation should

— Require a £25 *deposit from applicants to industrial tribunals*. This would restrain ill founded complaints and would be returned if the case was settled or withdrawn or if the application was successful

— Extend the *qualifying period* for the right to *written reasons for dismissal* from *6 months to 2 years* to bring it in line with the qualifying period for unfair dismissal itself

— Raise the number of hours of employment required to qualify for vital employment protection rights from *16 hours a week to 20 hours a week*. If employees had *5 years continuous service* the qualifying hours should be raised *from 8 to 12 hours a week*

— Exempt employers employing *less than 20 employees* from the legal requirements to include particulars relating to *disciplinary and grievance procedures* in the statutory particulars of employment

— Exempt employers employing *less than 10 employees* from the obligation to ensure *a right to return to the job to women taking maternity leave*

— Allow vocational training Boards to offer *one sex training*

— Restrict the range of duties for which trade union officials have a *right to paid time-off* to those matters falling within the scope of the employer — *union recognition agreement*

— Amend the 1981 *Transfer Of Undertakings Regulations*.

WAGES ACT 1986

This legislation continued to pursue the theme of de-regulation, more flexible wage setting and downward pressure on wages in the interests of flexibility. Young workers in particular were singled out for attack but restrictions on the powers of Wages Councils affected many low paid workers. Under the Act's provisions

- It became lawful from 25th July 1986 to employ those *under 21* on terms less favourable than those laid down in Wages Council Orders. Young people lost the limited protection Wages Councils gave them.

- The powers of existing Wages Councils were limited to setting *minimum* rates of pay and *overtime* rates.

- The *Truck Acts* which required workers to be paid in "coin of the realm" and the *Payment of Wages Act 1960* which allowed payment by cheque or direct transfer at *the workers request* were repealed from 1st January 1987. There would now be no barrier to employers including a term in contracts of employment on cashless pay.

- The *Truck Acts* had also protected workers against deductions from their pay and fines for poor workmanship. This was now replaced by a new provision by which *fines and deductions would be lawful if authorised by legislation or the written agreement of the worker.*

- The amount of any fine or deduction imposed on any one pay day was limited to *10% of the workers wages* although the 10% did not apply to the final instalment of wages.

- Employers could only impose fines or deductions in relation to cash shortages or stock deficiencies during the 12 months after the shortage or deficiency was discovered or could reasonably have been discovered.

- Complaints regarding these matters were now to be handled by industrial tribunals.

- Redundancy rebates were abolished for all employers except those employing *less than 10* workers.

THE SEX DISCRIMINATION ACT 1986

The key provisions of this enactment which rationalised the position of women workers were helpful in some aspects. But there were divided opinions on the removal of the controls on women's

Health and Safety

It was not just the legislation that the government put on the statute book that caused problems for workers in the 1980s. Its failure to provide adequate funds for the effective enforcement of *existing* legislation also made life difficult particularly for those working in sweated trades and poorly organised industries. By 1985 there was evidence that government policies were contributing towards increased numbers of breaches of wages council legislation and towards the creation of an 'anything goes' climate in relation to health and safety.

Between 1981 and 1985 the incidence of fatal and serious injuries per 100,000 employees rose by 42% in the construction industry; 47% in timber and furniture; 48% in the brick, pottery, glass and cement industries; and 54% in textiles. Over the same period the factory inspectorate was cut by 13.5%, leaving only 540 inspectors in place, while the number of workplaces requiring a visit increased by 23%. The number of improvement and prohibition notices issued fell from 5,271 to 4,655 and the number of prosecutions from 3,169 to 2,628. By 1986 the average penalty on conviction was £474.

During the same period the impact of the recession, the erosion of union bargaining power and the weakening of legislation protecting security of employment made it harder for workers to fight to make up for the inadequacies of the law and the lack of enforcement.

employment. In fact these changes, part of the government's deregulation policy, represented an attack on women workers. The formal freedom the Act gave women was in reality likely to produce greater exploitation. The removal of restrictions can give employers greater freedom to dictate unacceptable conditions to part-time women workers, those on fixed term contracts, those in badly organised industries, *those with little bargaining power.* Disadvantaged in the market, concentrated in low pay sectors, often without the protection of a union, dependent on individual negotiation they would be no match for the employer.

- It was now unlawful for an employer to set *different compulsory retirement ages for men and women.* It was also made unlawful for an employer to discriminate on grounds of sex in promotion transfer and training in relation to retirement.

- Women were now able to *complain of unfair dismissal up to the same age as men* i.e. the normal retirement age if this was the same for men and women or if there was no normal retirement age up to the age of 65.

- The *1975 Sex Discrimination Act* was extended to cover firms or partnerships with 5 or fewer employees or partners.

- The exemption for employment in *private households* in the existing legislation was limited.

- The need for organisations to be designated under the 1975 Act before they could lawfully run *single sex courses* was removed.
- Any term of a collective agreement employers or union rules or the regulation of professional or qualifying bodies which would result in a breach of the *Sex Discrimination Act 1975* or the *Equal Pay Act* was now made void.
- S.3 of the *Equal Pay Act 1970* enabling collective agreements containing provisions applying specifically to one sex to be referred to the Central Arbitration Committee was repealed.
- The provisions of the *Factories Act 1961* and *Mines and Quarries Act 1951* and *Hours of Employment Act 1936* which limited *women's hours and times of work were repealed.* And so were the restrictions on night work by men in the *Baking Industry (Hours of Work) Act 1954*

*   *   *

THE PRINTERS' TALE

Throughout 1984 Rupert Murdoch who owned *The Sun, The News of the World, The Times* and *The Sunday Times* negotiated with the print unions to transfer printing and production of his papers from Fleet Street to a new plant at Wapping. Murdoch wished to take advantage of developments in technology and communications, reduce staffing levels and union work controls. Murdoch was willing to go through the process of talking to the unions. But this was on the basis of presenting them with his terms on a take-it-or-leave it basis, using 'negotiation' as a stalling mechanism whilst preparing

---

Employment Training Schemes

In examining the government's erosions of the basic floor of employment rights it is important not to forget about the role played by the various training schemes. Programmes such as the Young Workers Scheme and the New Workers Scheme acted to subsidise employers, cloak the real levels of unemployment and by prescribing artificially low wages for scheme workers again attempted to exercise pressure on the terms and conditions of employed workers. For the most part workers on the schemes were not employees and therefore possessed none of the increasingly limited Employment Protection rights. Pressures were increasingly exercised to get young people particularly onto the schemes which were largely immune from legal control and the government announced that it would eventually take powers to determine the legal standing of trainees. The system can be seen as creating a showhouse for the government policies of deregulation and flexibility and transferring resources from the social security system and the jobless to the employers and the scheme controllers.

pre-emptive action. If the unions were going to Wapping then, as far as *News International* was concerned, they were not going on the old terms. As it became clear that this would be unacceptable to the unions, the company began to plan for a union-free Wapping.

Although the public pretext for the move, announced in 1985, was the printing of a projected new evening paper *The London Post*, News International privately planned to switch the printing of all its national papers to Wapping. By the summer of 1985 there were rumours that the plant was being prepared and staffed by workers recruited through the EETPU's Southampton office and that in return for undermining the negotiating efforts of their brothers and sisters in the print unions, the electricians' union was expecting sole negotiating rights and the chance to take over the print workers jobs at Wapping. Murdoch, clearly influenced by the success of Eddie Shah, hired Christopher Pole-Carew, formerly Managing Director of T. Bailey Foreman as adviser. An independent distribution system for News International papers was established with the co-operation of Murdoch's Australian partners, Thomas Nationwide Transport — who owned their own fleet of lorries — with 28 centres and 400 dispatch points throughout the country. Learning the lessons of the Dimbleby case, Murdoch also established a set of buffer companies between News International and its suppliers and customers. The newly created News International Distribution Ltd. would supply copies of *The Sun* to the wholesalers, not the parent company, News Group Newspapers, who printed *The Sun*.

This new structure would cause legal problems for the unions and in the build-up to the dispute News International received detailed legal advice on every aspect of the situation they were going into. Well in advance of the conflict, they were advised that "... if the moment came when it became necessary to dispense with the workforce the cheapest way of doing so would be to dismiss employees when they were participating in a strike or other industrial action".[6] Whilst in a dispute of this nature the employer obviously has the initiative and holds most of the aces, this strategic preparation contrasted with the unions make-do approach which, once more, stemmed, to some degree, from the divisions amongst them. The EETPU was fighting on Murdoch's side. Members of the NGA or SOGAT in the provinces historically had little in common with their higher paid brothers and sisters in Fleet Street.

By autumn 1985, with a sophisticated direct input system installed at Wapping by Atex, leading US computer specialists, Murdoch was ready to move. The unions were presented with extremely harsh terms which News International claimed were necessary if they were to compete with Eddie Shah's *Today* newspaper. In future, there would be no recognition of chapels and branches and no negotiations at local level. The unions must sign a 'no strike-no industrial action whatsoever' agreement and accept instant dismissal for any worker breaking it. There would be no closed shop, no union recognition for white collar and management grades, complete flexibility and freedom for management to change working methods — and no demarcations. The small print was even more revolutionary. Not surprisingly there was a failure to reach agreement and the unions balloted their members on industrial strike action. The move to Wapping was on and the unions called out their members from 24th January 1986.

Murdoch Uses the Legislation

The unions were once again going into dispute, where the odds were stacked against them any way, *divided*. EETPU members as well as some members of the NUJ were working in Wapping. Although a TUC investigation of a formal complaint brought by SOGAT and the NGA found the EETPU's behaviour to be, "detrimental to the trade union movement", the TUC fearing legal action by the EETPU if it sought to instruct that union to call its members in Wapping out, dragged its feet.

The EETPU was required to comply with six directives. The union was instructed that it should not assist further in recruiting for News International; that it should not take any more News International employees into membership; that it should inform its members at Wapping that they were carrying out work previously done by members of the print unions; that it should not negotiate separately with Murdoch; that it should in contrast seek to establish a framework for joint negotiations; and finally that it should reach no single union agreements, except as provided by the TUC. Evidence later came to light towards the end of the dispute which demonstrated the depth of the EETPU's early involvement with News International and its violation of these directives. Throughout the dispute the EETPU remained a dead weight on the efforts of the print unions to secure jobs and recognition.

With his alternative workforce relatively assured, Murdoch now sacked the 5,000 print workers and journalists who had refused to move to Wapping. In this he was protected by legislation removing unfair dismissal rights for those sacked whilst participating in industrial action. The unions, in response, picketed Wapping and sought to apply a complete boycott of the printing and handling of all News International titles.

Murdoch immediately unleashed a hail of writs focused on five major actions under the employment legislation. On the 27th January 1986, News International companies obtained injunctions against SOGAT restraining the union from instructing its members in wholesale depots not to handle the Murdoch papers. The following day Times Newspapers were granted an injunction against the NGA directing it to withdraw instructions to its members at Northampton Mercury Ltd not to print *The Times* supplements. Next, News International was awarded an injunction against the TGWU ordering it to lift its directive to its members not to cross picket lines. A second injunction against SOGAT restrained it from ordering its members not to co-operate with the *News of the World*. A fifth injunction was handed down against the Union of Communication Workers instructing it to call off its boycott of *The Sun*'s bingo cards scheme.

The specific rationale for each injunction was somewhat unclear but the court orders were based on a violation of the secondary action provisions of the 1982 Act and breaches of the strike ballot provisions of the 1984 Act — members of the print unions outside News International and members of other unions had not been balloted over support action.

SOGAT's failure to comply with the first injunction led to the union being brought before the courts on 10th February 1986. The union was fined £250,000 for contempt of court and its assets were sequestrated on the grounds that its leaders had expressed no regret for their contempt and evinced no firm, future intention to comply with the injunction. The NGA escaped with a £25,000 fine as it lifted, at the last minute, its directive to its members at Northampton not to work on *The Times* supplements (*News Group Newspapers Ltd v Society of Graphical and Allied Trades* [1986] Industrial Relations Law Reports 227).

The draconian nature of the new legal framework and its ability to strengthen the employer and undermine the unions in industrial disputes was once more apparent. There was not much point in the unions picketing the buildings vacated by Murdoch — yet picketing Wapping was unlawful. The law gave no support to the unions claim for recognition. Despite the fact they had balloted their members prior to the dispute, the law gave those members no protection when News International sacked them. Neither did the unions receive protection in attempting to inconvenience the company by encouraging action at their direct customers and supplier, apparently protected by s.17 of the 1980 Act. They fell into the same trap as the NUJ in the *Dimbleby* case.

S.17 protected sympathy action if it was taken against the *first* customer or *first* supplier of the employer directly involved in the dispute. But the wholesalers' commercial contract was with News International Distribution not with News Group itself. SOGAT could only take lawful secondary action against the buffer firm News International Distribution to disrupt *its* contract with News Group. SOGAT's attempt to take action to disrupt the commercial contracts between the wholesalers and an "outside" third company, News International Distribution, was not lawful secondary action covered by s.17.

In the same way the action by the NGA at the *Northampton Mercury* did not, in legal terms, disrupt the supply of goods between Northampton Mercury Ltd and Times Newspapers, the party to the dispute — this *would* be protected by s.17 — but between Northampton Mercury Ltd and News International Supply, a quite separate company in law, established as a buffer with the specific intention of getting around the law. Had the NGA induced its members at NIS to boycott News Group that *would be protected.* NIS was the *first* customer — *Northampton Mercury* was *not* as its contract was with NIS not News Group. Attempts to get NGA members at *Northampton Mercury* to boycott work which was, in reality News Group's but, in theory, NIS's was not protected by s.17. Once again the judges ignored the reality — News International Supply *was* Times Newspapers which, in turn, *was* News Group and News International — in favour of legal fictions specifically spun to beat the unions and win the dispute.

SOGAT had felt that at the start of the dispute they had no alternative but to risk sequestration in the hope of provoking solidarity action. But this action was not forthcoming on any significant scale — not even from wholesale workers who were members of SOGAT. The strike was not biting. Murdoch, albeit with some inconvenience, was getting his papers out and sold. With many of the unions officers not being paid, cars being seized and pension and provident payments paralyzed, the SOGAT leadership apologised in the High Court on 8th May and secured the return of the union's assets.

Murdoch Defeats The Unions

The decision to apologise for the contempt of court and end the sequestration intensified divisions between the union's national leadership and the militant London chapels. In early June, when Murdoch's final offer of four weeks redundancy pay and a review of recognition at Wapping after a year was turned down by the

News International workers and the SOGAT conference agreed that no action would be taken which would lead to the re-sequestration of assets, there appeared no easy way forward for the dispute. The leadership had, throughout, adopted a 'reasonable' approach which was contrasted with that of the miners. This involved controlling picketing, attempting to win public opinion, calling for a consumer boycott of News International and portraying SOGAT General Secretary, Brenda Dean, as the voice of moderation compared with the militant Murdoch. But the Audit Bureau of Circulation figures demonstrated that Brenda Dean's reasonable approach was having little impact on News International sales and by the summer of 1986 it looked as if the print unions would have as little success as the miners.

And the employment legislation again played a role in the final denouement. In July 1986, an injunction had been issued instructing the unions to call off the picketing at Wapping (*News Group Newspapers Ltd v SOGAT* [1986] Industrial Relations Law Reports 337). This was by now beyond the official strike leadership and picketing continued until the end of the year. In January 1987, News International declared their intention to return to the courts to begin contempt proceedings. SOGAT was advised that this action was likely to be successful and likely to lead to re-sequestration. On the basis of this advice it withdrew official support for the dispute.

Lessons

The Wapping dispute reaffirmed and strengthened the lessons of the *Messenger* dispute and the miners' strike. It demonstrated more fully than either that Britain now had the toughest labour laws in the western world. In most countries, as in the USA, strikers could not be dismissed in the fashion the News International workers were dismissed if their action was — as it was here — within the law. In most countries, as in the USA, News International would have had a duty to "bargain in good faith" with the unions. The dispute showed that almost any solidarity action essential to win such disputes would be rendered unlawful and that the unions would thereby be deprived of a powerful weapon. It showed that the unions still attached no legitimacy to the law and even after the miners strike were still prepared to defy it. It showed that employers such as Murdoch were now prepared to use the law to its full extent in contrast with the NCB or BSC two years before and had the support of the government in their endeavours. And it showed that

The Police And The Wapping Dispute

The Wapping Dispute, like the Miners' strike and the NGA-Eddie Shah conflict, was characterised by the use of mass policing against the pickets. It highlighted, once again, the determination of the government and the police to eradicate mass picketing as a feature of industrial disputes in the UK. It illustrated the difference between the state's response to key strikes in the 1970s and the 1980s and the impotence of mass picketing as a union tactic when it is confronted by a 'strong state' imbued with Mrs Thatcher's "law and order" philosophy.

On average more than 1,000 police were on duty during each week of the dispute — outnumbering the strikers 6:1. When there were big pickets more than 2,000 police were on duty at Wapping — on one occasion no less than 8 Special Patrol Groups were involved. The police again utilised the new tactics and technology pioneered in earlier disputes, road blocks were also used to prevent pickets reaching Wapping and 147 year old legislation was used to place restrictions on pedestrians and vehicles in the Borough of Tower Hamlets. The Home Officer stated in June 1986 that more than a £1 million had been spent on policing costs in the first six months of the dispute.

Between January and August there were 1,139 arrests. The original workforce totalled only 6,000 and whilst workers from elsewhere were represented on the picket line this is still an extremely high arrest rate. On average 65 people were arrested each week. Most of those arrested — over 80% — were charged with the small routine offences of obstruction of the highway and conduct likely to cause a breach of the peace. In a large number of cases the police offered no evidence but the pickets were "bound over to keep the peace". This procedure meshed well with the police tactics of charging the pickets and arresting at random. Owing to police violence many pickets suffered serious injuries including heart attacks. It was clear that if the civil law now plays an increased role in disputes the criminal law is always present where picketing is concerned and in fact does most of the donkey work in controlling a dispute.

Concern over the behaviour of the police developed throughout the dispute and peaked after the big January 1987 demonstration which produced 440 complaints against over 100 officers, including complaints from the BBC and individual reporters. 67 demonstrators were arrested and 65 were convicted. By the start of 1990 not a single police officer had been prosecuted.

Home Secretary Douglas Hurd rejected demands for a public inquiry and announced plans for new police powers! (see p.103) But in January 1990 the report of the Police Complaints Board leaked to the BBC found indiscriminate use of truncheons, inappropriate use of mounted police and inadequate supervision and control of police baton charges.

In January 1989 charges of perjury, assault and conspiracy to pervert the course of justice were laid against 24 Metropolitan Police officers. The case against the first six officers was thrown out in May 1989 by the Bow Street Stipendiary Magistrate because of delays in the prosecution process. It was 1988 before the officers were informed of the specific allegations against them and 1989, 2 years after the event, before they were charged. In December 1989 the High Court upheld this decision on the grounds that delays were unfair to those charged. 18 other officers were still due to appear.

These events strengthened the view of many trade unionists that the law works swiftly and efficiently against trade unions and pickets slowly and inefficiently, if at all, against police and employers.

the unions were only able to resist the employers most potent weapon, sequestration, for a relatively short period.

The dispute also showed the difficulties of attempting to box clever, bobbing and weaving with the law. When, for example, the NGA withdrew instructions to its members not to print *The Times* supplements to avoid sequestration but then announced it would swiftly reimpose the boycott, it was faced with a court hearing the following day and forced to back down.

The Wapping dispute reaffirmed the experience of the miners' strike, illustrating the degree to which the new legislation interacts with pre-existing law — such as the right of an employer to sack strikers — to foil union purposes. The dispute also illustrated the extent to which the courts, in contrast to their normal slow and distant workings, were now willing to take on speedily, intimate involvement in the day to day issues of industrial disputes.

The TUC, in contrast, were not — at least not in the full blooded sense proclaimed at Wembley. The News International dispute again demonstrated the irrelevance of the Wembley Principles as a means of combating the legislation. Four years after Wembley the unions no longer looked to the TUC to organise solidarity industrial action. If they took on the law now they did so independently. The TUC was involved in giving a range of support short of industrial action — but it had carried out this role in industrial disputes long, long before 1982 and it was now difficult to see what difference the Wembley Principles made to this role. The TUC's caution over the EETPU issue, partly because it feared legal action, emphasised the extent to which the law now influenced important union decisions. Coming after the EETPU's breach of policy over the ballots issue, the TUC's line encouraged divisions and defiance amongst its affiliates.

And internal divisions, stimulated by government policies and industrial trends and specifically encouraged by the government to weaken the unions, were a continuing handicap to the unions. If the Wapping dispute underlined the value of the legislation to employers who utilised the law, as Murdoch did, with strategic foresight and single-minded determination, it also underscored the degree to which the impact of the law, important as it was, was secondary to divisions within the movement. The role of the EETPU was clear — but throughout the dispute NUJ members kept working behind the Wapping barbed wire. Two out of the three NGA chapels asked to boycott the printing of *The Times* supplements rejected their leaders call. Throughout the dispute TGWU members at TNT kept carrying Murdoch's papers and most SOGAT members in the wholesalers continued to supply newsagents with *The Sun* and *The Times*. Although there were threats at TNT and at British Rail when railworkers refused to handle News International titles, there was overall, little stomach for extending and thus winning the battle.

Discussion Questions

1. Should trade unions be involved in politics? What are the advantages and disadvantages of being affiliated to the Labour Party?
2. Why do you think the campaign over the Political Fund Ballots in 1984-5 was so successful? What lessons can we learn from it to take into other campaigns?
3. Discuss the view that the argument put forward by the EETPU and the AEU for taking state funds for ballots was, after the defeat of the NGA and the miners, a convincing and urgent one.
4. "The failure of the TUC to take firm action over defiance of its policy on state funds for union ballots led to the divisions over 'no strike' deals and the eventual expulsion of the EETPU from the TUC." Comment on this statement.
5. Explain how the employment legislation operated in the Wapping Dispute. Was it the decisive element in the defeat of the print unions?

TABLE 2:
INJUNCTIONS SOUGHT BY EMPLOYERS MAY 1984-APRIL 1987

Date	Parties	Grounds	Outcome
1984			
May	Redbridge DHA v GMBATU NUPE	Picketing — not at own workplace	Injunction ignored — settlement agreed
June	Crown Agents v Civil Service Unions	Political strike	Injunction refused
Oct	Cammell Laird v GMBATU members	Occupation — order for repossession Contempt proceedings	Order ignored — 37 gaoled
	Shipping Co Uniform v Int. Tran. Fed	Ballot — none held before sec. action	Action lifted
Nov	Fed. London Wholesale Newsagents v SOGAT 82	Secondary action	Action lifted
	Ilford (Kodak) v GMBATU	Ballot — none held before strike	Ballot held overtime ban vote
	Safeway v GMBATU	Ballot — none held before strike	Ballot held strike vote
	Austin Rover v APAC, AUEW, EETPU, GMBATU, NSSM, TASS, TGWU, UCATT	Ballot — none held before strike Contempt proceedings	Strikers dismissed AUEW, EETPU repudiate strike, 4 other unions comply TGWU fined £200,000 for contempt
	M J Banks v NUM	Picketing — not at own workplace	Picket withdrawn
	R Read Transport v TGWU	Secondary action (blacking for miners)	Injunction withdrawn after settlement
	G Read Transport v TGWU	Secondary action (blacking for miners)	Injunction withdrawn after settlement
1985			
Jan	Everard v NUS	Secondary action (blacking for miners)	Action lifted
	British Rail v NUR	Ballot — none held before strike	Action proceeded No injunction sought Damages of £200,000 sought

Date	Parties	Grounds	Outcome
1985			
Feb	Daily Mail v SOGAT 82	Picketing — not at own workplace	Picket scaled down settlement agreed
	Press Comp. Systems v NGA	Secondary action (blacking)	Injunction ignored
	Stephenson Clarke v NUS	Secondary action (blacking for miners)	Action lifted
	National Bus Co v TGWU members	Picketing — not at own workplace	Injunction ignored
	Kempton & Keys Advertising v NGA	Not known	Not known
	Solihull Council v NAS/UWT, NUT	Ballot — none held before strike	Ballot held strike vote
Mar	W'hampton Ex & Star v NGA	Ballot — none held before strike	Ballot held strike vote
	W'hampton Ex & Star v NGA	Ballot — none held before sec. action Contempt proceedings	Injunction ignored NGA fined £15,500
	Crown v CPSA	Ballot — none held before strike	Action lifted
	News Group Newspapers v NGA SOGAT 82	Ballot — none held before strike	Not enforced settlement agreed
	Post Office v UCW	Ballot — none held before strike	Action lifted
	Brinks Mat v APEX	Ballot — none held before strike	Ballot held strike vote
Apl	Brighton Eve Argus v NGA, NUJ	Ballot — none held before strike	Action lifted
	London Reg. Transport v NUR	Ballot — none held before strike	Action lifted
June	Brinks Mat v APEX	Ballot — incorrect wording	Injunction refused Case dropped
	CPSA v APEX members	Ballot — none held before strike	Warning issued ballot held strike vote
July	Guardian Newspapers v NGA	Ballot — none held before blacking	Action lifted
	British Rail v NUR	Ballot — none held before blacking	Action lifted

Date	Parties	Grounds	Outcome
1985	Fin. Times v Eatwell (SOGAT 82 foc)	Secondary Action	Action lifted
Aug	Brit. Telecom v NCU	Ballot — none held before strike	Action lifted
	Mirror Newspapers v NGA	Secondary action (blacking)	Dispute settled by agreement
	Fin. Times v Dongworth (NGA foc and 18 members)	Secondary action (blacking)	
Sept	Scotsman v SOGAT	Ballot — none held before strike	Ex parte interdict lifted on appeal Agreed settlement
1986 Jan	Mirror Newspapers v SOGAT 82	Ballot — none held beofre lawful trade dispute	Injunction ignored after union complied Settle when foc sacked
	News Inter. v SOGAT 82	Secondary action (blacking wholesalers) Contempt proceedings	Injunction ignored SOGAT 82 fined £25,000 funds sequestrated
	Times Newspapers v NGA	Secondary action (blacking) Contempt proceedings	Injunction ignored NGA fined £25,000
	News Inter. v TGWU	Secondary action (instruction not to cross picket lines)	Injunction ignored but action not supported by drivers
	News Inter. v NGA, SOGAT 82	Picketing — not at own workplace	Injunction ignored
Feb	News Inter. v UCW	Secondary action (blacking for printers)	Action lifted
	N'hampton Mercury v NGA	Ballot — none held before secondary action called	
	British Rail v ASLEF, NUR	Ballot — none held before proposed secondary action (blacking for printers)	Warning issued Action not proceeded with

Date	Parties	Grounds	Outcome
1986	John Laing v Higgins and other	Picketing — not at own workplace	Injunction ignored but no union support
Mar	London Buses v TGWU	Ballot — incorrect procedures	Settlement negotiated
	Mirror Newspapers v SOGAT 82	Ballot — none held before strike Contempt proceedings	Injunction ignored Sequestration sought suspended to allow return to work
	Mirror Newspapers v SOGAT 82	Ballot — none held before union issued order not to cross picket lines Contempt proceedings	Injunction ignored workforce dismissed Court refused to act since workforce sacked
	Scottish Daily Record v SOGAT	Ballot — none held before strike	Ballot held strike vote
May	Townsend Thoresen v NUS branch officers	Ballot — none held before sympathy strike	Action lifted
	Townsend Thoresen v NUS branch officers	Ballot — none held before official sympathy strike	Injunction ignored after union complied
	Townsend Thoresen v NUS	Ballot — none held before official sympathy strike	Action lifted
	Falconer v ASLEF & NUR	Ballot — none held before secondary action	Private individual wins right to £153 damages against union
	Gtr London FA v Fire Brigade U	Ballot — none held before strike	Action lifted
June	News Inter. v SOGAT 82	Picketing — intimidation by numbers	Picket reduced to six
	News Inter. v NGA	Picketing — intimidation by numbers 128	Picket reduced to six
	Morfax v TASS	Ballot — none held before strike	Injunction refused Manual TU ballot for strike, TASS vote not material
	TNT Roadfreight (UK) v NGA, SOGAT 82	Picketing — not at own workplace	Unions complied but members ignore order

Date	Parties	Grounds	Outcome
1986	TNT Roadfreight (UK) v NGA & SOGAT pickets	Picketing — not at own workplace	Injunctions granted against two individuals withdrawn against three others after giving undertaking to court
Sept	Scene Printing v NGA branch officers	Secondary action (blacking)	Injunction ignored
	Mirror Newspapers v Harrison (NGA foc)	Ballot — none held before strike Contempt proceedings	Injunction ignored Undisclosed fine
	Monsanto v TGWU	Ballot — none held before strike	Ballot held strike vote
	Monsanto v TGWU	Ballot — none held before renewed strike	Injunction refused same dispute, no need for new ballot Strike unofficial TGWU not liable
	Barretts & Baird (& 8 others) v ICPS	Unlawful inducement of breach of statutory duty	Action lifted Injunction discharged on appeal
	Kent Free Press v NGA	Secondary action (blacking) Contempt proceedings	Injunction ignored NGA fined £4000 for contempt by two branch officers
Oct	R A Lister v TGWU	Ballot — incorrect wording	Action lifted settlement agreed
	Cornwall CC v NAS/UWT	Ballot — none held before strike	Ballot held strike vote
	Devon CC v NAS/UWT	Ballot — none held before strike	Ballot held strike vote
	Dorset CC v NAS/UWT	Ballot — none held before strike	Ballot held strike vote
	Hampshire CC v NAS/UWT	Ballot — none held before strike	Ballot held strike vote

Date	Parties	Grounds	Outcome
1986	Nth Yorks CC v NAS/UWT	Ballot — none held before strike	Ballot held strike vote
	West Sussex CC v NAS/UWT	Ballot — none held before strike	Ballot held strike vote
McCarthy & Stone v UCATT, TGWU	Ballot — none held before strike	Ballot held strike vote Judge refused to lift injunction because no longer a trade dispute.	Writ issued
1987 Jan	Dpt Employment v Thomason (CPSA officer)	Unlawful dispute — not connected with terms & conditions of employment	Action lifted
	News Inter. v NGA, SOGAT 82	Picketing — intimidation by numbers	Union agreed to reduce numbers
	Harrods v USDAW	Ballot — incorrect wording	Warning issued during negotiations
	Cunard v NUS	Secondary action (blacking)	Action lifted
Feb	Harlech TV v NUJ	Ballot — action longer than balloted for	Action shortened
Mar	Hereford & Worcs CC v NAS/UWT	Ballot — none held before strike	Damages claim £48,000
Apl	Caterpillar v Brannan & 807 others	Occupation	Interim interdict

Source: S. Evans, 'The use of injunctions in industrial disputes' *British Journal of Industrial Relations*, November, 1987.

CHAPTER 6

Another Brick in the Wall

Bad laws are the worst sort of tyranny — *Edmund Burke*

THE LEGISLATION AT WORK

The crumbling of the TUC position on boycotting public funds for union ballots was quickly reinforced as an increasing number of unions lined up to take the cash. The two in 1985 — the EETPU and the AEU — grew to nine in 1986 and 17 in 1987. There was a similar adaptation to the law by management and unions in other key areas.

Industrial Action

By October 1987 *Labour Research* reported there had been 194 legal cases involving industrial action with the largest number in one year being the 21 cases in 1986. Employers still seemed to be getting what they wanted through the interim injunction mechanism. In only a handful of cases did employers press home their advantage and seek damages from the union at a full trial. Whilst Hereford and Worcester County Council took action against the NAS/UWT teachers union to recover £48,000 in respect of a half day teachers strike, Austin-Rover dropped its claim against the unions over the 1984 industrial action on the traditional grounds that there was now an "improved industrial relations" climate.

TABLE 3:
Sectoral Distribution of Injunctions:
May 1984-April 1987

Printing	29
Shipping/Transport	18
Public Services	14
Engineering/Shipbuilding	5
Professional	3
Chemicals (incl.2 in same dispute)	3
Communications	3
Retail/Distribution	2
Construction	2
Coal	1
Total	80

Source: *Labour Research*

The impact of the legislation in the area of industrial action was real — but not to be overestimated. At the end of 1985, ACAS reported that they were aware of 94 strike ballots in the first 15 months of the 1984 Act's operation. In 1986 there were a further 152 ballots, bringing the total to 246. These statistics showed that there was an impetus towards compliance with the legislation where ballots were concerned. The unions remember, had no obligation to hold ballots on industrial action and only became liable in legal terms once the courts had issued an injunction after the union had "authorised" or "endorsed" industrial action without a ballot. But, as ACAS itself pointed out, the provisions were catching only a small proportion of action. There were more than 1,000 strikes annually plus many more incidents of other industrial action. In the majority of cases action was taking place in blithe disregard of the highly publicised legislation and employers were not availing themselves of their legal rights.

Moreover, the unions were showing in this area that they could at least live with the law — and sometimes turn it to their advantage. Of the total of 246 ballots on industrial action held by the end of 1986, 189 went in favour of the union position, 54 against and 3 were tied. Unions were winning the ballots but in *only 20 cases had some form of industrial action resulted.* Unions were using the ballots to strengthen their negotiating position and convince the employers that their members were serious. After a successful ballot a consequent strike or more normally the threat of a strike possessed, much to the annoyance of government and employers, a *new force and legitimacy.* It was clear that ballots on industrial action, whilst still small-scale in relation to the overall picture, were becoming as ACAS put it, a permanent part of the negotiating scene. In 1987 a further 280 ballots were held. In 251, or 90%, the ballot went in favour of the union's position. Turnouts were high — 75% votes were common and 53 unions had now been involved in statutory ballots.

In legal action in 1985 involving the National Union of Teachers it was made clear that a wide approach would be taken to what was involved in a breach of the legislation and injunctions would be issued, not only where no ballot had been held but where the wording did not cover the ambit of the industrial action and where the statement that it was in breach of contract was missing (*Solihull M.B. v NUT* [1985] Industrial Relations Law Reports 211). ASTMS attempted to minimise the impact of the requirement by a standard form which began 'obviously the usual breach of your contract of employment is involved'. In another case the Court of Appeal emphasised the importance of the *exact wording* of the ballot paper: a dispute sparked by the employment of five temporary workers had not terminated when they left as the union still wished to pursue the issue and the ballot paper referred to "industrial action in pursuit of the dispute with Monsanto plc over the employment of Temporary Labour". Moreover the court held that a commonsense attitude had to be taken to suspension of industrial action called after a ballot. If the action was suspended to allow negotiations, a second ballot was not required if action re-commenced within a reasonable period (*Monsanto plc v TGWU* [1986] Industrial Relations Law Reports 406). However, in another case involving APEX members at Brinks-Mat, the ballot had to be held again as the breach of contract requirement was missing from the ballot paper through a clerical error.

Applications for injunctions in cases where no ballot violation was alleged, likewise occurred in a very small minority of cases of industrial action. Here the employers' win rate in the courts was over 90% and in an even higher proportion of cases the injunction was complied with. It was clear that a growing number of employers faced with industrial action likely to be more than a passing cloud, or likely to cause financial problems, looked to the law as one weapon in their armoury — perhaps to be used in conjunction with others, whether inducements or threats of dismissal. Recourse to the law was usually a tactical matter. A case was more likely to be pursued, for example, where there were divisions within the union or where success for the union depended crucially on secondary action.

The Law against Shop Stewards

By 1987 there were also many examples of management attempting to influence the behaviour of trade unions by drawing the attention of members and lay representatives to the law or threatening its use against them.

On 7th November 1986 two NGA members at the Mirror Group, Tom Harrison and Laurence Wells were fined £15,000 for calling a chapel meeting in defiance of an injunction. Judge Mars-Jones stated that the men's contempt "undoubtedly merits a prison sentence".[1]

In 1987 members of the National Union of Seafarers took industrial action before a ballot had been held in accordance with the 1984 Act. P&O went to the High Court and secured an injunction not against the union but against Ken Turner, Secretary of Hull NUS, restraining him from giving any support to the action. He was later threatened with a suit for damages. A good example of the employer using the law to intimidate individuals occurred in January

1988 when British Coal threatened to use the legislation to stop secondary picketing and then wrote to all workers in the picketed pits stating that secondary action was unlawful and that they would sack anybody who participated in it.

A further development has been the threat of legal action against shop stewards. At Thorn-EMI four shop stewards were sent solicitors' letters which threatened them with a claim for damages of more than £40,000 for industrial action taken without a ballot, The employers only withdrew the threat after promises of future 'good behaviour' had been made. British Rail actually took legal action against six union activists at Kings Cross in preference to suing ASLEF after a decision was taken to support a Day of Action over the NHS dispute. They won an injunction and Mr Justice McKinnon not only ordered the six branch officers to withdraw their strike call "forthwith" but also instructed then not to issue any further calls for industrial action whilst the injunction was in place — apparently indefinitely. Support for the NHS workers was, of course, unlawful secondary action. For British Rail the injunction was not the end of the matter. Management had obtained it as a tactical prelude to victimisation. Five of the six were handed final written warnings stating in legal terminology that they would be "summararily dismissed if they again induced others to break their contracts of employment". Assistant Secretary Steve Forey was sacked on the spot.

Management then used the injunction to put the frighteners on the rest of the workforce to undermine support for Steve Forey. As members balloted for strike action to defend him, British Rail sent letters to all members of ASLEF at Kings Cross threatening to sue them individually for compensation should the ballot then being conducted result in strike action. This interference with the democratic process bore fruit. In the face of this intimidation the ballot was lost by 150 votes to 124.

Management, Individuals and the Closed Shop

Management were thus considering their ability to go to court far more than they did in the past and were using this power to a greater degree in flexible, forceful and imaginative fashion. Legal experts and line and financial managers appeared to be more involved in decision-making than in the past — compared with personnel managers. And the old management view that the use of the law against their own workforce could permanently sour industrial relations appeared to be no longer as relevant. From the union side there was some evidence that the existence of the legislation had buttressed the position of full time officers compared with lay representatives in decision-making about industrial action. Here again, the law must be seen in its interaction with other trends in industrial relations and the economic situation.

However, after the giddy heights of the miners' strike the government had less success in their cherished objective of mobilising *individuals* to use the legislation. The provisions on industrial action were, of course, drafted in such a way as to allow individual customers and consumers to go to law when inconvenienced by strike action. Such cases, however, remained extremely rare. The only reported example (*Falconer v ASLEF and NUR* [1986] Industrial Relations Law Reports 331), saw a commuter successfully obtain £153 damages from the rail unions for the expense and inconvenience he had suffered during a strike called without a ballot.

If employers were still exploring the use of the law in this area of industrial action there was, despite all the efforts of the government, little use of the legislation on the closed shop. This must, on the whole, be judged a rather complex failure. Between 1980 and 1987 years of orchestrated government concern, intense publicity and new rights for its alleged victims, there were only 14 recorded cases involving closed shop dismissals. Ten of these cases were bunched between 1983 and 1985 and were promoted or supported by the Freedom Association. The position 12 months after the second round of closed shop legislation took effect in the autumn of 1984, according to *Labour Research*

> ... suggests that non-unionists or those wishing to leave unions have shown little interest in the new 'freedoms' so generously given to them by the government ... This lack of evidence of a mass defection from the closed shop indicates that the balloting provisions for it were unnecessary.[2]

In early 1987 ACAS reported that ballots on the closed shop were also stuttering to a halt. There was a "falling away of interest in this area". In 1986 there were only 9 cases coming to the attention of ACAS bringing the total to 119 ballots. Again, despite the very high majorities required these ballots had vindicated the unions' stand on the closed shop. On their evidence workers *supported* the closed shop: 91 ballots had come out in its favour and in only 20 had the 80% plus vote not been achieved. However, the legislation had on the whole had very little impact. ACAS believed that out of more than 3 million workers still covered by closed shop arrangements only around 30,000 were covered by closed shops approved under the provisions of the legislation.

Union Ballots

By 1987 there was general compliance with the provisions of the 1984 Act on executive elections. Some unions such as NALGO did not change their rules when the Act received the royal assent but waited on successful complaints to the Certification Officer before introducing the required changes to rule. In 1986 the Certification Officer made nine declarations and in 1987 found four unions in breach of the requirements although by the end of 1987 there had been no applications to the High Court. The unions were, however, heartened by the success of previously 'non-political' unions like NALGO which won a ballot for the political fund by 77.4% to 22.5%, on a 67% turnout and the Institute of Professional Civil Servants which voted 81.7% in favour and only 18% against, on a 51% turnout. Conservative ministers indulged in sour grapes, sniped at the way the ballots had been conducted and promised that there was more legislation to come.

The TUC Campaign

By the time of the 1987 General Election, a little over five years since the Wembley Conference, any suggestion that the TUC would co-ordinate industrial action to protect an affiliate against an employer utilising the Conservative legislation would have produced hysterical laughter. Intervening events had cruelly exposed the rhetoric and bluff of the General Council. The TUC's campaign against the legislation now consisted of observing events rather than moulding matters, "keeping the operation of the 1980 and 1982 Employment Acts under close scrutiny". Whilst they also "assisted affiliated unions in dealing with difficulties, caused by the legislation",[3] this was technical assistance given in the context of a 'bending-the-knee' policy of practical compliance with the law. Out-manoeuvred on its domestic terrain, the TUC increasingly looked for succour to Europe and developments such as the EC *Social Charter.* Campaigning against what was to become the 1988 Act consisted of "lobbying employers, Conservative MPs and the House of Lords on the dangerous, consequences of the proposals".[4] The unions had travelled a long, hard, humbling road since 1982.

THE 1988 EMPLOYMENT ACT

In the autumn of 1986 Tom King was replaced by Lord Young as Secretary of State For Employment and junior minister Kenneth Clarke promised the Conservative Party Conference new legal measures on the closed shop, industrial disputes and union elections. In the build up to the General Election a Green Paper *Trade Unions and Their Members* was published. After listing the governments achievements since 1979 the document promised a further package which would paper over cracks which had emerged, fill in the gaps and take matters a stage further. The government were still convinced that anti-union measures remained popular with the electorate. But it was noticeable that the Green Paper produced a lukewarm or hostile response amongst both employers and the media.

Nonetheless, in October 1987, in the aftermath of the General Election, pursuing the now familiar pattern of a continuing cycle of employment legislation through each Parliament, the government published a Bill in which the Green Paper's provisions largely survived intact. Lord Young justified the need for further legislation by remarking:

> We have observed closely the impact of our legislation. In general, progress has been marked and encouraging. However, some unions have declined the opportunity to put their house in order and union members have not always felt able to take a stand and ensure that abuses are corrected. It is, therefore, clear that we need now to take another step both to strengthen the rights of individuals within a union and to reinforce their ability to enforce those rights.[5]

In other words if the unions successfully resisted or found ways round the legislation or, if allegedly oppressed individuals failed to use it, the government would introduce further legislation to make life still more difficult for the unions. As the TUC pointed out, quite apart from the content of legislation, successive rounds were:

> imposing a burden of administrative law and detailed statutory regulation on unions which is not borne by any other equivalent organisation ... The government should let union members decide for themselves on their union's rules and constitutional arrangements.[6]

Alistair Graham of the Industrial Society gave voice to the concerns of "progressive" management and indeed many other employers when he stated:

> If the Government presses ahead with its reforms many of us will begin to question what sort of trade unions this government wants to see, if indeed it wants to see any at all.[7]

Nonetheless, the Bill wended its way through Parliament and received the Royal Assent on 26th May 1988. It came into force in May and July 1988.

Ballots On Industrial Action
(s.1, 3, 4, 5, 17, 18)

The Act introduced three key changes to the 1984 Act's provisions.

Union Members: The 1984 Act provided that unions would lose their immunity against legal action if they *induced* workers to take industrial action in breach of their contracts of employment *without a ballot*. The right to take legal action in these circumstances however was given only to *employers*. The 1988 Act extended this right to *union members*. This was seen by the government as extending the rights of the individual and as doubling up the pressure on the union. Remember that "induce" is wider than "instruct" and this allowed unions to be sucessfully sued in a wide range of situations.

Strike-Breaking: Occasionally unions have to take disciplinary action — usually a fine sometimes expulsion — against members who work normally during a strike or industrial action, do the work of strikers, refuse to pay a levy or cross picket lines. The Act now introduced a right *not to be unjustifiably disciplined*. This gave union members the right to take a case to an industrial tribunal where they had

— failed to participate in or support a strike or industrial action even if it was official, constitutional and backed by the majority of workers in a statutory secret ballot
— made allegations that the union or full-time officers or other representatives of the union acted contrary to the union rules or broke agreements or the law
— brought legal proceedings against the union or alleged that union support for industrial action was against the law
— sought advice or help from the Certification Officer, the Commissioner For the Rights of Trade Union Members, or any other person in relation to the above matters
— personally encouraged or assisted others in failure to participate in legal action, making allegations about the union or, seeking help from the Commissioner
— refused to comply with any penalty imposed in relation to the above
— intended to do any of the above.

This provision was said by the government to "give members freedom to make up their own minds whether or not to support industrial action". But, in terms of any conception of democracy, members were already given the right to make up their own minds by being given the right to vote in a ballot in industrial action. The right to ignore the result if it went against the way they had voted is a right to ignore democracy. It makes a mockery of the idea of a ballot. What is the point of having a vote if everybody is then free to ignore it? It is difficult to see the logic in terms of democratic theory of branding as "unjustifiable", action intended to penalise those who refuse to be bound by democratic decision-making.

In practical terms, the widespread utilisation of this right would reduce collective action, the essence of trade unionism, to chaos, with individual decisions being substituted for collectivism. Unions were now prohibited by law from upholding their rules even though those rules met the tests of reasonableness and natural justice.

Separate Ballots: Where a ballot involved unions at different places of work they could, under the 1984 Act, be simply counted together to produce a single overall result. However, in a confusing provision, the 1988 Act states that this should continue to be the position where all the members involved share a "common distinguishing factor". Members share a "common distinguishing factor" where, for example, all those voting in the ballot represent all the union members in a particular grade or occupation employed by that employer. Or where all those to be balloted share terms and conditions of employment which are distinguished from those of employees not being balloted and determined by the same established bargaining arrangements. If these conditions do *not* apply then the votes of workers at different workplaces must be counted and declared separately.

Codes of Practice
(s.18)

The Secretary of State For Employment is given the power to issue statutory Codes of Practice to promote what he considers desirable practices in relation to unions' conduct of ballots and elections. The government announced its intention of quickly issuing a Code of Practice on ballots for industrial action.

The Closed Shop
(s.10, 11)

In the 1980 and 1982 Acts the government had erected complex machinery for creating approved closed shops. The 1988 Act renders this carefully constructed edifice redundant after allowing only three years to see if it worked or not! As a replacement for the ballots in the previous legislation, which as recently as 1984 were seen as the token of democracy, a means of restoring to ordinary members the right to make up their own mind, the government has substituted by legal *diktat* a simple *ban on the post-entry closed shop*. The reason is that the provisions of the earlier legislation were seen not to have worked as members made up their own minds not to use them in the fashion the government required. As we have seen, there were few ballots and of these the majority went in favour of maintaining the closed shop. Despite this clear evidence of what workers wanted, the government's guidance to this part of the 1988 Act states

> the effect of the new provisions is to remove all statutory support for the closed shop. Unions will no longer be free to operate any sort of closed shop practice which denies jobs to, discriminates against or forces the dismissal of non-unionists. Dismissal for non-membership of a trade union will automatically be unfair.[8]

This statement is not quite true. The Act did not affect the *pre-entry* closed shop. Prospective employees could still lawfully be refused a job on the grounds of their non-membership of a trade union. But the Act did hit the post-entry closed shop by
— making any dismissal, or discrimination short of dismissal, against an employee on the grounds of non-membership of a union automatically unfair in all circumstances
— making it unlawful to organise or threaten industrial action to establish or maintain any sort of union closed shop practice by withdrawing the immunities from any such action. This could affect pre-entry closed shops. It took the 1982 Act which prohibited secondary action to achieve this purpose a stage further: *any action to achieve a closed shop* by an employers' *own employees* was now prohibited.

Political Fund Ballots
(s.14, 15, 16)
The 1984 Act had allowed ballots on the creation or maintenance of a political fund to be conducted by a variety of methods: by post, or at the workplace or by a mix of both. Now such ballots must be *held by the postal voting method only*.
— Previously complaints about the conduct of political fund ballots had to be taken directly to the High Court. The Act now provided that they could also be taken up with the Certification Officer.
— The Act also required independent scrutiny of political fund ballots as well as a scrutineer's report to be made available to all members.
These provisions represented a further affirmation of the Conservative belief that postal ballots produce Conservative results: the 1985-86 round of political fund ballots had been run by the

unions at the workplace, the results next time round with postal voting might turn out very differently.

Union Elections
(s.12-15)

The Act extended the statutory election requirements from *voting members* of a union's executive committee to

— The chief executive officers of the union such as the *General Secretary* and the *President* or their nearest equivalent.
— All those who under the rules or practice of the union may *attend and speak at meetings of the executive committee* unless they attend or speak only to provide factual information or technical or professional advice on matters incidental to the committee's functions.

All those covered by these provisions must in future be elected *every 5 years*. Moreover, as in the case of political fund ballots (but not ballots over industrial action) ballots for executive positions must now take place by *the postal method only* and must be supervised by *independent scrutineers.*

As with the political fund ballots the scrutineers must be free from interference by the union. They will supervise the production, circulation and return of the ballot papers. The scrutineers will also draw up a *report* on the details of the election, covering such matters as the number of votes cast, the numbers cast for each candidate, the numbers of papers spoiled. The union must notify details of this report to members within three months by, for example, circular, or publication in the union journal. *All members are entitled to a full copy of the report on request though the union may charge for this.*

The Act lays down certain exceptions to the requirements on ballots for union elections

— If an executive member or officer to whom the Act would otherwise apply has been elected in the 5 years previous to 26th July 1989 (the Act's implementation date) they can stay in office for a full 5 years from the date of their election even though that election did not meet the requirements of the 1984 Act
— 'Special Register Bodies' organisations such as the Royal College of Nursing which are registered as trade unions but which see themselves more as 'professional associations' are excluded from these provisions
— Special arrangements are made for Executive Officers reaching retirement age, those with only a limited term of office and the

situation where a new union is created by amalgamation or transfer of engagements.

These measures represented a further step in the government objective of gradually introducing postal ballots for all levels of appointments in trade unions.

Election Addresses (s.13)

— Candidates for elections covered by the legislation have now a legal right to prepare an election address and have it distributed with voting papers, at *no cost* to themselves, to all those entitled to vote.

— The union can set a maximum length for the address and a deadline for receipt of copy after the closing date for nominations.

— The union cannot modify the content of the address.

— Any legal liability for its contents lies with the candidate for office. Complaints regarding this new right may be made to the Certification Officer or directly to the High Court.

Further Obligations On Unions (s.6-9)

Access to Accounts: The Act places a duty on unions to keep their accounts *available for inspection for a period of six years.* Within *28 days* of a members request to make them available the union must arrange for an inspection, allow the member to be accompanied by *an accountant*, who must however agree to confidentiality. The union must also facilitate the taking of copies or alternatively supply copies or extracts. The union can make a reasonable charge for administrative expenses. If it does not comply with these requirements the aggrieved member can take action in the High Court.

Union Trustees: Members were also given the right to take legal action against their union's trustees if they apply or permit the application of union funds or other property for unlawful purposes — or if the members believe the trustees *intend* to do this. Previously union members could only take action in the courts if the trustees were in contravention of union rules. Now, as in so many other cases, specific breach of the rulebook is not necessary. On a member's application the courts can now require the trustees to take specified steps to protect or recover union property, appoint a receiver for union property or remove one or more of the trustees.

If the court order is not complied with the court *must* remove all the trustees unless good grounds are shown.

Indemnification: In the past unions have paid the fines of officers, representatives and members who were penalised by the courts for carrying out union policies. Now it is unlawful for a union to provide such an indemnity for anybody fined for contempt of court, or any other criminal offence, except those designated by the Secretary of State. The union *can indemnify members against claims for damages at civil law.*

If the union pays a member's fine the indemnity can be recovered from the fined member. Any other member who objects can take the matter to the High Court which can authorise recovery.

The Check-off: In the past there have been vague complaints that those who wish to stop being members of a trade union find barriers placed in their path and experience particular difficulties in stopping deduction of dues at source by their employer. Despite the lack of any persuasive evidence on this point, the Act provides that an employer who receives written notification that an employee has ceased to be a member and that the union is aware of this, must stop deducting union subscriptions from the date specified in the letter. If that is not practicable he must stop the deductions as soon as administrative arrangements can be made. The employer does not have to receive the union's authorisation. If the employer does not comply with these requirements the employee can apply to an industrial tribunal under the *Wages Act 1986* for a *declaration* that unlawful deductions have been made and for a *refund* of the money unlawfully deducted.

These provisions, as the TUC has argued, impose additional cramping administrative burdens, not applied to other organisations, to the unions. They introduce a great element of legalism and a greater element of expense as with the provisions on accounts to the activities of unions. In *Taylor v NUM (Derbyshire Area)* [1985] Industrial Relations Law Reports 65, 99, a case arising from the miners' strike, the High Court authorised an accountant to spend three days inspecting the books of one area of the union which only had 10,000 members. The disorganisation the Act's provisions can impose on busy unions needs no underlining. They provide, as with the provisions on trustees, for a greater degree of outside control of unions. They are intended to further facilitate an exodus from the unions, as with the provisions on deduction of dues at source. They are intended to strengthen tendencies to caution and compliance with the legislation, as with the requirements on indemnities, intended to put the frighteners on union activists and encourage obedience through fear. Whether they will work in this fashion is, of course, quite another matter.

Civil Servants and Crown Employment (s.30)

Case law in 1987 had created doubts as to whether certain categories of civil servant were employed under a contract of employment. If this was so, many of the key provisions of the legislation would be inapplicable to those employed by the crown (the government) and those employed by other crown bodies. If civil servants did not have contracts of employment then their union could not be sued for inducing them to break contracts of employment. There would be no need for civil servants to be balloted prior to industrial action as that action could not be in breach of contract. If the crown could not make contracts then the provisions on union membership and recognition requirements in commercial contracts could not apply.

This section of the Act attempts to ensure that there is no alternative to the legislation for thousands of government workers. It provides that for all civil servants and others employed by the government on terms that do *not* constitute a contract of employment those terms will nevertheless *be deemed to constitute a contract of employment* for the following purposes

— those arising from the liability of any person who induces another to break or interfere with the performance of a contract or who threatens such a breach or interference
— those arising from the law on strike ballots and union membership agreements
— those arising from the right given to union members not to be unjustifiably disciplined.

Civil servants and those working for other crown bodies are also specifically included in the right to have arrangements for the deduction of union subscriptions stopped. This act also applies to government employment the prohibition placed upon recognition requirements in contracts for the supply of goods or services contained in the *1982 Employment Act.*

This section of the Act illustrates again the speed and determination with which the government acts to close any loopholes in the legislation opened up by the courts. The government offered to fund an appeal by the Inland Revenue officer, Vaughan Bruce, whose High Court case opened the loophole and when this did not succeed they once again simply changed the rules of the game. The judges, it seemed, were only right when they agreed with Mrs Thatcher.

Getting The Member To Sue
(s.2, 19, 20, 21)

One of the key problems with employment legislation from the government's point of view has been the resistance of what they see as the sane and decent ordinary members to the array of inducements proffered to stimulate them to take legal action against their unions. How to get the member into court has been a continuing puzzle to the government.

The Commissioner For The Rights Of Trade Union Members: One problem in getting the member to take legal action has been the time, expense and aggravation involved. Unless the disgruntled member is lucky enough to come across a philanthropic outfit like The Freedom Association, inertia is generally preferred to litigation. Now union members can seek the assistance of the new Commissioner who can pay for any legal advice and representation required and make arrangements for its provision. The Commissioner has a *discretion* to decide whether or not to help. Help *must* be provided where a member has won a declaration from the Certification Officer against the union about a union election, membership register or political fund ballot and it appears to the Commissioner that the applicant has a reasonable prospect of success in any proceedings. Help *may* be provided even where success appears unlikely in court if the proceedings raise *a point or principle*, are *complex* or raise a matter of *substantial public interest*. The Commissioner can help with cases going to court arising out of complaints by members against their union which relate to

— ballots on industrial action
— the right to inspect accounts
— indemnities to union officers or representatives
— proceedings involving union trustees
— political funds
— union executive elections
— such other proceedings, being proceedings against a trade union, an official of a trade union or the trustees of the property of a trade union *as may be specified in an order made by the Secretary of State.*

No assistance can be granted to help with complaints to industrial tribunals or to the Certification Officer.

Access To The Courts: Until 1988 the courts could refuse to hear a case brought by a member against a union if the member had not fully used any procedures for pursuing the grievance laid down in the unions rulebook. The Act ends this discretion and *prohibits* the courts from dismissing or adjourning proceedings on the grounds that the internal domestic procedures have not been used. If the applicant has applied to the union for the matter to be resolved according to the rulebook and the application to the court was made more than *six months after the day on which the union received the member's application* then the court *must* hear the complaint. In other words unions have six months to deal with problems through their own procedures before the courts intervene.

These provisions would appear, in their desire to get the union member to court, to sacrifice Conservative philosophy for union bashing. After all, the Conservatives are the party of self reliance and individualism opposed to state intervention and its discouragement of individual initiative. They have opposed the Equal Opportunities Commission and the Commission For Racial Equality on these grounds. Yet in this case they are spending taxpayers' money in extending 'the nanny state' and making an exception to their general policy of benignly neglecting the legal aid system. There is, for example, still no legal aid for applicants to industrial tribunals. The other two Commissions were only established after mountains of research had been used to hammer out the need for public intervention to counteract long entrenched patterns of racist and sexist discrimination. *There is not even a small molehill of evidence of trade unions discriminating against their members* to justify the breach with conservatism this initiative represents. The new *six month limit* on internal resolution of grievances also singles unions out from other similar organisations. It clearly encourages resort to the courts and legalism at the expense of conciliation and voluntary settlement of grievances, approaches hitherto espoused by Conservative politicians.

A broad principle of public policy in the UK has been to leave as far as possible to independent organisations, whether the British Medical Association, the Law Society, the Women's Institute or, the Engineering Employers Federation, the right to enforce their own rules in their own sphere. The 1988 Act marks the definite exclusion of the unions from this principle. It is now very obvious that the domestic affairs of unions are to be made subject to a far greater degree of legalism. Provisions, such as that allowing members to go to court whilst their grievance is still being dealt with by the union's internal procedures, strike at the rules of several important unions — the NUM is one — which ban members from legal action until they have exhausted the domestic process. These provisions can only impair efficiency, and involve unions in more time-consuming and expensive litigation. But they also undermine union self-government and, taken together with the new right to ignore the results of ballots, they are intended to undermine democracy something the government claims it wants to encourage.

The Training Commission

The Act replaced the Manpower Services Commission with the Training Commission. It enabled the Secretary of State for Employment to introduce new payments for those awaiting a place on the Youth Training Scheme and gave the Secretary of State powers to determine the employment status of those on government training schemes.

RESPONSES

The main thrust of the 1988 Act had been advertised as tidying up and plugging the gaps. Added together, and to the previous framework, the measures represented an important increment to existing policies. The provisions relating to unjustifiable discipline and the Commissioner For The Rights Of Trade Union Members were themselves of major significance and represented a qualitative development in the regulation of union activities. The government were also attacking, on other fronts, *The Teachers' Pay and Conditions Act 1987*, abolished collective bargaining in the schools and gave the Secretary of State powers to impose terms and conditions by order. In early 1988, having as they saw it, cleaned up the printing industry the government, in the wake of a campaign in the Murdoch press attacking the unions in broadcasting and carricaturing feather bedding practices — the aim was deregulation of broadcasting and a chance for the press magnates to cash in — referred 'restrictive labour practices' in television, broadcasting and film production, to the Monopolies and Mergers Commission under s79 of the *Fair Trading Act 1973*.

However there were clear indications that for many of its supporters some of the provisions of the 1988 Act represented "a bridge too far". Condemnation of the "unjustifiable discipline" section united all the employers organisations from the CBI and the EEF to the IPM. Even the Freedom Association and the Association of Conservative Trade Unionists opposed it. The IPM summed up the feeling of many in management

> the use of the law to deny any opportunity to discipline members when they infringe rules which go to the heart of the contract between the union and its members is coming close to denying the body any legal standing. This is a far cry from action to ensure that trade unions are democratically run.[9]

TABLE 4:
Legal action initiated by employers 1987-88

Date	Union	Employer or party bringing action	Remedy sought	Grounds	Outcome
August '87	TGWU	Mersey Docks & Harbour Board	injunction	B	injunction sought to demand union ballot on unofficial action
December '87	TGWU	Golf Links Hotel Isle of Man	injunction	P	picketing said to contravene Isle of Man 1936 law
	TGWU	Isle of Man Breweries	injunction	P	legislation used following success of previous action (above). Dispute eventually settled with government commitment to review existing restrictive laws
January '88	NUM	British Coal		P	considered using legislation to halt secondary picketing but instead issued threatening letter to employees
February '88	seven unions	Austin Rover		B	employer finally announced that it would drop action for damages with each side paying own costs
	NAS/UWT	Hereford & Worcester CC	writ	B	claim for damages for 1986 strike settled out of court
	NUS	P&O	injunction	P	employer argued that picketing unlawful
	NUS	Sealink	injunction	S	contempt of court fine of £7,500 for not calling off national ferry strike
March '88	NUS	P&O	injunction	B	order to union not to declare votes on national ballot

B = Boycott; P = Picketing; S = Strike

Date	Union	Employer or party bringing action	Remedy sought	Grounds	Outcome
	GMB/AEU	Thorn–EMI		B/P	threat to sue for damages of £42,000 for action without ballot and unlawful picketing
	ASLEF reps	BR	injunction	S	order to withdraw strike instruction and not to call further strikes while injunction in force
	ACTT/other	Secretary of State			investigation into restrictive labour practices under Fair Trading Act 1973
May '88	NUS	Sealink		S	fine £150,000 and sequestration
	NUS	P&O		S	fine £150,000 on complaint that unlawful action still affecting ships
	NUS	P&O		P	opposition to lifting of sequestration on grounds of intimidation of strike breakers
July '88	NUS	P&O		P	further contempt for failure to dissociate union from mass pickets
	UCW	Post Office	injunction	P	order on union not to instruct members to boycott "team briefings"
	NUS	P&O		P	new fine of £25,000 for ongoing contempt of court

Source: *Labour Research*, September 1988

EQUAL PAY

The trade unions *were* having some success in 1988 in the field of equal rights. Julie Hayward, a canteen assistant, had lodged her case under the Equal Value regulations as long ago as February 1984. The industrial tribunal accepted the report of an independent expert on her claim for equal value with a joiner, a painter and a thermal insulation engineer and found in her favour. Later, however, the employer returned to the tribunal arguing that although Julie Hayward was engaged on work of equal value with the men and although her basic wage was lower than theirs, she was not employed on less favourable terms *overall*. This was because, unlike the men, she had a paid meal break, extra holidays and a better sick pay package.

Arguments as to this ensured that Julie Hayward's case went right through the court system and it was more than four years later, in May 1988, that the House of Lords gave judgement. They decided that *a woman who can point to a term in her contract which is less favourable than a term of a similar kind in a man's contract is entitled to have that term made not less favourable even though she enjoys other benefits and advantages which the men do not*. Julie Hayward was entitled, therefore, to the same basic wage as the men. They, in their turn, could bring similar claims to secure parity on the fringe benefits such as holidays and sickness (*Hayward v Cammell Laird Shipbuilders* [1988] Industrial Relations Law Reports 257).

In another important case, in July 1988, Rene Pickstone and four other women employed as "warehouse operatives" claimed their work was of equal value to that of "checker warehouse operatives". The problem was that a number of men were employed as warehouse operatives. Freemans, therefore, argued that Rene Pickstone and the other women could not bring an equal value claim against men in another occupational group because they were engaged on like work with and paid the same as the men in the "warehouse operative category".

The House of Lords found for the women. They decided that the *fact that a woman is employed on like work with one man does not stop her from claiming equal pay on the grounds of equal value with another man*. An employer cannot, therefore, undermine the regulations' intention by appointing a token man to an essentially female group. Mixed groups can use the women as a means of raising wages all round. The women can claim equal value with men earning more in a different occupational group. If they succeed then the men in their own group can claim parity with their women colleagues on the grounds that they are engaged in like work (*Pickstone v Freemans plc* [1988] Industrial Relations Law Reports 357).

If by 1988 judicial interpretation of these regulations gave unions some hope in the battle against low pay they were still suffering reverses in industrial action where legislation was clearly acting against their interests.

*   *   *

THE SEAFARERS' TALE

The background to the 1988 shipping strikes was very similar to that of the miners' strike or the News International dispute: they were about restructuring and reorganisation. Faced with the threat to their businesses from the channel tunnel, due to be completed in 1992, the shipping companies, with P&O in the van, put forward plans for radical reductions in staffing levels and changes in hours and working practices. The National Union of Seafarers saw the employers package as a recipe for job loss and speed up involving working longer hours for less pay and holidays and skimping on safety requirements. In December 1987 P&O, for example, were demanding 400 job losses and an increase in the working day from 12 to 18 hours with single shifts at sea of up to 72 hours. The NUS claimed that under the P&O offer crews were being asked to work 28 extra 24 hour shifts each year for no additional payment. Many of the seafarers' perks such as leave, food, shift overlap and shorthand allowances would be cut. Workers would lose the equivalent of £12 a week and the company would save £6m a year on its annual wage bill. Despite accidents such as *The Herald of Free Enterprise* disaster the union claimed the employers were further cutting safety margins by, for example, speeding-up the turn-around time of the ferries.

The ignition spark for the dispute came in early 1988 when a Sealink subsidiary, the Isle of Man Steam Packet Company, sacked 16 seamen from the *Tynwald* who were striking over changes in working conditions. Believing that all their members were facing a similar threat and intending to stop the employers' restructuring offensive in its tracks, the National Union of Seafarers, on 30th January 1988, called a national strike to support the sacked workers. This was described as "a shot across the bows of other employers considering radical changes to working agreements in the shipping industry".[10]

The Legislation Intervenes

The NUS immediately came into conflict with the law. From the union's point of view and from the point of view of the intelligent passenger on the Clapham Omnibus, the national strike was *primary* action because all NUS members were facing the same general threat. What was happening at the Isle of Man was also happening or threatened at Dover or Harwich. From the vantage point of the courts, action based on this view by members at Dover or Harwich was *secondary* action and unlawful. The High Court on 1st February granted injunctions to Sealink and P&O instructing the NUS to withdraw its call for a national stoppage. The NUS's primary dispute was with the Isle of Man Steam Packet Company. Therefore, s.17 of the *1980 Employment Act* opened it up to a legal order restraining it from inducing P&O workers at Dover and Sealink workers — despite the fact that the struck company was a Sealink subsidiary — at a variety of ports, from breaking their contracts of employment and taking sympathetic secondary action. Even though all NUS members were threatened the law forbade a national strike because terms and conditions were not formally determined by national bargaining — despite employer co-ordination in practice. As far as the law and the courts were concerned the NUS were not in dispute with P&O or Sealink. As in previous disputes, the law was playing a role in splitting up and isolating workers, maximising divisions, making the rational impulse to unity more difficult and, thus, adding several aces to the employers' already strong hand.

For the best part of three days the NUS defied the injunction. General Secretary Sam McCluskie said the strike would continue and he was prepared to go to gaol. However, as legal advice that persistence in this position would make the sequestration of the union's assets inevitable was fully absorbed, union leaders swiftly changed position and meetings of the national executive and the ferry ports committee called off the stoppage. As many NUS ferry members in a variety of ports were still on strike, P&O and Sealink returned to court.

A P&O action urging sequestration for contempt was withdrawn but on 11th February in the High Court, Mr Justice Michael Davies fined the NUS £7,500 for contempt and ordered it to pay substantial costs. Mr McCluskie should not have called a strike he knew to be illegal and his remarks had been imprudent, the judge felt, but he was under pressure from militants who wished the strike to continue. However, the union was in contempt because once an order was made by the court its leaders could not wait until bodies such as the national executive had met. The executive officers of a union had to act immediately to implement an injunction. This was required whatever the unions existing policies or democratic arrangements and whatever the effect in terms of internal tensions between strikers, acting in accord with democratically agreed union policy and general secretaries, acting as policemen at the behest of the courts. Having made clear since 1983 the dire consequences of contempt, the courts were now using the strict liability rule — contempt had to be ended the minute the courts said so — ignoring the difference between, say, a union and a company in order to develop the policing role of union leaders. Whether this was the best way of getting workers back to work was questionable. But in putting down a marker for the future the courts dealt gently with the NUS in this case.

You Can't Even Hold a Ballot!

Having got off the legal hook in February the NUS was quickly back on it. By March P&O workers at Dover had remained on strike and the company accepted that their own demands for changes in working conditions and the employees' resistance meant that the dispute at Dover now constituted primary action within the definition of a trade dispute. However, pressure from the 2,300 Dover workers, sacked by P&O after six weeks on strike, led the NUS leadership to return to the question of a national strike. This time they attempted to work within the law by balloting all their 21,000 members — deep sea as well as ferry workers. The union prepared a ballot paper which made no reference to the P&O dispute. Instead it simply asked for industrial action over the crisis in the shipping industry, the erosion of the UK merchant fleet and the general attack on working conditions. In other words the NUS were attempting what the judges in previous cases had described as the artificial construction of a trade dispute.

The attitude of P&O was that if the unions could try to develop the law they could go one better. On 27th March the High Court, in a novel development of the legislation, granted P&O an injunction *prohibiting the NUS from holding a ballot.* Mr Justice Michael Davies described the proposed ballot as "an ingenious and ingenuous attempt to get round the law". An injunction would be granted because the proposed action by all NUS members would be sympathetic action unprotected by s.17 of the 1980 Act. The judge also went some way with P&O's argument that the ballot was an *incitement* to unlawful secondary action. He refused to move to sequestration but made a sequestration order that would lapse within 28 days if there was no further contempt by the NUS. This would be "a way of readily testing the *bona fides* of the union".[11]

The final step in this phase of activity came on 31st March. The NUS returned to court in an unprecedented move to request the judge's permission to hold a ballot because of new evidence. James Sherwood, Chair of Sealink's parent company, had stated publicly that if P&O won their dispute with the NUS, Sealink would be looking to implement similar cuts in jobs and changes in working practices. However, the court stuck to its guns and refused permission to ballot on the grounds that the NUS disputes, or possible disputes, with P&O and Sealink were separate and distinct.

This episode raised again basic questions about the role of the courts in disputes and their development of the legislation. Holding a ballot and, even more, gaining a *'yes'* vote in the ballot could have firmed up the union's weakening negotiating position. Surely the union should, within the legislation, have only attracted an injunction if, as a result of a successful ballot, the leadership had called for what the courts considered unlawful secondary action. It is only with difficulty that *the ballot itself* can be seen as an inducement to workers to break their contracts. The ballot might have been lost. It might have been won but the union, as in many other cases, might not have acted on it but returned strengthened to the negotiating table. It is difficult to see how *the ballot itself* was unlawful. In branding it as such the judge was going too far, too soon. And, of course, undermining the union strategy for advancing the dispute. The statement by James Sherwood of Sealink underscored once more the tension between the legal fiction of separate disputes and the reality that UK ferry workers were confronting a common predicament which the legal fiction and its coercive consequences made it more difficult to deal with.

A further token of the degree to which the law was now regulating the fine detail of industrial disputes and incubating further litigation was given by the Midland Bank. Receiving "unusual" instructions from the NUS regarding movement of funds and fearing that it would get caught up in sequestration manoeuvres, the Bank applied for and were awarded an injunction prohibiting the union from taking money assets out of the country. The suspended sequestration order constituted another innovation — a Sword of Damocles hanging over the heads of the union leaders to guarantee good behaviour. It seemed likely that this flexible "putting the union on probation" approach would see service in future disputes.

Sequestration Again

But in this case where the union possessed decreasing purchase with the increasingly alienated strikers, sequestration was not long in coming. At the end of April Sealink, whose UK fleet was almost at a standstill because of supportive action for the Dover strikers, went back to court claiming contempt for breach of the injunction granted to it on 1st February. The judge on 3rd May, fined the NUS £150,000 and ordered the sequestration of all its assets involving the seizure of £2.8 million in funds, the closure of national and local offices, the freezing of staff wages, the impounding of union cars, the cutting off of telephones and the suspension of its pension fund. The judge stated that "the time for pussyfooting is over. The law and the authority of the court must be upheld".[12] Yet if it was the authority of the court that was put at stake by the union's contempt it was very questionable why the judge should have allowed extended negotiations between Sealink and the NUS to take place before Sealink decided whether or not to pursue its application for sequestration. The court only decisively terminated matters on 3rd May. Both Sealink and the NUS were interested in an alliance which would strengthen Sealink which would then employ sacked seafarers against its bitter competitor P&O.

Once again the NUS switched tack and Sam McCluskie again announced his defiance of the law and called for national action in support of the Dover strikers. This led to the union being fined a further £150,000 on 11th May and warned of even bigger fines if it continued to give sustenance to its members taking action to support the Dover strikers. The same day Sealink threatened to dismiss all its employees who remained on strike. On 13th May, in another *volte-face*, the NUS ordered all those taking sympathy action back to work. They claimed that the odds were now simply too great and that the strike was crumbling. The former point may have been true but there was little evidence for the latter. In early May 5,000 of the 5,200 NUS ferry members were on strike and ferries were halted in 17 ports. The real problems for the union were to some degree the ability of P&O to increasingly staff ferries with an alternative workforce, the lack of support from TGWU dockers and lorry drivers but essentially its inability, because of the legal position, to give leadership and sustained continuous organisation to the undoubted desire of seafarers in other ports to support the P&O stoppage. However, there can be little doubt that the constant twists and turns the use of the legislation engendered gradually produced disorientation and demoralisation amongst potential supporters of an all out national strike.

Certainly by June, it appeared that the union leadership had lost a lot of its stomach for the fight. On the 23rd May the action by Sealink members at an end, the NUS returned to court to end the sequestration. Sealink, at whose behest the order had been made, did not oppose the union's application but P&O did! They now shifted the focus back to Dover arguing that the picketing there was unlawful. Mr Justice Michael Davies agreed that this was so — on the basis that more than six pickets was unlawful. In another novel use of the law he allowed the Sealink sequestration order to be "transferred" to P&O — despite the fact that the original injunction granted to P&O against the NUS in February had been issued in very different circumstances. That order had been made on the basis that the action at Dover was secondary to the dispute between the Isle of Man Steam Packet Company and the NUS. Now it was accepted that there was a primary dispute between the NUS and the P&O — so why should the NUS be penalised for breaches of an injunction the basis of which was no longer applicable?

The Dover Strikers Left Isolated

Successive attempts by the NUS leadership to get the sequestration order lifted failed because of the continued mass picketing at Dover. The NUS were fined further sums of £25,000 — and £10,000 in a Scottish court — for failing to get the picketing called off. The judge stated that pickets 500 and 600 strong were

> neither lawful nor peaceful. To describe this as peaceful picketing either in law or in fact would be a hollow mockery of the English language. It is an attempt by weight of numbers coupled with gestures and words unlawfully to try to get people to stop work.[13]

Sam McCluskie visited Dover to urge restraint and, on 26th July, Mr Justice Michael Davies, convinced that the union had done its best, decided the sequestration order would be lifted in 3 weeks if the NUS continued to disassociate itself from the mass picketing and there were no further complaints of unlawful action. Of course, deprived of more potent methods, the mass picketing was all the Dover strikers had left to attempt an uphill fight to win the dispute. When the union got back its assets it was liable for fines of £350,000 and legal costs estimated at over £900,000. It played no further role in attempting to extend the dispute. Isolated, the Dover strikers stuck it out well into 1989 but they were heading for inevitable defeat. The logic of the law had by 1988 successfully worked through. First the TUC had been pressured into leaving individual unions to fight alone. And then those individual unions had been pressured into leaving their members to fight alone.

The strike of the Dover seafarers went on. It was finally called off on 9th June 1989 after 16 months. It had nearly bankrupted the union and led to a suicide and split families. NUS Research Officer Mike Gibson said

> There is a mixture of pride and anger. Pride that they stuck it out for 16 months and anger that they were only beaten by the Government's industrial relations laws which meant they could not lawfully spread the dispute.[14]

Discussion Questions

1. Looking back how would you evaluate the operation of the 1980, 1982 and 1984 Acts and other ancillary measures on the eve of the 1987 General Election?
2. Draw up a report on the successes and failures of the TUC campaign against the Employment Legislation from 1980 to 1987.
3. "The Conservative legislation on ballots was counterproductive. It *helped* the unions and worked in their interests". Do you agree?
4. What do the provisions of the 1988 Act on ballots for union elections and the closed shop tell you?
5. "The Seafarers' dispute demonstrated that by 1988 the UK had one of the most tightly regulated and one-sided systems of employment law in Europe". Critically discuss this statement.

CHAPTER 7

Wider Still and Wider

Law is a bottomless pit — *Dr Arbuthnot*

The government was pleased that the P&O dispute had once more demonstrated the potency of the legislation and its potential for development by the courts. It was slightly discomfited by the reaction to the 1988 Act. There was further embarrassment for the Conservatives. Difficulties were experienced in appointing a Commissioner for the Rights of Trade Unionists. Eventually in November 1988 a 58 year old barrister Ms Gill Rowland accepted the position, a £1.2 million budget and an office in Warrington. In 1989 it was reported that the first report of the new Commissioner had been delayed as "there had been a limited amount of applications".[1]

When the Monopolies and Mergers Commission reported (see p.139) it recorded that it had found no evidence of union restrictive practices in TV and radio. The report was described by *The Financial Times* as "a significant reverse" for the Employment Secretary Norman Fowler. Condemnation of the 1988 Act was now coming from all sides. The Catholic Church weighed in. A Catholic Truth Society pamphlet *A Threefold Cord* noted the overwhelming power modern technology and company structures gave employers to maintain production in industrial disputes long enough for the strikers to exhaust themselves. It concluded that unions needed disciplinary powers to ensure 100% support — "absolutely necessary" — as well as the right to picket and take secondary action. The Act's "right" to ignore democratic decisions was criticised: "if a member of the Cabinet were to vote against government policy that member would be shown the door very quickly".[2]

For ordinary trade unionists the floor of rights was creaking even more. There were far more people living on social security and more people living in poverty than at the start of the decade. In 1986 the Child Poverty Action Group stated that more than 9 million people were living on or below supplementary benefit levels. In 1978 a single man, previously on average earnings, receiving unemployment benefit at standard rate, received around 24% of his former pay, whilst a single man on unemployment benefit with earnings related supplement received around 47% of his former pay. Ten years later, with the abolition of earnings related benefit and other legal changes, a single man formerly on average earnings, now on unemployment benefit, received only 18.9% of his earnings. A married man with two children, previously on average earnings, receiving unemployment benefit in 1978 would receive 46.4% or 66.6% (earnings related) of his earnings. By 1988 this figure had declined to 34.6%.[3]

Amongst wage earners those at the top of the tree had increased their share of earnings at the expense of those at the bottom of the pile whose share had declined. Half of all income was going to the top quarter of taxpayers and the gap between rich and poor — and the problems of the poor — were increasing. The share of pre-tax income going to the top 25% of taxpayers had gone up five full points since 1979, whilst the income share going to the bottom 70% of taxpayers fell from 50% to 45% between 1979-89.[4]

Changes in legislation on unemployment, social security and employment protection had facilitated these changes. There appeared to be no dramatic changes in the weak Employment Protection position as measured by tribunal statistics. In 1987 66% of unfair dismissal cases were lost by workers compared with 67% in 1987. The 'win rate' as a percentage of all unfair dismissal applications was 10.6% in 1987, as against 11.6% in 1986. The median award was £1,805 and reinstatement was recommended in around 1% of cases heard. There were only 33 hearings under the Race Relations legislation and 28 under the *Sex Discrimination Act.* Under the latter, 80% of those who won their cases received less than £1,000 in compensation. ACAS received some 1,700 applications in 1987 under the equal value regulations but many of these were multiple claims and in only 27% of the cases going to a full hearing was success achieved. Even aspects of recent legislation, such as these regulations, which could be perceived as favourable to the Labour Movement were, in practice, of limited value and there was a decline in the number of cases in 1988. Moreover, a careful study of the hidden social, financial and career costs of bringing a tribunal case in the 1980s demonstrated the severe limitations of hard won victories.[5]

Those able to use the law in this way represented, with increasing exclusions from the legislation, a shrinking proportion of the workforce. As deregulation proceeded, there were signs of the courts and tribunals firming up protection for those remaining within the scope of employment protection and a rehabilitation of the individual contract of employment for 'core' workers.[6] So some curbs were placed on the burgeoning of employer prerogative (*Rigby v Ferodo Ltd* [1987] Industrial Relations Law Reports 516). High ranking, autonomous, public sector employees were granted injunctions to restrain dismissal (*Powell v London Borough of Brent* [1987] Industrial Relations Law Reports 466) and the courts' undermining of the procedural protection ACAS proposed in disciplinary matters was modified (*Polkey v A.E. Dayton Services Ltd* [1987] Industrial Relations Law Reports 503).

For the majority of workers, however, the legislative offensive had taken a heavy toll. In 1989, in a glare of publicity, the government's record on employment legislation was savaged by the International Labour Organisation which found that Britain had broken international conventions on eight counts. It cited the ban on sympathy action, the freedom allowed employers to sack workers on strike, the union ban at GCHQ, the denial of negotiating rights to teachers and the acceptance by the courts of employers' manipulation of company law as witnessed in the *Dimbleby* and Murdoch cases. The ILO condemned the government failure to act against the blacklisting of employees and it specifically singled out two provisions of the 1988 Act — the ban on unions paying members fines and the restriction on unions' rights to discipline members. The legal framework developed since 1979 was unbalanced and unfair, violated freedom of association and required a thorough review. At the same time it was noted that almost 30% of the cases which came before the European Court of Human Rights between 1980 and 1986 emanated from Britain. We topped the list, far outstripping West Germany, and had a higher percentage of cases upheld against the government than any other country.

Despite this international condemnation the government shrugged off criticism and sought to further slake its insatiable thirst for union bashing by unleashing yet another wave of restrictions.

RESTRICTIONS ON EMPLOYMENT OF YOUNG PEOPLE AND THE REMOVAL OF SEX DISCRIMINATION LEGISLATION, 1987

This consultative document was published at the end of 1987 with suggestions for possible follow-up legislation to the 1988 Act. It proposed certain changes in the law regulating the employment of women and young people and revision of sex discrimination law required by European developments.

CONSULTATION PAPER ON INDUSTRIAL TRIBUNALS 1988

Despite the undermining of individual rights and changes in tribunal procedure which made application and eventual success in the case more difficult for individuals the government were still obsessed with the idea that the tribunals' time and the taxpayers' pockets were exploited by litigation happy punters pursuing unwinnable cases. Going on from *Building Businesses Not Barriers*, this paper now suggested a system of £150 deposits prior to a hearing, the replacement of pre-hearing assessments by pre-hearing reviews, giving tribunal chairs greater powers and the addition of interest to tribunal compensation 28 days after the award. On 31st October 1988 Under-Secretary of State for Employment Patrick Nicholls informed the House that tribunal procedure would be changed as soon as Parliamentary time allowed.

THE SOCIAL SECURITY ACT 1988

This measure followed government policy in toughening things up for the jobless to increase pressure on those working. Supplementary benefit was replaced by *income support* targetted at particular groups. The system of additional allowances was replaced by the *Social Fund* through which claimants had to bargain for grants or repayeable *loans* with only a fixed sum available for all needs. And Family Income Supplement was replaced by a new Family Credit. There were also changes in unemployment benefit with 2 years contributions rather than one years contributions now being required to qualify.

THE EMPLOYMENT ACT 1989

Norman Fowler's second piece of legislation — the bill was published on 30th November 1988 — is a ragbag of miscellaneous and piecemeal measures taken from *Building Businesses* and the consultative documents on young people and industrial tribunals.

Employment Protection Rights
(s.9-16)

Written Particulars of Employment

The *Employment Protection (Consolidation) Act* required every employee to be given written particulars of important terms and conditions of his or her employment within 13 weeks of starting work. The legislation provided for these particulars to include a statement of disciplinary rules and details of any disciplinary procedures.

The 1989 Act now removes the legal obligation to provide these details if the employer together with any associated employer has less than 20 employees at the date a worker's employment commences. If the figure later goes above 20, then only new entrants will be entitled to the particulars of discipline.

Time Off for Union Duties

Under s.27 and 28 of the *Employment Protection (Consolidation) Act* officials — lay representatives of a recognised trade union — were entitled to reasonable time-off with pay for certain purposes. These purposes were the carrying out of duties as an official concerned with industrial relations between the employer and any associated employer and their employers and training in any aspects of industrial relations relevant the carrying out of these duties. The training had to be approved by the TUC or by the employee's union.

Tribunals and courts gave a broad interpretation to the meaning of "industrial relations". They did not accept that union representatives should only be entitled to time-off to deal with problems arising from matters for which the union was recognised or that "industrial relations" should be limited to "collective bargaining". So representatives were entitled to time-off to attend meetings preparatory to negotiations, meetings to discuss issues which unions might later seek to negotiate about and training courses dealing with issues for which the union was not recognised for negotiations by the employer.

The government thought that this gave shop stewards and other workplace representatives too many rights. From 1989 the right to time-off was limited

— to the situation where union representatives are carrying out duties concerned with the matters listed in s.29(i) of the *Trade Union and Labour Relations Act 1974*

— where the union is recognised by the employer for negotiating over these matters

— or where the union is not recognised for negotiations over these matters but the employer has agreed that it may perform functions on behalf of employees in relation to these matters.

The matters specified in s.29(i) are very basic industrial relations matters

- terms and conditions of employment
- recruitment, non-recruitment, dismissal and suspension of workers
- allocation of work
- matters of discipline
- membership or non-membership of a union
- facilities for union officials
- machinery for negotiation and consultation.

The Act, thus, limits the rights of workplace representatives. *Industrial relations* is now very much defined in terms of *collective bargaining.* And the developmental aspect, allowing representatives time-off to deal with issues they *wish* to negotiate about is removed. If you don't negotiate about pensions then you cannot get time-off to *plan how* to negotiate or to *prepare* to negotiate. This freezes change and strengthens the *status quo.* Employers are given lots of room for manoeuvre in defining exactly what shop stewards can and cannot do. And the tendency of the legislation to limit union activities to the workplace is strengthened by the elimination of any reference to *associated employers.*

Written Reasons for Dismissal
When the government progressively raised the qualifying period for unfair dismissal they seem to have forgotten about the ancillary right to receive reasons for dismissal in writing and this continued to be available to all employees with six months continuous employment. The six months is now raised to 2 years in another small blow at employment protection rights.

Redundancy Payments
In the past, the state redundancy payments scheme embodied in the *Employment Protection (Consolidation) Act* had been tied to the 'traditional' retirement ages so that when a man reached 64 and a woman 59 the redundancy payment was reduced by one-twelfth for each completed month calculation ceasing on the man's 65 and the woman's 60 birthday. In 1988 the courts found this to be in violation of Article 119 of the Treaty of Rome.

All employees men and women will now be disqualified from receiving a redundancy payment on reaching the age of 65 and the tapering provisions will apply from their 64th birthday. The only exception is where there is a *normal retirement age* in particular employment of less than 65 which applies equally to both men and women. In that case employees will lose their right to a state redundancy payment when they attain that normal retiring age. This is a small but useful increment to sex equality even if it is within an environment where the rights of both sexes are being progressively reduced.

Redundancy Rebates
In another example of the government's policy of freeing employers from 'petty restriction' these rebates, restricted to employers with less than 10 employees by the *Wages Act*, are abolished completely.

Insolvency
Under the present law the Department of Employment cannot make payments to employees under the provisions of the *Employment Protection (Consolidation) Act* dealing with money owing until they have received certain statements from the receiver or liquidator. This has led to long delays and the new act allows payment where the Department considers there is likely to be an unreasonable delay or where they feel that they can work out what an employee is owed without a statement. Finally if payments are made to employees affected by insolvency out of the Redundancy Fund any claims on the Fund these employers may have will pass to the Secretary of State For Employment.

Industrial Tribunals
(s.20)
The powers of industrial tribunals are specified in special regulations made by order-in-council. The 1989 Act simply states that the Secretary of State will have powers to make new regulations introducing *pre-hearing reviews* of tribunal cases. In such a review worker or employee can be required to pay *a deposit of up to £150* if they wish to continue to pursue the proceedings. Details of these new powers will be embodied in regulations. But it appears likely that the £150 will be held against an award of costs when a pre-hearing review finds a case *unreasonable, frivolous or vexatious.* This provision differs from the original idea of an automatic deposit in every case. Nonetheless it will place new difficulties in the path of applicants.

All in all the Act's provisions on employment protection represent another series of small holes in the basic floor of rights.

Sikhs and Safety
(s.11)

Sikhs, under religious obligation to wear a turban, are exempted when working on construction sites from any legal requirements to wear a safety helmet and any associated requirement. Sikhs and their employers are protected from actions in tort for any loss, injury or damage arising from failure to wear a safety helmet.

Employment of 16-18 Year Olds
(s.8)

The removal of regulatory legislation was again intended to help in setting lower standards by undermining even poor minimal standards. Once again it was the poorly organised youth in low paid industries who were targetted for de-regulation

— Restrictions on the employment of 16-18 year olds in relation to hours, holidays and night work contained in the *Young Persons (Employment) Act 1938*, the *Shops Act 1950*, the *Mines and Quarries Act 1954* and the *Factories Act 1961* are abolished
— The requirements on employers to keep a register of 16-18 year olds in their employment are abolished
— The power of local authorities to make bye-laws with respect to the employment of young people is abolished
— The prohibition on young women working near brine evaporation or glass annealing processes (s.73 *Factories Act 1961*) is abolished.

Other specific restrictions on the employment of young people — on offshore installations, for example, remain.

Employment of Women
(s.1-10)

Whilst formally tidying up certain aspects of discrimination, the thrust of this part of the act was to further de-regulate the employment of working women and "shake-up" and deteriorate wages and conditions in the interests of flexibility. Once again the most grievous impact of de-regulation was likely to be on those who most needed the very limited statutory protections

— The *Sex Discrimination Act 1975 s.51* stated that where an discriminatory act was required in order to comply with a statute passed before the *Sex Discrimination Act* or with a statutory order made under such a statute at any time that act would constitute discrimination under the Sex Discrimination Act. The 1989 Act now repeals this exception

— s.7(2) of the *1975 Sex Discrimination Act* which established a defence of *genuine occupational qualification* where a job needed to be done by a man because of restrictions the law imposed on the employment of women is also repealed

— s.51 of the 1975 Act is, however, replaced by a new section which does allow discriminatory acts in employment or vocational training if they are necessary to comply with legislation passed before the 1975 Act and they protect women in relation to pregnancy, maternity or other circumstances giving rise to risks which specially affect women

— Laws which protect women and which are therefore excluded from action under the *Sex Discrimination Act* cover

● the ban on women working within 4 weeks of childbirth

● the ban on women working in lead processes

● the ban on women working on ship and aircraft while pregnant

● the ban on women working on certain processes in the pottery industry

● the protection given to women against exposure to ionising radiation.

— The 1989 Act makes it lawful to discriminate in certain educational appointments where an instrument restricts certain jobs to one sex — for example head teachers who are required to be members of a religious order. But a requirement that fellows of Oxbridge Colleges must be men (which has been upheld in case law) will no longer be allowed.

— The Secretary of State for Employment is given powers to issue orders making discrimination authorised by any Act prior to the 1975 Act or any instrument later made under such an Act lawful even if it is on the face of it caught by the 1989 Act.

— Restrictions on women operating winding apparatus and conveyors in mines and quarries are abolished.

— Restrictions on women working underground in mines are repealed.

— Restrictions on women and young people lifting heavy loads in mines and quarries are extended to cover men.

— Restrictions on women cleaning machinery in factories are removed.

— A range of provisions in statutory instruments protecting women in a range of employment, jute processing, potteries, tin plate manufacture are also repealed.

The Training Commission

The Act abolishes the Training Commission established by the 1988 Act and scheduled to be replaced by an employer-led system of industrial training.

SOCIAL SECURITY ACT 1989

This measure followed the *Social Security Act 1988* which required two year's contributions rather than one year's in order to qualify for unemployment benefit. It kept up the attack on the unemployed

— unemployed claimants henceforth must not only be *genuinely available for work*. They must also be able to demonstrate week-by-week that they are *actively seeking work*.

— For 13 weeks after they become unemployed claimants would have the right to accept only a job equivalent in terms and conditions to their previous post. At the end of that period they would be expected to take a *lower paid job* or run the risk of forfeiting unemployment benefit.

— In order to re-qualify for unemployment benefit when starting work again employees would have to work more than 16 hours per week in thirteen of the 26 weeks prior to the date of claiming. This would hit part-time workers.

DRAFT CODE OF PRACTICE ON INDUSTRIAL ACTION BALLOTS 1988

In 1987 the government had refused to accept a draft *Code of Practice on Discipline* produced by ACAS on the grounds of its length and complexity. Junior Employment Minister Kenneth Clarke opined "I believe the Code should be a reasonably short and sensible document". In late 1988, the government themselves published a draft code on industrial action intended to be a gloss on the detailed provisions in the legislation which ran to no less than 53 pages and 103 sections. The code stated

— Unions must inform employers of their intention to hold a ballot and give employers time to respond.

— They should take into account the views of the employer on which workers should be balloted.

— They should enclose with ballot forms a statement on the statutory duties of unions in holding ballots.

— They should allow employers to scrutinize the statement of reasons for the ballot given to members and allow the employer to provide an accompanying statement.

— Ballots should only be considered once all procedures have been exhausted.

— Ballots should be held at a time when they are least likely to damage 'good industrial relations'.

— The wording of the questions to be voted on should be given careful consideration and should not be misleading.

— Ballots should not be held in many situations without the union conducting a straw poll to see if a majority of the members really want a ballot.

— Ballots should not be held where there is no real intention to take *lawful* industrial action and where the real purpose is simply to strengthen the unions' hand in negotiations.

— Ballots should normally be postal ballots.

— Independent scrutineers should be appointed to deal with all aspects of the balloting process.

— If the vote in the ballot is *for* industrial action unions should only consider taking action if there has been a turn-out of at least 70%.

— If the vote in the ballot is for industrial action unions should only consider acting on it if there is "a very much more substantial majority" than 51% for industrial action.

— If there is an intention to take industrial action the employer should be given adequate notice "to ensure that there is no risk to the health and safety of employees or the general public".

— Information about the ballot should be provided to all likely to be affected by any consequent industrial action.

It was clear, firstly, that this draft code represented a further attempt to interfere with the right to strike and further abuse of the legal process. The legislation on ballots said nothing about majorities more than 51%, or turnouts of at least 70%, or about exhausting dispute procedure, or about pre-strike ballot opinion polls. The government was once again using the freedom the Code of Practice form gave it to *extend the law,* rather than to *explain it* and suggest how it might work in different circumstances. In some cases — the attempt to prescribe against using ballots as negotiating ploys — it was using the Code to seek to plug gaps in the law the unions had exploited. In other cases it was attempting to compensate for its own legal caution — it had passed over the chance to make strike ballots, like union election ballots and political fund ballots, fully postal in the 1988 Act. Or perhaps it was laying the ground for future legislation by attempting to familiarize industrial relations practitioners with certain conceptions in the more flexible form of the Code it would later concretise in legislation.

Secondly, the Code provided numerous evidence — if such evidence was by now required — that its purpose was not to give the unions back to their members but to keep production rolling. Throughout the document there is a continuing concern with *the rights of the employer* — this in a process which must inevitably be directed against the employer and view him in antagonistic terms. There is a strong element of giving the unions' opponents a strong say in the unions' strategy, an element which if accepted by the unions could weaken their bargaining position and strengthen that of their opponents. The suggestions on pre-strike ballots and 70% minimum turnouts also raise again the question marks over the government's conception of democracy.

The third problem is the expensive bureaucratic and time-consuming system which would emerge if the unions were to study the Code and adapt their procedures to its suggestions. As the TUC commented, strict adherence to the letter of the Code "could virtually rule out industrial action". As ACAS noted more diplomatically, many of its suggestions are "potentially impracticable". The Code has not only been criticised by ACAS but by the CBI, the EEF and the IPM. Opinion in mid-1989 appeared to be that it would only be proceeded with after substantial modification. But stranger things have happened in the crazy world of Conservative employment law.[7]

EMPLOYMENT FOR THE 1990s

The White Paper *Employment for the 1990s* was published in December 1988. It was focused on the government's concern that rates of pay were inadequately related to performance, that wages were in many areas artificially high and that concepts such as the "going rate" for a job, comparability of earnings between groups and increases based on cost of living increases were out of date and disastrous to economic recovery. It insisted: "Moderation of pay is essential for competitiveness and jobs". In order to continue to introduce greater flexibility into the labour market it was vital for the government to continue to resist EEC initiatives on worker rights and in particular proposals for workers participation. And it was vital for them to continue to press forward with their programme of sustained labour market deregulation.

The body of the White Paper dealt with:

The Closed Shop: The government pledged itself in the coming months to examine the operation of the *pre-entry* closed shop previously neglected in their reform programme. The paper felt that government reforms had reduced the coverage of the closed shop but more needed to be done. Restricting the supply of labour for particular jobs the pre-entry closed shop artificially drives up labour costs producing "higher prices, lower output and inefficient use of the nation's resources". The pre-entry closed shop, in particular, placed unacceptable limits on the freedom to choose. The White Paper stated that "The Government will take any further legislative steps that are needed on this or any other aspects of industrial relations which constitute a barrier to employment". But employers must help by taking action against the closed shop and winning employees over to the goals of competition and profit by schemes for employee involvement particularly profit sharing.

Training: The centrepiece of the White Paper was a proposal to hand industrial training over, to a far greater degree than hitherto, to the employers regardless of the fact that their historic neglect of this area had made an important contribution to economic decline. Over the next four years the government planned to gradually create 100 employer based local Training and Enterprise Councils. The Department of Employment would invite local groups of employers to submit proposals for local TECs. Each TEC would then sign a contract with the Department of Employment's new Training Agency to provide in each area training programmes for young people, the unemployed and those wishing to change jobs as well as providing in-company training and establishing close links with the education system.

The Councils would be allocated funds of between £15 and £50m a year and supported by Training Agency staff. They would monitor local labour markets and survey the whole range of skills training. Two-thirds of the members of each TEC would be high-ranking managers from the private sector. The Training Agency would take over the staff of the Training Commission and report directly to the Secretary of State as well as collaborating with the TECs it would work with a National Training Task Force. The brief of this body would be to stimulate improved training schemes, commission special studies of training needs, foster the development of the TECs and develop a national system of vocational qualifications and training standards. It would be established for four years until the TECs were in place and have 12 members drawn from leading figures in commerce and industry.

WAGES COUNCILS: 1988 CONSULTATION DOCUMENT

This document accompanied the White Paper and was informed by the same objective of labour market deregulation. The Government, the document stated, felt that the 26 Wages Councils setting minimum hourly pay rates for workers over 21 in low paid industries should now be abolished. The councils, it felt, had not curtailed their role despite the changes in the *1986 Wages Act.* Covering 2.5 million workers and setting hourly minimum rates between £1.95 and £2.38, the Councils, the government argued, inhibited pay flexibility by increasing rates by a uniform percentage. These artificial rates then had a knock-on impact on the pay of other workers and it meant that pay continued to be above the market rate required to fill jobs.

The abolition of the councils might lead to some reduction of wages but it would be limited and with the improvements in the system of social security it would be unlikely to increase poverty. The government stated that it was responding to pressure from the CBI for abolition of the Wages Councils in sectors such as hotels and catering and a reduction in the coverage of the system might be an alternative to total abolition.

In an immediate response to the consultative document the Low Pay Unit pointed out that abolition would leave the UK as the only country in Europe with no minimum wage protection. It argued that Wages Council rates had increased no faster, often more slowly, than average earnings. There was a real problem of non-enforcement with 1:4 relevant employers not paying the rates and abolition would produce a spiral of wage cutting and real hardship.

REMOVING BARRIERS TO EMPLOYMENT 1989

There was no let-up in the flow of proposals to further restrict union activities. The Green Paper, *Removing Barriers To Employment* published in April 1989 returned to the now well-worn themes of the closed shop and secondary action

- The complex clause 17 of the 1980 Act had outlawed many forms of sympathy action. But as we have seen it had given protection where action was directed against a customer or supplier who had a contract with the party in dispute where the principal aim of the secondary action was to disrupt supplies to or from the employer in dispute and where the action was likely to achieve that purpose. The Green Paper proposed that future legislation should simply *abolish s.17, outlaw all secondary action and limit lawful industrial action to the employer directly in dispute.*

The Green Paper cited the threat secondary action to pressurise employers to recognise unions or abide by the terms of national agreements could represent to inward investment. It specifically mentioned the abandonment by Ford in 1988 of an attempt to open a plant in Dundee: "Regardless of whether they are lawful or unlawful under the present law, there is no good reason why any threats of this kind or the organisation of action of this kind should enjoy immunity".

- The law on secondary action and ballots on industrial action with the growth of flexibility, free-lancing and self employment should be extended to cover not only employment but the self employed

- The only exception to the outlawing of all secondary action should be protection for pickets who, when picketing their own workplace, induced employees of direct suppliers or customers to break their contracts of employment

- The Green paper expressed surprise and annoyance at the fact that its research showed around 500,000 workers were still covered by the pre-entry closed shop. As we have seen the government had hesitated over dealing with this thorny problem. If, on the model of sex or race discrimination, you made it unlawful to refuse a job to the non-unionist you risked drawing attention to a whole range of other discriminatory practices at the point of entry to employment — most obviously and nearest home the blacklisting of union members. The introduction of rights for job applicants is always messy and discrimination difficult to prove.

Nonetheless the government now grasped the nettle. The Green Paper suggested the introduction of *a statutory right for prospective employees not to be refused employment on the grounds that they were not or had refused to become union members once employed.* The right would be similar to those provided by the *Race Relations* and *Sex Discrimination Acts* with compensation around £9,000. A similar right would not apply to those refused employment because they *were* union members

- The Commissioner for the Rights of Trade Unionists was in business but hardly overburdened by requests for help. The Green Paper now proposed that the Commissioner's brief would be extended to enable her to assist union members in proceedings against their union which arose from complaints about the operation of the union rulebook — if the case raised an "issue of substantial public interest".

- To give a complainant "more assurance" and "to increase public awareness" the Commissioner should be enabled to personally appear in court alongside the individual litigant.

There could be little doubt that these proposals, centrally those on secondary action and the closed shop, represented some of the gravest challenges to trade unionists in a decade of constant challenges.

EUROPEAN COMMUNITY SOCIAL CHARTER OF WORKERS RIGHTS

In 1988-89 the government was also busily opposing the European Commission's attempts to get EC countries to endorse a Charter of Workers Rights intended to give a social dimension to the moves towards a single market in 1992. The Charter consisted of a series of broad committments on fair wages, employment protection rights, working time, holidays, paid leave and health, safety and welfare and workers participation. It supported the right to organise

---

BLACKLISTING

The International Labour Organisation criticised the British Government for its failure to deal with blacklisting of workers on the grounds of their trade union or political activities. Almost simultaneously the government announced its intention to legislate to stop discrimination in recruitment against those who are not union members whilst insisting it would do nothing to help those refused work because of their union membership and activities.

This demonstrates again a clear double standard as there are well documented cases each year of companies blacklisting union activists. The right wing *Economic League* established precisely for this purpose maintains detailed lists of thousands of union "militants" and political activists — the figure of 250,000 has been quoted and apart from the principle of the thing many are inaccurate and out of date. In 1988 *Labour Research* published a list of 360 companies which paid for the services of the Economic League and Labour MP Maria Fyfe unsuccessfully introduced a *Blacklists (Access to Information) Bill* which would have extended the *Data Protection Act 1984* to enable union activists to see files held on them by groups like the Economic League.

Despite the comments of the I.L.O. and a mass of other legislation the government obviously has no intention of dealing with this abuse of civil liberties. In 1989 two campaigns — the Anti-Blacklisting Campaign and League Watch — were set up to publicise and counteract the activities of the blacklist organisations.

collectively in trade unions and to be recognised for collective negotiations by employers. It also urged that the right to belong and not to belong to a trade union should be safeguarded (see p.218). Ratification of the Charter would leave member states with a number of ways of meeting the Charter's objectives. The philosophy of the Charter obviously clashed with Conservative policies of de-regulation. Mrs Thatcher condemned the Charter as Marxist and Mr Fowler assured other heads of government that the UK would do all possible to block its adoption. The TUC enthusiastically embraced the Charter and the President of the Commission Jacques Delors was rapturously greeted at the 1988 TUC.

LOCAL GOVERNMENT AND HOUSING ACT 1989

Certain specified senior staff in local authority employment as well as all those earning more than the then £19,500 point on the pay scale (amended from an amazing £13,500) were prohibited from becoming a member of another authority or an MP. The time local authority employees could take off work to perform duties as a member was restricted to 208 hours a year. Members of local authorities who are also members of relevant trade unions may not represent the authority in industrial relations negotiations. Once again the unions declared their intention of challenging these provisions in the European Court of Human Rights.

*   *   *

THE RAILWAYWORKERS' TALE

The unions, meanwhile, were meeting the challenge of the existing legislation in the field. Spring 1989 with inflation moving over 8% to catch up with average earnings, falling unemployment, high interest rates affecting mortgages and the government in trouble produced a spate of strikes. The rail unions were in dispute over British Rail's attempt to break up national bargaining and its refusal to improve on a 7% pay offer. On the London Underground there were two disputes, one over pay for driver-only crews, the other over the employer's *Action Stations* proposals, an attempt to alter working practices and discipline and promotion procedures.

Of particular concern to the government — also to the union leaders — was the re-emergence of unofficial industrial action. Two one-day 'wild-cat' strikes organised by unofficial line co-ordinators described in the press as "a faceless group of individuals" stopped the London Underground and were met with fury but inaction by management who could apparently find no-one to use the law against. They were not to be frustrated for very long. In an attempt to regain control of the situation the NUR and TSSA balloted their underground members on an all out official strike over the *Action Stations* proposals. There was a 7:1 majority in favour and the NUR called a stoppage from midnight on Sunday, 7th May.

The Law Takes A Hand

On Thursday, 4th May the employers were granted an injunction stopping the NUR strike. The union called off the stoppage, NUR General Secretary Jimmy Knapp observing that unions were living in a legal nightmare: "We are rapidly reaching the position in this country where it is not possible to call a strike and remain within the law".[8] This comment appeared justified. Previously employers had been able to take successful legal action where the unions had not held a ballot or had called for secondary industrial action. This judgement was aimed at primary action where the union had done everything it thought was required to stay within the law. When the employer's barrister was asked by Mr Justice Simon Brown at the start of the proceedings whether there was any legal precedent for the action he was forced to answer 'no'. Nevertheless, the judge granted the employers an injunction on the grounds that the question that NUR members were asked was unclear, inconcise and confusing. The NUR ballot paper asked

> Do you agree to support the executive committee in their fight to maintain the current agreement on seniority and to resist the imposition of organisational changes, unsatisfactory attendance procedures and compulsory tendering by taking strike action?

This might seem as clear as daylight to you and me but the court went a long way with the argument of London Underground that it was not certain that there was a trade dispute over all the issues mentioned. Even if there *was* a dispute over each of them they were separate issues and could not be classified as one dispute. Members were not given the chance to decide whether or not they wished to strike over promotion but not compulsory tendering. The form was drafted in a confusing way and the union had piled in extraneous issues when the real bone of contention was seniority (*London Underground Ltd v NUR* [1989] Industrial Relations Law Reports 341).

Mr Justice Simon Brown's judgement that it was not certain that the union was in dispute over all four issues and that the form was incorrectly phrased was a novel development. The 1984 Act says nothing about the form and content of the ballot — apart from the need for the statement that strikers will be in breach of contract. However, it was suggested that in framing their argument about the form and phrasing of the question the lawyers for London Underground had been influenced by the suggestions in the *draft* Code of Practice on Industrial Action Ballots — and this point had been taken by the judge. Such was the impetus of the anti-union juggernaut that proposals were being translated into *law* even before they had been laid before Parliament as a Code of Practice! Certainly the courts were taking yet a further step towards complicating the law controlling union activities and banning strikes. The judgement was particularly harsh in view of the overwhelming majority for an all out strike.

Back To Square One

The efficacy of this kind of judicial law-making for the employers was that the union was now back to square one and they had won an important cooling-off period in which to work on the union members. Instead of appealing the NUR decided on another ballot, this time of all their members so that they could link the tube and the BR disputes. This time the members were balloted on a series of strikes and other sanctions on all the issues. 75,000 members voted for an overtime ban and 24 hour strikes against BR's imposition of the 7% deal and its plans to end national negotiations, 29,675 to 20,704 for strikes and 34,988 to 15,762 for an overtime ban. 10,000 members voted 4:1 on a 60% turnout for strikes against the Underground's *Action Stations* plan and 2,000 train crew members voted 11-1 for strikes over pay linked to driver-only trains.

The delay of another month — the result of the second ballot was announced on 13th June — appears to have intensified not dissipated the dissatisfaction of the workers. However to nobody's surprise, when the NUR called a 24 hour stoppage for 21st June, BR sought a High Court injunction on the grounds that the ballot had been improperly conducted. The resort to the law was announced as the union representatives were negotiating with BR at ACAS shattering the talks. Jimmy Knapp accused BR of deviousness, deceit and negotiating under false pretences. He also made the point that the resort to law by the employers at every twist in the dispute made the organisational tasks of the union more difficult but also militated against a negotiated solution. This time the employers luck had run out. BR's evidence that "several hundred people did not have the opportunity to vote" in breach of the legislation was, Mr Justice Vinelott found, "largely indirect". There was no evidence that these people had been interviewed by BR and no evidence for finding that they had been *deprived* of an opportunity to vote. Moreover, any "inadvertent failure" in a balloting operation of this size would not invalidate the ballot unless it was on a far larger scale than appeared likely here. No injunction would be granted (*British Railways Board v NUR* [1989] Industrial Relations Law Reports 345).

The Court of Appeal

BR immediately appealed and the Court of Appeal granted them a hearing with amazing rapidity the morning after — 19th June. To BR's chagrin Mr Justice Vinelott's decision not to grant an injunction was upheld. The Court stated that the ballot had been conducted with the Electoral Reform Society and after legal advice and all reasonable precautions had been taken. The court stated that "where there was a balloting operation of this size in an industrial context there were inevitably a number of people who were entitled to be balloted but who were not due to reasons such as an inability to trace them due to changes of address". The duty placed on the union by s.11(6) of the 1984 Act was only a duty to ensure *so far as was reasonably practicable* that all had a duty to vote. At the very best BR's evidence suggested that up to 200 members might not have had the opportunity to vote but the NUR had gone "to great lengths" to make ballot papers available to all.

> Against that background there was no evidence that so far as was reasonably practicable those who were entitled to vote did not have the opportunity of voting subject to trifling errors (*British Railways Board v NUR* [1989] Industrial Relations Law Reports 349).

End of story. Not quite. There was a final twist in the railwayworkers' tale. In the first action to be supported by the Commissioner For the Rights of Trade Union Members a member of the NUR, claiming ballot irregularities, sought a High Court injunction a few hours before the 24 hour stoppage was to go ahead. The case failed to meet the deadline but the Commissioner Gill Rowlands commented "one man could have stopped the strike". The case came up on 25th June before the next of the one day 24 hour strikes. The judge dismissed the application and ordered the Commissioner to pay the unions costs.

The BR dispute was eventually settled on 27th July. The unions won a limited victory with a wage increase of 8.8% and important modification of the plans to move away from national bargaining. The dispute confirmed that unions had now reluctantly accepted the law and were working within it — with some success. The employers had scored an initial triumph with the law and demonstrated once more how far reaching it was and what difficulties it could cause the union. Nonetheless the tactical acumen of the union leadership in steering the dispute around these difficulties armed with — perhaps the key factor — a powerful case understood by the public ensured that the law's impact on the end result was minimal.

*   *   *

THE DOCKERS' TALE

The government's abuse of the normal conventions of legislation was highlighted when on 7th April 1989 a White Paper *Employment in the Ports: The Dock Labour Scheme* appeared and the Dock Work Bill intended to meet the objectives discussed in the White Paper was published simultaneously. The White Paper rehearsed a range of arguments against the Dock Labour Scheme: it created labour surpluses and inefficient working practices, boosting wages, restricting the number of jobs, shackling management. Britain's competitors and ports not covered by the scheme were far more efficient. The White Paper commented without a hint of black humour that there was no need for the employment protection the scheme involved, given the "far-reaching system of employment law established over the economy as a whole". A mere 10 days later the Bill had received its second reading.

The Dock Labour Scheme established in 1947 to end the casualisation of dock work — something only completed in the 1960s — was an object of particular antagonism to a government pledged to the extension of casualisation, or flexibility as it is now euphemistically termed. Even worse, the unions' 50% representation on the National Board and 20 Local Boards gave the unions (by 1989 just the TGWU) control over hiring and firing, safety and welfare facilities and training. Employers were required to continue paying registered dockers even when there was no work unless the docker agreed to redundancy. It was a criminal offence to use anybody other than a dockworker registered by the relevant board for dockwork and redundancy payments were very high. The supplementary Jones-Aldington arrangements, introduced in 1972, also established that employers would retain any registered dockers for whom there was no work and accept additional workers allocated to them by the Boards when a closure occurred. However, certain ports had been excluded from the scheme and these had proliferated — to 35 in 1989 — and their share of business increased. There were 80,000 registered dockworkers in 1947 and 9,400 in 61 scheme ports in 1989.

For the dockers the scheme gave them a powerful element of control and job security which lent dignity and civilisation to their lives at work. The scheme represented to the government the perfect embodiment of the bad old days. It represented everything they were trying to change. The Port employers facing competition from the non-scheme ports wanted job cuts, wage reductions and a far freer hand in the organisation of work. The guarantees of job security and general conditions the dockers enjoyed were out of step with what employers were trying to achieve everywhere else in industry particularly with 1992 looming.

The employers had been attempting to convince the government to abolish the scheme for many years. They approached the government twice unsuccessfully in 1988 to urge abolition. At the end of 1988 the right-wing Centre For Policy Studies published a report *Clear the Decks: Abolish the National Dock Labour Board Scheme* written by Tory MP David Davis. For the government the decision was purely a matter of timing. A paper by the National Association of Port Employers in 1987, *Repeal of the Dock Labour Board Scheme: Industrial Action — An Analysis* stressed the necessity for "good presentation of the overwhelming case against maintaining the scheme". It emphasised the need "to secure public support for Her Majesty's Government and public antagonism towards the docker's blind and damaging desire to keep the scheme open at any cost". It stated on abolition of the scheme: "It is considered inevitable that a national strike will take place with a maximum duration of six weeks in the majority of ports". It judged that the dockers would be unlikely to get support from workers elsewhere. The document explored a number of ways of minimising the impact of a strike — 70% of cargo going through UK ports was still handled by registered dockers — such as stockpiling and transfer of cargoes and demoralising the dockers. And it noted that *"Employers in both scheme and non-scheme ports have indicated firm resolve to use the courts to enforce legal protection against secondary action".*[9]

Given this degree of forward planning many felt that the government's announcement represented a calculated gamble. Given their unshakeable believe that the trade union card was amongst the highest in the electoral pack, they wished to play it to revive their sagging fortunes. A dock strike in defence of restrictive practices and led by 'dinosaur' Ron Todd could embarrass Labour and check their resurgence in the polls. Moreover, such a dispute could be won far easier than the Miners' Strike had been and as a bonus it could deflect attention from the role of poor economic performance in Britain's disastrous trade figures.

However, there was evidence that the decision had been taken well in advance and the shipping concerns and key exporters and importers had been alerted by Ministers in 1988. The publication of the Centre For Policy Studies report had been accompanied by a series of disputes, such as that in Glasgow where employers refused to use registered dockers for loading certain ships. In December 1988 a conference of TGWU port delegates voted to endorse a call for a ballot on a national strike.

A Difficult Struggle

Be that as it may, the TGWU leadership acted with caution once the announcement of abolition came. They wanted to support the dockers — but not at any price. They realised that the forward planning of government and employers, the existence of the non-registered ports and divisions amongst the registered ports had undermined the bargaining power of the dockers. They were not prepared to bankrupt the TGWU in what they saw as possibly an unwinnable struggle involving a tiny fraction of members. They knew that the employers would almost certainly utilise the legislation at the first opportunity. Sequestration was a neutron bomb to any union but in the TGWU, with its far flung, disparate membership, putting its assets into hock for 9,000 workers whose very distinct traditions had often marked them off from the union's mainstream — increasingly so as their internal clout had diminished — could prove very unpopular and explode internal tensions.

In legal terms the first problem was that if the union supported a strike explicitly directed against the abolition of the scheme this might be found by the courts, on the model of the *Mercury v POEU,* case to be a political strike directed against government policy and falling outside the definition and the protection of a *trade dispute.* Even if the TGWU could surmount this hurdle it was clear that the quickest way to win the strike was to attempt to enlist the aid of dockers in non-scheme ports, lorry drivers and seamen. There might also be a need to picket some scheme ports in response to employers tactics such as sackings. All of this, of course, was unlawful secondary action and to support it would be to court sequestration.

The TGWU leaders decided to go for the option of an official action confined to the scheme ports. They felt that the legal position gave them little alternative — but a strike confined to the scheme ports looked at worst unwinnable, at best, uphill all the way. The smart money saw the dockers following workers in other declining industries, such as coal and steel, to defeat. Whilst the TGWU leaders accepted that, putting the best complexion on it, this strategy involved playing matters longer they were heartened by a Department of Trade and Industry circular which claimed that in the event of a strike in scheme ports

> sectors heavily dependent on imports of raw materials or components could face problems quite quickly. Steel, vehicles, chemicals, newsprint and textiles could all be hit.[10]

Pursuit of this limited strategy meant ensuring that the strike clearly possessed an industrial content. It also entailed keeping a close eye on the clock. Once the scheme was abolished the employers hand would be strengthened. For example they would be able to sack dockers far easier. It also meant winning over the dockers' representatives who wanted an immediate stoppage and who might, if this got off the ground, quickly resort to secondary action. To this end Ron Todd persuaded both the TGWU executive and a reluctant port committee and dockers delegate conference to delay a strike ballot until negotiations had taken place with the employers. These negotiations, intended to bring the dispute within the industrial sphere and the legal definition, focused on the union's demand for a national umbrella of terms and conditions to replace the scheme when abolished. By implicitly accepting abolition the union intended to empty the dispute of any political content in relation to later legal interpretation.

Not surprisingly the talks failed but the union had established its position. On 20th April the TGWU announced a strike ballot. Its leaders Ron Todd and Bill Morris stated on several occasions that they intended to conduct the dispute "totally in accordance with the law".

The Legal Offensive Begins

On 8th May the port employers began legal proceedings to have the threatened strike declared unlawful. Four days later the TGWU assured the court that it would await the outcome of legal action before seeking to implement a 'yes' vote in the strike ballot. The result of the strike ballot announced on 19th May showed a 3-1 majority in favour of striking but the union held its hand until the High Court decision was announced on 27th May. The medium pace of the High Court in this case contrasted with its speed in similar litigation. However Mr Justice Millett decided that there was definitely a genuine trade dispute between the TGWU and the Port employers as to the terms and conditions of employment of the dockers after the scheme was abolished. A national dock strike would, therefore, be protected against legal action and there was a negligible prospect of this view being overturned at a full trial of the issue. Confident that that was that the TGWU accepted the court's order to hold their hand while the employers went to the Court of Appeal (*Associated British Ports Ltd v TGWU* [1989] Industrial Relations Law Reports 291).

On 7th June, in one of the most astounding decisions in an astonishing history of novel interpretations of the law on industrial conflict, the Court of Appeal overturned the High Court and issued an injunction against the TGWU restraining the strike. The decision was described in a *Guardian* editorial as driving "a container lorry slap through existing understandings of labour law", "a bit rum" and given the TGWU's painstaking attempts to stay with the law as generally understood "the humiliation of responsible trade unionism". The Labour Party spokesperson Michael Meacher echoed Jimmy Knapp in the rail dispute stating "this extraordinary judgement demonstrates that it is becoming impossible to hold a lawful strike".[11]

The Judges Make New Law

The Court of Appeal did not question Mr Justice Millett's reasoning on the question of a trade dispute. They stated, however, that further consideration should be given to clause 8 (5) b of the Dock Labour Board scheme. It was arguable, they felt, that this clause placed on dockers a *statutory duty to be available for work and not to strike.* If the TGWU asked them to strike the union would then be liable for inducing breach of a statutory duty and this was not protected by the law *even if it was done in contemplation or furtherance of a trade dispute.*

It was little short of amazing that despite four national dock strikes and scores of sectional stoppages since the war no docker, employer, lawyer, or judge, had raised this question of a statutory duty — not during the 1960s strike, not over Pentonville, nor the ensuing national docks strike, not even over the two strikes by dockers during the 1984-85 miners strike. It was even more amazing that the Court of Appeal should accept such nonsense on stilts. It meant that dockers had *never* had any right to strike and that the same might follow for numerous other groups of workers whose employment was statutorily defined.

But worse was to come. The employers had overcome the first hurdle to obtain an injunction — the court accepted that there was *a serious issue* to be tried. They now had to show that *the balance of convenience* favoured making a legal order. Mr Justice Millet had like previous judges simply considered whether the employer or the union would suffer most damage if the strike was halted. Given that the existence of a trade dispute was as plain as a pikestaff and that any arguments, thin as they were, about the dockers' statutory duty would soon be laid to rest by the abolition of the statutory scheme he felt that the balance of convenience favoured the union. This, according to the Court of Appeal, was claptrap as the judge had only considered the interests of the two parties, neglecting a third interest — *the public interest.* As Lord Justice Stuart-Smith put it

> There is no doubt that a complete stoppage would have a major impact on innocent third parties and the economic well being of the nation (*Associated British Ports Ltd V TGWU* [1989] Industrial Relations Law Reports 305).

Nothing in the four major statutes enacted by the Conservative Government or the past practice of the courts directed them to consider this issue. The concept of "the public interest" has, of course, always been a Trojan horse for partisan conceptions of what is right and what is wrong — my idea of what is in "the public interest" may very well be very different from yours. On the whole, over the years the judges have rarely seen "the public interest" as embodying the interest of millions of trade unionists and their families. Similarly, here, they did not take account of the economic well being of the dockers and other workers who might be effected by the dispute as part of the nation. Nor did they balance against the inconvenience a strike would cause the damage banning a stoppage would cause to the right to strike. And there is presumably, despite all that has happened, still in Britain in 1989 a "public interest" in the right to strike.

But the most worrying point about the judgement was the freedom it would give the courts to ban future strikes. The government would not need to introduce legislation limiting the right to strike in essential services, for the introduction of "the public interest" when weighing the balance of convenience in applications for injunctions would do the job-and more-for them. In fact if the tests of *impact on innocent third parties* and *economic well being of the nation* were used in the sense that the judges normally used them, then those groups of workers still allowed to go on strike would be as rare as snow in Australia on Christmas Day. The final irony of ironies was that the port employers were using the Dock Labour scheme to stop industrial action intended to maintain that very scheme the employers wanted to abolish!

The Dockers Walk Out

Many of the dockers had by now had their belly-full of the legal process which they saw with a lot of justification as simply stitching them up and stalling a strike. Moreover, the clock was ticking away. The TGWU still keenly aware of the dangers of sequestration urged the dockers to hang loose whilst an appeal was taken to the House of Lords. However, it was quickly apparent that the House of Lords would not be able to hear the case before the 28 day period in which strike ballot protected industrial action had expired. Moreover, the Dock Work Bill abolishing the scheme was now scheduled to receive the Royal Assent in mid-July.

In the ports, employers were attempting to defuse the situation by a mixture of carrot and stick. They were attempting to negotiate local agreements to replace national arrangements when the scheme went. They were drawing workers' attention to the generous redundancy payments on offer. And they were pointing out that once the scheme went then workers could be sacked for participating in industrial action and under the general law would not be entitled to a penny in compensation. Moreover, key importers had started building up stocks prior to the announcement of abolition and their efforts had intensified from April. Cargoes had been diverted to non-scheme ports and Rotterdam, Antwerp and Hamburg. The delays engendered by keeping within the law and the licence that had given the judges were daily diminishing the prospects for a successful strike.

By Friday, 9th June dockers had walked out at Liverpool, Tilbury, Bristol and Lowestoft — ignoring a plea from Ron Todd to await the appeal to the House of Lords which could not set a date for a decision. George Lake, Chair of one of the Tilbury TGWU branches expressed anger at the Court of Appeal judgement and stated that whilst he had supported the tactics of the union leadership, the dockers now had to act themselves

> ... the strike ballot will expire in eight days time. Time is not on our side. We do not know when the House of Lords hearing will be and we cannot wait that long. I am fully convinced now that dockers will never be allowed out on official strike.[12]

On 19th June stewards from 11 ports met and agreed to call an unofficial national strike. Eight ports employing almost a third of the 9,400 registered dockers were already strike bound. However, the strike failed to gather further impetus. Hull and Southampton continued to work. Ron Todd told ITN that the strikers were wrong. They should accept TGWU policy and hold fire until the union had freed itself from the "legal shackles". As the port employers threatened legal action and future dismissal against the strikers and the union, the strike crumbled and ended on 19th June when Liverpool and Tilbury voted to return to work.

The House of Lords Judgement

The spotlight now switched back to the courts. On 21st June the House of Lords overruled the Court of Appeal, allowed the TGWU's appeal and discharged the injunction. Their revisions were short and sweet. Lord Goff said it seemed "a startling proposition" that there existed a statutory duty of the kind that the Appeal Court had accepted. He noted that "No such contention had ever been advanced before". Clause 8 (5) provided that a registered docker shall —

> (a) carry out his duties in accordance with the rules of the port or place where he is working; and (b) work for such periods as are reasonable in his particular case.

It was (b) that the employers and Appeal Court had relied upon to suggest that dockers had a statutory duty higher than that applied to other workers and no right within it to strike. But, the House of Lords pointed out, "the rules of the port" were to be found in local and national agreements made under the scheme which determined the basic terms of dockers' *contracts*. Clause 12 of the original scheme explicitly stated

> ... it shall be an implied term of the contract between (a RDW) available for work and a registered employer that the rates of remuneration and conditions of service ... shall be in accordance with the national or local agreements ... in force.

The dockers' obligations to work and the hours they were to work were laid down in detailed local agreements which were implied into their *contracts* of employment. Clause 12 took precedence over and developed s.8 (5) (b). Dockers had *contracts* just like any other workers. And dockers were free to go on strike — within the confines of the legislation — just like other workers. A dockers' strike would be primary action and called after a ballot which met the requirements of the 1984 Act. There was therefore no justification for an injunction (*Associated British Ports Ltd v TGWU* [1989] Industrial Relations Law Reports 399).

The dockers were finally free although it had taken far more than one bound. The reality they now faced was galling. As the courts had slowed the dockers down so the government had speeded the Bill up. Guillotined in the Commons, it received the Royal Assent on the 3rd of July, thereby enhancing the freedom of manoeuvre of the port employers.

The Lessons of Defeat

The Dockers' Tale confirmed that by the end of the decade major disputes were being conducted within the law. The requirements of the legislation had been strictly adhered to — at times the TGWU leadership seemed to accept more than the letter of the law — by Britain's biggest union which as late as 1985 had coined the phrase 'Business As Usual'. The dispute also confirmed, taken together with the rail dispute, that employers would now utilise every possible technicality to take the unions to court and that at least some of the judges would be prepared to cut their legal cloth to meet their requirements. The disputes of 1988 and 1989 demonstrated that no matter how draconian the legislation the judges could make it worse! Judicial law-making was alive and kicking and for the duration of the Court of Appeal judgement most strikes in the UK could well have been found to be unlawful. The Law Lords baulked at this conclusion. They felt that the sweeping and unsustainable development of the law by the Court of Appeal could only bring the judiciary into disrepute.

The fact that the Appeal Court reached

> the clear and unambiguous conclusion that clause 8 could not have the meaning and effect attributed to it by the employers with the result that there was no legal basis for the injunction since there was no serious issue to be tried (*Associated British Ports Ltd v TGWU* [1989] Industrial Relations Law Reports 399).

was a damning indictment of the professional competence of senior judges. Yet for a time the Appeal Court judgement *was the law* and it played its role in undermining the efficacy of the unions action. In this dispute everything, from the dockers' point of view, was too late and that included the judgement of the House of Lords.

If the Railwayworkers' Tale had shown that in certain circumstances unions could achieve their objectives within the law, the Dockers' Tale demonstrated the opposite — at least in relation to a set piece all out national strike. In a situation where both sides were racing against the clock, one to get the scheme abolished, the other to hit the employers hard and build an effective stoppage capable of being sustained before the scheme was abolished, speed was of the essence. In a situation where the odds were anyway heavily stacked against the dockers, the delays and the conflicting interpretations and the switch of focus from building the strike to dealing with legal problems all contributed to sap the initial impetus to strike action. A legally induced delay of three months from the announcement of the abolition of the scheme to the start of the national action was disastrous to the prospects of the strike and helped to exacerbate differences within the union and between ports, to confuse and demoralise the rank and file and to further increase the odds against a dockers' victory. The utility of the law combined with forward planning and the other weapons in the employers' armoury had been demonstrated by the time a national dock strike commenced on 8th July. As the *Financial Times* commented: "The three month delay in calling the national strike has presented the Transport and General Workers Union with an enormous problem in organising effective industrial action".[13]

The acuteness of this judgement was to be confirmed by the future disintegration and defeat of the four week strike. By 28th July faced with dismissals — 16 shop stewards at Tilbury had been sacked — and threats of dismissal and consequent loss of redundancy pay, the strike was weakening. The employers' estimate — probably not very far off the mark — was that 4,120 dockers were on strike, 2,500 were working and 2,577 had taken redundancy. On that day the Dock Delegates Committee voted overwhelmingly to support the General Secretary's recommendation to continue the strike. But over the weekend dockers at Hull and Southampton voted to return and on 1st August, with a majority working, the TGWU national executive in an about turn voted 18-12 to end the national stoppage. When Liverpool went back a week later it was all over.

The weakened bargaining power of registered dockers, the government's speed in rushing the abolition legislation through Parliament in the context of a carefully planned strategy; the fact that once the scheme had *gone* the focus for the strike disintegrated as few dockers saw any possibility of restoring it; the lure of redundancy payments up to £35,000; and the fear of losing them through dismissal, these were the key factors in the defeat of the strike. The use of the legislation and the role of the judges enabled them to be effectively deployed and combined and undermined the efficacy of counteraction. It thus played an important role in the Dockers' Tale.

UNOFFICIAL STRIKES AND PUBLIC SERVICES

Unofficial action by north sea contract workers and London steel erectors, as well as by train drivers and dockers, prompted the government to threaten further legislation. In response to the "wildcat" strikes on the docks Employment Secretary Norman Fowler suggested that there might be a need in the government's reform of industrial relations for further controls over this kind of action. *The Independent* reported on 10th June 1989 that one measure believed to be under consideration and due for publication in a consultation paper over the next few months is a statute which would force unions to discipline or even expel unofficial strikers to prove they were not being backed by the leadership.

As the one day rail strikes began to bite, Mr Fowler suggested that there might be a particular need to look at "strikes against the public". The TUC opposing such proposals argued that they would be likely to divorce the rank and file from their leaders and stimulate militancy. John Banham, Director-General of the CBI, gave guarded support stating that if there were any signs that unofficial action was becoming more widespread and intended to get round the existing law then there would be a case for new legislation. And of course the judgement of the Court of Appeal in the Docks dispute still smouldered in the Law Reports. In 1980 a Conservative Government had taken key Court of Appeal judgements overruled by the Law Lords and used them as a basis for legislation. This exercise, some Conservatives thought, might bear repetition in 1990.

CODE OF PRACTICE ON INDUSTRIAL ACTION BALLOTS

In September 1989 the Department of Employment published a final draft of the Code on industrial ballots (see p.159). The new version was reorganised the better to distinguish law and advice. Many of the more extreme suggestions in the first draft were amended and the language was toned down. For example, the requirement that every employer whose workers might be given entitlement to vote should be given notice by the union involved was now subject to "so far as practicable". The support for postal balloting was less prescriptive. The detailed list of information to be presented on the ballot paper was removed, although the examples of ballot papers in the Code still included all the points on the previous list. The requirement that the employer be given the chance to put his case in the ballot is removed and so is the most controversial statement that unions may not feel industrial action justified unless at least 70% of those involved voted 'yes'. The Code is another example of the government putting forward very extreme measures to gain the bonus of the "be thankful for small mercies" effect when they are eventually toned down. It came into effect on April 11th 1990.

UNOFFICIAL ACTION AND THE LAW 1989

As a direct response to the hot summer of 1989, Employment Secretary Norman Fowler announced to the Conservative Party Conference on October 10th that there would be further legislation to outlaw unofficial action. His speech underlined yet again the dynamics of Conservative policy-making on employment law in the second half of the decade. Legislation was being developed in response to specific challenges to the government as and when they occurred rather than as part of prior, calculated strategy. And legislation was being developed to keep the "union problem" on the boil, to limit the impact of opinion polls demonstrating that the unions were increasingly popular and manufacture a return to the antipathetic public attitudes of the "Winter of Discontent" which the government saw as vital to its electoral fortunes. The Cabinet was particularly concerned at the degree of public support for the railwayworkers. Legislation limiting industrial action in "essential services" was seen as a "hot chestnut" in terms of definition and enforcement. Moreover, limitations on industrial action in "essential services" might suggest trade-offs in terms of the establishment of pay review bodies, or an acceptance by the government of binding arbitration for groups of workers affected by bans on industrial action. These mechanisms were devices the government wished to limit to those already covered — not extend to new groups. Action instead on "unofficial stoppages" aimed at curbing the "wild-cats" might strike an old chord and mobilise resentment against unions and strikes, a resentment the Conservatives suspected was merely slumbering rather than eradicated from the public mind. Even the sober *Financial Times* headlined "Fowler plans curbs on wild-cat strike action".[14]

The *ad hoc* nature of Conservative policy was emphasised when Mr Fowler introduced his Green Paper *Unofficial Action and the Law* on October 11th 1989 by emphasising that the purpose of its proposals was to ensure that action, such as that mounted by the tubeworkers in 1989, or that threatened by the TGWU over Ford's plans to open a new plant in Dundee in 1988 would not be countenanced in the 1990s.

The Green Paper demonstrated yet again the degree to which legislation was based upon political considerations and antagonistic stereotypes of the unions rather than detailed research. For its sermon on the extent of unofficial strikes and their impact upon employers, the government relied on the *Donovan Report* published precisely 21 years earlier. It asserted that unofficial stoppages constituted a continuing problem in the motor industry and the docks but were now also affecting "essential services" such as the railways and the post office. The degree to which this was a response to earlier government policies and legislation was not analysed. In a particularly brazen justification for further legislation to control secondary action, reminiscent of legal policy-making on the closed shop, the government stated: "The law as it stands is complicated and it could well be difficult for those involved to determine in the absence of a court judgement whether there would be immunity for organising certain secondary action".[15] The government was now, in the most cynical fashion, accepting criticisms made of its legislation by the unions almost ten years before — criticisms which throughout the decade it has fiercely rebutted — only to use these criticisms to tighten, not liberalise, the position on secondary action.

As well as proposing to deal with unofficial action and secondary stoppages the Green Paper also suggested legislation to give employers a freer hand in selectively sacking the ringleaders of industrial action undertaken without union support.

The government allowed its by now customary extended period for consultation over these vital proposals. Interested parties were given some six weeks to respond. Not surprisingly the proposals were condemned by the Labour Party and the TUC as attempting to revive the ogres of wild-cat strikes and untrammelled union power to distract attention away from higher interest rates and rising inflation. It was also argued that the consequent legislation would be difficult to apply in practice. The CBI gave qualified support but noted that there would be difficulties in utilising some of the new measures. The EEF also gave the Green Paper a cautious welcome. But the British Institute of Management had strong reservations and the IPM felt that the consequences of legislation might be more arbitrary sackings by unscrupulous managers and more unofficial action. If unofficial strikers *were* repudiated by their unions one essential control in a dispute would be lost. Interestingly, whilst Stuart Bradley, the Managing Director of Associated British Ports who had had to deal with unofficial action in 1989 felt that the proposals, if acted upon, would persuade workers against such methods and stabilise industrial relations, Roger Straker, Personnel Director of London Underground and involved in the tubeworkers dispute, felt that these measures could create martyrs, stiffen resistance and make it more difficult to ensure a return to work once an unofficial dispute began.[16]

THE EMPLOYMENT ACT 1990

Despite these differences the government pressed ahead. On November 21st 1989, just a little over five weeks since the publication of the "consultative" Green Paper and a week before the consultation period was to end, it was announced in the Queen's Speech that a sixth major piece of employment legislation would be introduced in the forthcoming session of Parliament. Exactly a month later, with the Cabinet having had less than three weeks to examine the results of the consultation exercise, the Bill was published. Norman Fowler indicated that it would be the last piece of union legislation this side of a general election. On January 3rd 1990, Norman Fowler resigned as Employment Secretary to devote more time to his family but his assurance that the new Employment Bill would be the Tories "last tilt at the unions" was repeated by his successor Michael Howard. Hardly had Mr Howard's breath cooled his soup however, before there was talk in Conservative circles of plans to tax strike pay. This proposal was incited by the engineering union's payments to members involved in industrial action over the '35 hour week'.

The 1990 Act is based on proposals outlined in the two 1989 Green Papers *Removing Barriers to Employment* and *Unofficial Action and the Law*. It deals once again with the rights to union membership; the closed shop; legal action against trade unions by their members; unofficial industrial action; dismissal of strikers; and limits of secondary action.

The Closed Shop and Non-Membership (s.1-3)

Having legally undermined the basis of the post-entry closed shop in the Acts of 1980, 1982 and 1988, the government has now legislated against the *pre-entry closed shop* — the situation where existing union membership was a pre-requisite for employment. Research published in late 1989 claimed that the numbers of workers covered by the closed shop had declined to 2.6 million of whom half were subject to pre-entry closed shop requirements.[17] The previous legislation had applied to action taken to ensure those already *employees* were union members. The new Act deals, for the first time, with the issue of *recruitment* to jobs. It is based upon the idea that the closed shop destroyed jobs, raised costs and depressed profitability — a view the government took in *Employment for the 1990s*. The analysis was borrowed from the work of Professor Metcalfe which was later challenged by further research. It was ultimately, of course, dependent on wider and contentious economic and political judgements.[18]

The new Act gives those *refused employment on the ground that they were not, or refused to become a member of a union*, or of a particular union, or of a particular section or branch of a union, a right to take the employer to an industrial tribunal. The new right also covers workers suffering discrimination if they fail to become a union member.

The Act specifically refers to job advertisements. If an advertisement is published which indicates, or might be reasonably understood as indicating, that the employment is only open to union members then a worker who does not meet these requirements, applies for the job and is refused employment shall be *conclusively presumed* to have been refused employment for failing to satisfy the condition or requirement laid down in the advertisement.

Where the recommendation of workers for jobs is controlled by a trade union then anybody who is not a member of a trade union and who is refused employment will be presumed to have been refused employment because of their non-membership of a union and will be able to claim discrimination. The provisions also apply to Employment Agencies. In future it will be unlawful for an Employment Agency to restrict its services in finding employment for workers, or supplying employers with labour, to trade union members.

A *refusal of employment* covers the situation where an employer causes an individual to withdraw, or cease to pursue an application, or makes a spurious offer of employment, the terms of which no reasonable employer intent on filling the post would make. It also covers refusing or deliberately omitting to entertain an application or enquiry and refusing or deliberately omitting to offer employment.

A tribunal, if the case is proven, may recommend that the employer take action "which the tribunal consider to be practicable for the purposes of obviating or reducing the effect on the complainant of the act complained of" — for example, they may recommend that the non-unionists be employed. If a recommendation is not complied with compensation may be increased — up to a level of £8,925.

Rights to Union Membership

The government wished to use the new legislation to undermine the pre-entry closed shop. But they were faced with problems if they simply outlawed a refusal to employ on the grounds of non-membership of a union but left employers completely free to refuse to take on workers on the grounds that they *were* members of a trade union. The government's original view was that rights to union membership were not comparable to rights to non-membership. This was because of their belief that the first tends to increase labour costs and the second tends to diminish them — in the words of Employment Minister Patrick Nicholls "...a major objection to the pre-entry closed shop is its adverse economic effects. There would be no comparable effects where employers declined to recruit union members".[19] Nevertheless political expediency and the articulation of *both* rights in the EEC Social Charter led the government to change course. To balance the situation the Act gives prospective employees who are trade unionists a right not to be refused employment on the same criteria as apply to non-unionists.

Suing the Union
(s.10, 11)

As we have seen the Commissioner for the Rights of Trade Union Members had been established by the 1988 legislation and become active the following year, dealing, however, with a tiny number of complaints scarcely justifying the £1 million costs involved. In accordance with their general approach, the government, having established the new commissioner as part of the scenery of industrial relations, now wished to extend her role. In addition to the commissioner's ability to assist those taking legal action against their union over ballots for industrial action; inspection of union accounts; trustees' use of funds; ballots for internal union posts; and ballots over the political fund — the Act now gave the commissioner new rights. She will now be able to aid an applicant to bring a case *involving a breach by the union of requirements laid down in its rulebook* where this involves an issue of *substantial public interest.*

This new right granted to the commissioner would cover situations where the union had failed to observe rulebook requirements relating to
— nomination of candidates for office or to attend meetings concerned with union policy
— selection or election of candidates for office or to attend meetings
— discipline, expulsion or the imposition of other penalties
— the authorisation or endorsement of industrial action and strike levies
— ballots of members

— application of union funds or property
— the composition of union bodies.

The commissioner will now be able to appear in any legal proceedings alongside the individual applicant as a party to the case and those seeking the commissioner's assistance will be protected from any consequent action by their union.

Secondary Action
(s.4)

The complicated provisions of s.17 of the 1980 Act had given workers some protection where they were taking industrial action to prevent or disrupt the flow of goods or services to or from a supplier or customer of the employer in dispute, where certain requirements as to the purpose of the action and its likely contribution to the success of the primary dispute were met.

The Act *removes immunity from all forms of secondary action,* so that workers at a struck plant seeking to get workers at the plant of a customer or supplier not to handle delivery would be open to legal action for damages. So would any union authorising or supporting the action. This represents the culmination of the government policy of limiting disputes to the employer directly involved.

Moreover, the prohibition on secondary action will apply not only to those working under a contract of employment but also those — independent contractors, the self-employed — working under a *contract for services.* Moreover, all the earlier legislation requiring ballots before industrial action will now apply not only to employees but also to freelances — those employed under a contract for services. The logic of this is that if, for example, the NUJ wanted to call a strike of its members on a newspaper or magazine then they would have to ballot not only those employed but, also any freelance workers they reasonably believed might be induced to take industrial action.

Unofficial Action
(s.6, 7)

Complex provisions of the Act make unions responsible for the actions of anyone empowered by rules to *authorize or endorse* industrial action; the union executive committee, general secretary or president; any other committee of the union; any official of the union, lay shop stewards as well as paid officers. Responsibility and legal liability for the actions of all union personnel thus covered will apply, notwithstanding anything in the union rules stating, for example, that shop stewards have no power to *authorize or endorse industrial action.* And a union cannot evade responsibility for the actions of its officials or other activists by changing its rules. Even further, it is provided that if any official is part of a strike committee or co-ordinating committee, part of any group authorizing or endorsing industrial action, or even if *any member* of that group authorizes or endorses such action although the official is not involved, then the union will be deemed to have authorized or endorsed the industrial action. The only way it can escape being deemed to have authorized or endorsed industrial action is if it *specifically repudiates* the action. This may well alienate and demoralize its members and stimulate internal divisions.

Repudiation must come from the union executive or the President or General Secretary if the union is to escape legal action. However, such repudiation will be ineffective unless *written notice* of the repudiation is given without delay to the officers, shop stewards or committee organising the unlawful industrial action. Moreover, the union must then 'do its best' to give written notice of the fact and date of the repudiation

— to the employer(s) of every member involved
— to every member who the union has reason to believe is taking part in industrial action as a result of the action of union officers, shop stewards or committees.

The written repudiation given to all members must read as follows

Your union has repudiated any call(s) for industrial action to which this notice relates and will give no support to unofficial action taken in response to it (or them). If you are dismissed whilst taking unofficial industrial action you will have no right to complain of unfair dismissal.

Repudiation will be ineffective if the union executive, President or General Secretary later behave in a manner inconsistent with the terms of that repudiation.

The judgement in *Express and Star Ltd v NGA* [1985] Industrial Relations Law Reports 455 (see p.73) is now codified and extended by legislation to hit the unofficial striker. Where industrial action occurs in the absence of a ballot, the employer will now be able to push the union into the picture in a more formal fashion although it is difficult to see what impact this would have in cases such as the tubeworkers' action in 1989 — apart from stiffening already existing divisions between the rank and file and their unions.

Ballots Again
(s.5, 7, 8)

Voting papers are now required to specify the identity of the person authorised by the union to call upon members to take part or continue to take part in industrial action. This must be the executive committee, the President, the General Secretary, or another committee official specifically authorised. Whatever the result of the ballot, industrial action will not be protected by it unless it is called by the person specified on the ballot paper, after the date of the ballot and within four weeks of that date.

The Act also states that voting papers must now name an independent scrutineer on voting papers for political fund and union election ballots. Before that scrutineer begins to operate the union must send out a notice with the name of the scrutineer to every member so far as is reasonably practicable and utilise all other means it normally uses to publicise matters of general interest to bring the name to the notice of members.

Dismissal of Strikers
(s.9)

However, the second weapon to be used against unofficial strikers in the event that action by the union fails, brings the employer directly into the picture. In future where the industrial action is unofficial the normal rules on dismissal (see p.61) will be relaxed. In the belief that, as *Unofficial Action and the Law* puts it, these rules constitute "a major constraint on an employer's ability to take steps to safeguard his business and the jobs of other employees against unofficial action" the 1990 Act makes it easier for employers to sack strikers. This despite the condemnation of the *existing legislation* by the ILO as inconsistent with any real right to strike (see p.152).

— Any workers taking part *in unofficial action* such as the leaders or shop stewards may be *selected out* for dismissal and will have no right to take a case to an industrial tribunal

— Any industrial action in support of those selectively dismissed in unofficial action even if that solidarity and action is called after a ballot and authorised by the union will be unprotected by the immunities and will be open to legal action by any employers or other persons affected

— Action will not be deemed unofficial and covered by these provisions if all those taking part are non-trade unionists.

This section of the Act was described by the *Financial Times* as having "worrying implications". An editorial stated "It appears invidious when coupled with the narrowing of the right to strike in support of a person dismissed in such circumstances and breaches the principle of equal treatment by an employer".[20]

Other Changes
(s.13-17)

The Act, in addition, made a number of minor changes to the law. It provides for revision of Codes of Practice by ACAS or the Secretary of State for Employment. The Redundancy Fund will be wound up and assets transferred to the National Insurance Fund. And children can now be employed for work experience from the start of the term preceding the school year in which they have the right to leave school.

Discussion Questions

1. Has Conservative Employment legislation helped moves towards a more flexible labour force with a core of highly paid secure workers and a mass of peripheral, low paid, casual workers?
2. Critically examine the provisions of *The Code of Practice on Ballots*.
3. "The European *Social Charter of Workers Rights* is one of the unions' best hopes for a fair and balanced Employment Law in the 1990s". How far is this true?
4. "The industrial disputes in the summer of 1989 demonstrated that trade unions after 10 years of Thatcherism were still strong and could get around, or live with, Tory employment laws" Discuss this statement with reference to the disputes on the docks and the railways.
5. Draw up a report on the *1990 Employment Act* and how it is likely to influence union objectives and methods.

CHAPTER 8

Yesterday's Gone

Elect a Labour Government and distrust them thoroughly! — *R.H. Tawney*

LOOKING BACK

As the 1990s dawned it was clear that on the legislative front at least, the Conservatives had won and the unions had lost. The line taken by the left-wing executive of the NUR and the TGWU leadership during the docks dispute showed that even tactical defiance of the law was now a thing of the past. And the cases kept coming. By 1990 it was usual for employers to look for the legal angles and possibilities in any important industrial dispute. Legal action now occurred on a scale far greater than during the 1945-79 period if still in a minority of all disputes.

In September 1989, for example, British Coal was granted an injunction prohibiting the NUM from picketing Betteshanger Colliery which the union argued was closed in breach of the consultative procedure. In October 1989 British Aerospace took action in the High Court against a number of engineering unions using obscure rules of the Confederation of Shipbuilding and Engineering Unions to argue that strikes for a reduction of hours were unlawful. Whilst this action was largely unsuccessful the employers during the ambulance dispute of 1989-90 were able to use the courts to prevent crews operating independent services. And in January 1990 the Court of Appeal ruled that a 24-hour strike by Post Office counter staff was unlawful because the ballot had been held too long ago and the question on the ballot paper did not comply with the requirements of the 1984 Act. At its Biennial Delegate Conference in 1989, Britain's biggest union, the TGWU, generally regarded as the mainstay of the left, finally came into line and agreed to apply for state funds for internal ballots. A TUC affiliate, the Electrical Power Engineering Association, was even challenging the Certification Officer in the High Court for *refusing* to grant it public funds for a ballot to elect its representatives! Wembley was once again almost completely associated with football.

TUC policy, having gone through the three phases of limited evasive action, 1979-82; co-ordinated opposition, 1982-83; and disintegration of opposition and acceptance of the legislation in practice, 1984-87; had by the end of the decade settled on a dual track. The TUC combined powerless protest as new measures rolled off the conveyor belt with an understanding that there was little that could be done in practice to oppose the impact of legislation this side of a Labour Government. Its powers to co-ordinate the actions of its affiliates, developed so carefully to enforce incomes policies and oppose legislation, had been undermined. The TUC had suffered a serious defeat. What it said or did had little effect on the P&O, NUR or docks disputes. By 1990, it was relying more and more on public opinion and the EC to stem the tide of legislation and, ironically, on opposition from employers. The reservations that the CBI and the IPM registered over the draft *Code of Practice on Ballots*,were eagerly seized upon, although a scrutiny of the small print demonstrated that opposition was not to the idea of a code but the length, organisation, and over-prescriptive tone of the draft. Similarly, the CBI's doubts over the plans to scrap wages councils — on the grounds that in certain sectors they could be useful and there should be a sector-by-sector review — were warmly welcomed. However, whilst there was certainly in some quarters a feeling that the legislation had gone far enough — 63% of managing directors polled by the magazine *Chief Executive* thought so — Conservative governments had generally taken little account of the hesitations of employers.

What was particularly worrying for the unions was the fact that, having got the smell of union weakness, the government was not placated but stimulated and was now seriously engaged in a game of 'remorseless pursuits'. The amount of law and its reach, looked at from the standpoints of even the early 1980s, was mind-boggling. The new proposals on secondary action and the closed shop promised even more difficulties for the unions. And there were hints of yet more to come — the statement in the draft Code on Ballots that ballots should await an exhaustion of disputes procedures, for example, suggested a return to the long neglected issue of making collective agreements legally enforceable.

The legislative saga had weakened the TUC industrially and politically. Yet in some quarters a mood seemed to be developing by the end of the decade which implied that the unions could live with the legislation; whether this was related to Labour's plans — or lack of them — for its future repeal, is another matter. Certainly, defiance was still possible — when the law took aim at *individuals*. In April 1989, in a dispute involving workers at the Isle of Grain channel tunnel construction site, 400 workers were named in an injunction — and ignored it. It had no effect on the dispute over bonus pay and a little later Trans Manche Ltd. conceded the workers' claim. When the *union* and its assets were involved it was different. Disputes like that involving the NUR led experts to opine that the unions could achieve their objectives by wriggling within the law. But that was a dispute involving *one* monopoly employer and it was over pay. Where, as in the docks dispute, a more heterogeneous workforce is involved in a dispute about wider terms and conditions, wriggling successfully within the law may be much more difficult. Moreover, the element of judicial creativity, which caused such important delays in the dock dispute, is inescapable and cannot be budgetted for with any precision.

By the end of the decade the weaknesses in the floor of rights were being reflected in legal statistics. The extension of the qualifying period for unfair dismissal, from 6 months in 1979 to two years in 1985, was represented by a fall in tribunal applications: in 1987-88 there were only 34,233 applications compared with 41,244 in 1979. Moreover, of the cases proceeding to a hearing only 9.61% were successful compared with 10.8% in 1986-87. Only 83 — 1.1% — received an award of reinstatement. Similarly, equal pay claims dropped by two-thirds and the applicant was successful in a mere seven cases. There was a small increase in the number of race discrimination cases but in only 40 out of 320 cases proceeding to a hearing was the applicant successful. Only 166 Sex Discrimination cases proceeded to a hearing and in only 48 was the applicant successful. 1989 actually saw an increase in unfair dismissal claims but, despite this, the median award of compensation decreased to £1,732. By any reasonable standards it was now possible to term the legal floor of individual rights in the UK as, without any exaggeration, a scandal, compared with the position in other EC states. And the Thatcherite woodpeckers were far from finished drilling holes in what remained. The CBI concluded a year long review of the Equal Pay for work of Equal Value Regulations by urging they be weakened — independent experts, for example, should only be used with the agreement of applicants *and employers.*

If unions have learnt to live with the law, it is on the law's terms not theirs. The unions have had success with strike ballots. But the 1988 and 1989 disputes, for example, illustrated that winning a ballot may mark the beginning, not the end, of legal intervention. *Living with the law means accepting a restrictive framework inimical to the success of union organisation and action and this must not be glossed over.* In its attack on collectivism and union organisation, its control of internal union operations, its limitations on industrial action, its confinement of union activity to the workplace or enterprise, and its undermining of workers rights through the policy of deregulation, the Conservative legislation makes a contribution to the creation of a union-hostile environment.

From the government's point of view there is still some cause for concern. We have seen that the use of the law by employers remains a rarity and workers have been even more reluctant to use it. The result has involved thrusting the state, through the new commissioner, more into the arena. Unions have managed to draw the sting of key measures on the closed shop and strike ballots, although this has simply prompted further legislation. Where things *have* changed in industry, economics have had more to do with it than law — the closed shop is a good example. A recent series of papers from the universities of London and Oxford, based on the evidence collected by the government's *Workplace Industrial Relations Survey*, concludes that economic factors rather than the introduction of legislation prompted changes and increased productivity in industry in the period 1980-84.[1]

Against this, the government can argue that the legislation was never intended to stand alone; it was developed as *one component* in a wider package of political and economic measures — as we outlined in our introduction. If unemployment and the recession of the early 1980s were crucial, together with rising wages for those in work since 1983, the laws, they can claim, have still played an important role in changing trade union behaviour. In the docks dispute, for example, the entire strategy of one of the most intransigent opponents of the legislation was predicated on what that legislation would and would not allow. And despite the new role of the judges in scrutinising the detail of important disputes, you don't need to go to court to use the law. There is an increased involvement of lawyers in the planning of both management and unions and an increased awareness on both sides of industry that, whatever they would *like* to do, unions now mould their behaviour to meet the requirements of the law. This, rather than the number of cases reported, bespeaks the success of employment legislation.

A balanced view would grant the government success over the legislation but not in the inflated terms they often claim. In the end, Mrs Thatcher's success was due to careful tactical steering within an overall strategic approach, and not a little luck, but perhaps, most of all, to her determination to break decisively and clearly from the 1945-79 social democratic consensus over full employment and 'restrained' state intervention in major disputes. She kept her nerve when unemployment soared and did little. The behaviour of the government of her predecessor Heath, over Saltley Gates, or the Pentonville 5, contrasted with her own use of the police and the law. However, success has been mixed, clear victories partially due to the influence of legislation — but with one or two setbacks. Moreover, the formal success of the Conservative Goverment's employment laws has to be balanced within and against the wider failure of Conservative economic policy. By the end of the Thatcher decade her government was faced with balance of payment problems; soaring interest rates; embarrassments over privatisation policy; the failure of its attempts to cut wages — by 1990 average earnings were increasing at over 10% — and an apparent inability to curb inflation and generate sustained growth. The CBI reported that orders were falling, prices were being squeezed by competition and profit margins by rising costs and high interest rates. The rate of earnings increase, *The Financial Times* claimed, needed to be reduced by 4-5 percentage points.

The required legal framework was on the statute books and operating. It had not paid the expected dividends in terms of its fundamental purpose, a serious contribution to the solution of the UK's deep seated economic problems. By 1990 the economy was *deteriorating* not *improving*: the UK was facing a serious recession. The proof of the pudding for Mrs Thatcher was to lie in the bitter eating. It was the failure to achieve her economic objectives — in the realisation of which employment legislation was expected to play an important ancillary role — which combined with discontent over the poll tax to precipitate her removal and replacement as Prime Minister by John Major.

In the Green Paper *Removing Barriers to Employment* the government stated that employment legislation had "made an important contribution to the improvement in the employment scene". There is no evidence to back this statement. As to specifics, research in progress suggests that the Conservative policies have meant higher wages in unionised workplaces in return for increased productivity and job cuts. The "union mark-up" over non-unionised enterprises has continued and overall the legislation has had a limited impact on unemployment and labour efficiency. It has also forced unions to tighten up their organisation and discipline and measures such as strike ballots have introduced a more cautious but more strategic and well supported approach to industrial action and negotiation.[2]

Perhaps the most important lesson we can take from the experience is that whilst those who argued — in the wake of the *1971 Industrial Relations Act* — that restrictive employment legislation could not take root and sucessfully operate to constrain union activities were wrong, the contribution that even *successful* employment legislation can make to the transformation of deeply embedded culture and practice in industry *is inherently limited.* This would appear so even when it is introduced in tandem with the shock of high and sustained unemployment. Even the break from the post-war consensus has failed to turn the tide. The Conservatives this decade have written a book of employment laws yet the emergence of new problems and new loopholes has prompted further and further additions and proposals almost monthly. Perhaps a complete bible will be required but the doubt now nagging at even Conservative minds must be that the potency of this weapon has been over-estimated.

The unions, on any account, would certainly still be far better off *without* this legal framework. They tried to stop it reaching the statute book and they lost. And they tried to stop it operating and they lost. They have accepted it and, in so doing, limited its impact in certain ways. But their very acceptance has limited the optimal mobilisation of union resources and power in important circumstances. The legislation has had a strong impact on secondary action. Where trade unionists in a primary dispute have been determined and united it has had little impact. Again, the delays and confusion it engenders have been circumnavigated in one case, say the railway dispute, but not in another, say the dock dispute. It appears to have influenced union methods but not end products such as wage increases, unless we assume that in unfavourable circumstance they would, without legislation, have been running since 1982 at *treble* rather than, as they have been, *double* the rate of price increases. The legislation seems to have had little overall impact on the decline in union membership, or the rate of wage increases. None the less we need far more evidence to finally judge the impact of legislation on trade unions and industrial relations.

Economic and political factors, not legal factors, would seem to be primary. And where the legislation has played a part in changing the behaviour of trade unionists, with the possible exception of ballots, this change appears to have been wrought through fear of the consequences — injunctions and sequestration — rather than even a broad acceptance that the standards the law requires are fair and just ones. Its impact cannot be separated from the wider political and economic events of the 1980s. Any success which has depended to this degree on a mixture of state coercion, high unemployment, and a greater differentiation of the labour force between the unemployed, the semi-employed, the low paid and those who have had real wage increases in the Thatcher years, is unlikely to constitute a permanent revolution.

*   *   *

THE WHITE COLLAR WORKERS' TALE

NALGO is a union which did well during the 1980s, emerging from the recession with some 750,000 members. Like its fellow TUC affiliates, however, it suffered problems because of the new employment legislation. Unlike other unions NALGO's main difficulties centred on its rules and arrangements for internal democracy.

As a union which developed with a strong "professional association" ethos, the NALGO Executive appointed its General Secretary. He was seen as very much an Executive Officer and until 1965 did not even have the right to speak at Annual Conference. As a multi-occupational union seeking to reconcile and mesh together the interests not only of different groups of local government workers, but also of employees in the NHS, water, gas, electricity supply and other industries, NALGO sought to make special arrangements to ensure that all interests were adequately represented at national level. Approximately two-thirds of the unions's 70 person national executive were elected annually by the membership as a whole on a district basis after nominations by branches. To avoid local government domination the chairs of NALGO's eight subsidiary national service conditions committees — when they were not otherwise elected to the executive — were appointed to it. Arrangements were also made for the appointment of additional members of the national service conditions committees to the NEC where there was an overall imbalance producing under-representation. Under the *1984 Trade Union Act* all voting members of the executive had to be *elected* (see p.81). Under the *1988 Employment Act* a union's chief executive officer — in NALGO's case the General Secretary — had to be elected (see p.133). NALGO, therefore, faced problems as its rules did not comply with the requirements of the law.

Like several other unions NALGO took no immediate steps to change its rules when the 1984 Act became law. Instead it adopted a 'wait and see' policy of 'least compliance'. However, individual members protested and, in 1985 and 1986, a number of complaints were brought before the Certification Officer — in one case by a member of the Conservative Trade Unionists Organisation. NALGO attempted to resolve the difficulty by withdrawing voting rights from the appointed members of the NEC but events were overtaken by the 1988 Act which required all executive members and officers to be elected by ballot. NALGO decided to abide by the legislation but the dilemmas of union democracy were illustrated when the NEC decided to place before the 1989 conference proposals for a confirmatory ballot. This entailed the NEC selecting a General Secretary and *then* placing his name on the ballot paper, to be confirmed by the membership in a vote. Whilst this represented an ingenious means of getting round the legislation and whilst it could be argued that it maintained the traditional modicum of democracy — the NEC was itself directly elected and answerable to the members as to who it appointed — this notion of democracy was no longer acceptable to the annual conference.

In an interesting example of the way in which the Conservative legislation on elections has meshed in with wider ideas of democracy, and demonstrated the limitations of some traditional union mechanisms — why should not the whole membership pick the Chief Officer rather than the electoral college of the NEC? — the position of the NEC was overturned by the 1989 Annual Conference. With confirmatory balloting thrown out the NEC still tried to maintain as much of the original position as possible and it interviewed three of the four original candidates for the position in the 1990 ballot — the fourth declining the opportunity — and nominated an NEC candidate in the run-off.

NALGO was also facing problems in the area of union discipline, essential to any effective industrial action. In the summer of 1989 half a million town hall workers began a series of rolling strikes. A June national one-day stoppage was followed in July by a two-day and then a three-day all out strike by local government white collar workers. The strikes were over the employers' refusal to increase a 7% pay offer. The offer also had important strings attached. The employers wished to undermine national bargaining and under the terms of the offer national grading appeals would be done away with and councils would be entitled to fix hours of work and unsocial payments. In the ballot on industrial action 186,365 NALGO members, 59.26%, voted to strike and 128,132, 40.74%, voted against — on a high turnout of 61.7%.

Whilst these figures showed a clear majority support for action and were encouraging, particularly as the two most recent ballots over local government pay had been *against* action, they also demonstrated that many members were still unsure about the situation. However, the strikes drew a remarkable response. In the atmosphere of militancy of mid-1989 the majority of NALGO members struck — although some defied the majority decision of their brothers and sisters, perhaps stiffened a little by "the strike breakers charter" in the 1988 Act which legitimised such violations of democracy. Thousands of local government workers joined

NALGO — 1,100 were reported to have signed up in the North East alone after the first one-day strike and picket lines were well supported. The rolling stoppages were then followed by indefinite strikes by key groups of workers which involved 15,000 NALGO members from 325 branches hitting local government revenue. In what was probably the largest ever strike by computer staff, the processing of payments of rent, rate collections and poll tax registration were disrupted. Despite every precaution being taken to exclude their intervention the Employment Laws were soon in action. Ravenshead Glass Co. failed to get an injunction against eight NALGO members on strike in St. Helens who supervised the stamping of beer glasses to comply with weights and measures legislation on the grounds that the supply to the pubs would soon dry up — with calamitous consequences!

The action was soon biting. Whilst all NALGO members had lost money in the six days of earlier stoppages, the selective strikers received full take home pay. Some of the councils were, in contrast, quickly in financial difficulties, despite the small number of staff involved. A typical example was Chester-le-Street in Durham where only eleven NALGO members were on strike. The fact that they were able to close down the computers and switchboard, cutting off income from council house rents and rates, motivated the council along with others in a similar plight, to write to the negotiators urging an increased offer. When negotiations commenced on August 10th the employers caved in completely, offering an 8.8% increase with no strings attached and 9.5% to the lowest paid NALGO members. NALGO's success was established by the condemnation of the settlement by David Hunt, the Minister for Local Government, who pronounced himself "astounded" by the employers climbdown which he saw as reminiscent of the bad old days of the 1970s.[3] NALGO had demonstrated once again the power of carefully thought out, strategically calculated industrial action to bring home the bacon, despite a decade of Conservative legislation aimed at rendering it ineffectual.

But some clearing up remained to be done. Agitation commenced in the branches for action to be taken against those who had refused to accept the strike ballot. The demand for discipline often came from moderates who had voted against industrial action but accepted the democratic verdict of the majority, those new to the union and those on strike for the first time. Why, they asked, should those who had refused to fight for a wage increase — indeed had by continuing to work made that fight and the eventual victory harder to achieve — simply pocket the 8.8% wage increase produced by the sacrifices of their colleagues? Why, 8.8% better off, should the strikebreakers continue to enjoy the benefits and privileges of membership of the union whose democratic decisions they had refused to accept? Many experienced NALGO members appreciated the difficulties of disciplining the strikebreakers. In retaliation, the latter could then take the union to law under the 1988 Act which provided that members have a right not to be disciplined for ignoring the result of a ballot on industrial action and receive awards of over £14,000. But they felt that this consideration was outweighed by the loss of confidence new activists would feel if nothing was done about the strikebreakers. The situation was even more inflamed by the fact that NALGO activists had been disciplined by the employers for their activities during the strike. In Tower Hamlets, for example, when the strike ended the branch secretary Derek Relph was suspended and faced dismissal because of allegations that he had attacked strikebreakers on the picket lines. Why, many asked, should those who had stabbed their union in the back get off Scot free, whilst those who had been in the local leadership of the struggle suffered for their activities?

In September 1989 the NALGO Local Government Group voted to accept the need for discipline and the NEC rejected the call for a special conference to change the association's rules to halt disciplinary measures. But anger against the strikebreakers benefitting from a pay rise they had not helped to win expressed itself in branches beginning proceedings for expulsion against the dissidents. NALGO Headquarters circulated branches with a draft letter to be sent to strikebreakers which sought to avoid the crunch. It stated "While not seeking to undermine your right to remain in NALGO, I would ask you to consider seriously whether it is appropriate for you to remain a member of the union in the light of your unwillingness to abide by the wishes of the majority". This definitely did *not* do the trick with many local activists who viewed it as ineffectual or supine. By the end of 1989 some 400 members had been expelled for crossing picket lines and over 50 had complained to industrial tribunals under the 1988 Act. Bitterness against the blacklegs intensified when it was reported that the Tory Westminster City Council had made available £20,000 for disciplined members to take the union to court — leading to complaints to the District Auditor — and that Tower Hamlets councillors had offered to foot the bill for a private prosecution against Derek Relph.

However when, in the first case heard, a South Tyneside industrial tribunal found that NALGO had breached the 1988 Act by expelling eleven local members, the NEC, in early 1990 ordered branches, under Rule 40, to reinstate the now more than 600 members who had been expelled by 26 branches for working during the dispute. If the branches maintained the expulsions then their disciplinary powers would be suspended by the Executive: they themselves would be liable for any compensation awarded the former members, although the NEC suggested that the strikebreakers might be offered national membership. This issue threatened to continue as a source of internal conflict within NALGO, an infection planted by the provisions of the *1988 Employment Act.*

The White Collar Workers' Tale illustrates that unions which avoid frontal confrontation with the law over industrial action can find themselves in difficulties as the law slips in at the back door. Action by individual members against their union which attracted particular attention from Conservatives during the miners' strike remains a potent weapon for disrupting union action, particularly when it falls within the confines of the "strikebreaker clause" of the 1988 Employment Act. Unions, like NALGO, which seek to discipline those who ignore strike instructions will face claims for serious damages. Yet the failure by a union faced with legal claims to exercise discipline over those who refuse to abide by democratic decisions can only disrupt collectivism and undermine the efficacy of future industrial action. The dilemma is a difficult one — particularly perhaps in white collar unions — and unions will have to steer as adeptly and cunningly as they can between the horns of accepting the right of members to ignore ballots, with its potentially disastrous consequences for membership mobilisation, and discipline and expulsions which can attract serious legal sanction.

THE LAND OF 'IF'

Could things have been different? Could the unions have stopped the legislation getting off the ground had there been more strategic thinking and effective leadership, particularly from the TUC in the early 1980s? Why were the unions able to halt the *In Place of Strife* proposals in 1969 and immobilise the *Industrial Relations Act* in 1972 yet fail so lamentably to damage Mrs Thatcher's measures a decade later? Is it still too late for the unions to defeat the impact of the law through industrial action as we enter the 1990s?

Once again, we need more research on these important questions but it seems that had the unions wished to mount a repetition of the events of 1969-1972, then it would have been most likely to achieve success in the period 1979-82. By the summer of 1980, for example, prices were rising at an annual rate of 22% and wages by more than 20%. Mrs Thatcher was the most unpopular Prime Minister since opinion polls began. The moderate 'wets' were still numerically strong in the Conservative Party and the cabinet. By the winter of that year Sir John Hoskyns and other close advisers went to see the Prime Minister and said to her "If there is ever going to be any sort of U-turn on policy you absolutely must think about it now!"[4] A further crisis blew up in the cabinet in March 1981 and it was at this time that, as John Biffen accepted, the government did back down in the face of a developing miners strike. The Minister responsible, David Howell, pressurised the Coal Board to withdraw plans for pit closures murmuring: "I did not come into politics to act like a kamikaze pilot".[5]

If the government was to be hit hard then it had to be in its first two years, the period when Heath had been forced into a U-turn. If there was a time for a successful resistance it was this time. The irony was that the period from 1979 until Norman Tebbit's proposals for the 1982 Act were placed on the table at the end of November 1981 was essentially the period of the more conciliatory Jim Prior. The 1980 Act *was* limited and the TUC was still hoping there would be no qualitative upping of the legislative ante. They were interested in placating the government and, as we have seen, underestimated its impetus and philosophy. *When the time was best, the TUC was not prepared for vigorous action.*

The events of 1972-4 had terrified the TUC as well as the politicians. They had embraced a close relationship with the state even more firmly afterwards. Throughout the period 1979-82 they never broke off links with the government, indeed fought attempts within the movement to do so. They were prepared to countenance a degree of direct action but never at the expense of talks with the Tories. The TUC had boosted the role they played in the defeat of the Industrial Relations Act. It was in reality a limited one. The TUC of 1979-82 was a flabby bureaucratic machine, disorientated by the failure of 1970s corporatism, essentially committed to waiting out Thatcherism in the hope that Labour would be returned in 1983/4 and concerned that direct action against the government could diminish that prospect. The chances were slimmer than slim that the TUC would call for direct action to bust the legislation. The question would only even arise if trade unionists were already on strike in strength and the TUC saw the need to recapture the initiative. This was true in this period or in any other.

By the time the TUC had got into some sort of shape at Wembley in the spring of 1982, the situation had changed: the government's political fortunes had improved. In Buenos Aires, General Galtieri was flexing his muscles. On the home front the dramatic increase in unemployment, particularly in the unions' strongholds in manufacturing, was beginning to make its impact felt whilst for those in work wages were rising faster than prices. The more aggressive posture adopted at Wembley came when it was perhaps already too late in the day.

Had the trade union leadership done its homework and understood the ambitions of Thatcherism and if we accept that there *was* a possibility in this period of union muscle motivating a U-turn, there are at least two other questions. *When* would a union offensive have been mounted? A legal occasion, such as Pentonville, did not present itself, owing to the precautions the Tories had taken with the drafting of the Act to ensure that there would be no martyrs this time around. The occasion for confrontation would, therefore, have had to be over some less emotive industrial issue, less likely to attract solidarity action, perhaps over the 1980 steel strike. As such, even a union victory would not have *directly* affected the legislation, although it may well have influenced the possibility of a further round.

Secondly, had the TUC shown more determined leadership in these years — improbable as the prospect was — would the troops have answered the call? Here we must remember that, whilst the TUC ran a campaign of co-ordinated opposition and education in relation to the 1971 Act, individual unions such as the AEUW supported strikes before it reached the statute book. And the breakthrough in the summer of 1972 was not initially led by the TUC. Strike action in support of the five dockers imprisoned in Pentonville as a consequence of defiance of the Industrial Relations Act was initiated from below, stimulated by shop stewards and branch officers. A rolling strike already was underway by the time the TUC stepped in and called for a national 24-hour stoppage. The fact that *the union ranks did not take action themselves* in the 1980s as they did in 1969 or 1972 demonstrates the weaknesses that had developed at rank and file level. *It was this failure that was the key to the success of the legislation*: in the absence of direct action from below the TUC's role could have been budgetted for.

For by the early 1980s, the position was very different. In 1972, the rank and file were confident in the context of 20 years of full employment and slowly increasing living standards. Whilst cracks were appearing in the post-war boom, they were producing aggression rather than demoralisation. The unions had stopped *In Place of Strife*, Heath had already backed down over state aid for Rolls Royce, and the UCS sit-in symbolised a mood of strong militancy. By 1980-81, in contrast, the union rank and file had seen real wage cuts and growing unemployment during the Social Contract. Shop floor organisation, the key to earlier successes, was weaker than it had been. Disillusionment with Labour and its perennial incomes policies had led a key group, the skilled manual workers, to desert in significant numbers and vote for Mrs Thatcher in 1979. There was a feeling that the world was a grimmer place, the new government was tougher than its predecessors and there were no easy solutions — a mood Thatcherism chimed with, particularly as unemployment developed from 1980. Against this, we have to set the fact that we know who won, and this affects judgements. Mrs Thatcher's deep unpopularity, the continuing strength of trade unionism, the staunch resistance in strikes in this period, the success of the big demonstrations against unemployment and the move to the left in the Labour Party, were straws in a wind blowing in the opposite direction. How far weak unimaginative leadership strengthened demoralising tendencies, or correctly cut its coat according to the cloth available, we shall never know.

Certainly, the prospects of successful resistance were rendered more difficult after the 1983 election victory. Now Thatcherism had stabilised and it possessed the ballast of its successful circumnavigation of earlier difficulties. The differences between Mrs Thatcher and Ted Heath were now clear. Working within, if wishing to revise the post-war consensus, he was not prepared to unleash mass unemployment and the full extent of state coercion to discipline the working class. Faced with this dilemma, he changed horses. Mrs Thatcher, aiming at *terminating* the post-war consensus, was prepared to fully deploy economic policy and state coercion to decisively defeat the organised working class. Moreover, from 1982-83 onwards, Mrs Thatcher had very useful cards in her pack: there were both high levels of unemployment *and* wage increases above inflation for those with jobs.

None the less, as we have seen, there were strong arguments for saying that, even at this stage, it would have been preferable to have stood and fought by extending the *Messenger* dispute into Fleet Street and further. It is difficult to see how a defeat in action could have damaged the unions more in relation to the legislation than the defeat they suffered through inaction. After the NGA dispute, certainly after the miners' strike, it was clear the game was up. The prospects of wider solidarity action, which was the only thing that stood a fighting chance of immobilising the legislation, were negligible. A union which defied the law single-handed would simply be taken over by the state.

This appears to be the position today: the accumulated defeats of the 1980s and the general acceptance of the law mean that it cannot be successfully *confronted*. Although trade unionists should keep their eyes open for opportunities, it appears unlikely things will change to the degree required to afford them. Change, if it comes, will come through electoral reverse for Conservatism and a Labourist alternative highly influenced by EEC development.

Some disagree. The Socialist Society's 'Alternative Policy Review' argues

> 8.5 million trade unionists are still affiliated to the TUC despite the decline in membership and the serious damage done to shop floor organisation. It is absurd to argue that a movement of this size has no alternative but to comply with outrageous laws which remove the most basic democratic rights and which are blantantly manipulated to the advantage of the employers. If the courts had to face industrial action as a result of their actions they might start to temper their decisions. This would begin to undermine the credibility of the laws and lay the basis for a more generalised industrial challenge to them.[6]

This is certainly true in the abstract but it falls to pieces when confronted with the reality of recent disputes. Had the TGWU, for example, defied the injunctions granted against it in the docks dispute, or called lorry drivers and dockers in non-registered ports to take industrial action the inevitable consequence would have been the sequestration of its assets. Had it then called directly for wider industrial action to make the judges temper their decisions, or called on the TUC to organise such industrial action, the response would have been negligible. The TGWU, like the NUR or the NUS, did indeed have no alternative but to comply with the legislation, unless we are talking about years of sequestration. Open, clear-cut defiance is only on when it will spark a wider response. In none of the cases where sequestration has occurred has there been any wider response from other groups of workers. Yet it is only when confronted by such a wider response, as in the Pentonville case, that the judges *will* temper their decisions sufficiently to undermine the legislation.

This is not to recommend inaction and straightforward compliance, or to argue that the game is up forever. Trade unionists can achieve results in specific circumstances through tactical shrewdness bobbing and weaving with the legal attack. It is to recognise that a difficult situation is not helped by simplistic sloganising about all-out defiance or general strikes — sloganising which apparently applies eternally to every struggle despite the different circumstances shaping 1990 compared with 1982, 1972 or 1926. Nor by the argument that, recognising the imbalance of forces, still asserts that, in the conditions of the 1990s, unions should risk sequestration, lose their assets 'go underground', 'start all over again'. Union leaders should give leadership. They should attempt to manoeuvre around the legislation to ensure that the objectives of industrial action are achieved. But this is increasingly difficult. At times it may be possible to tactically ignore or even take on the law on a very short-term basis. Conditions for this will be more favourable where the rank and file move into action themselves. But where the ranks do *not*, as in the 60s and 70s, act themselves but wait on their leaders, the difficulties of taking on the law are massive. Union leaders can explore alternative methods — and these were, perhaps, to a degree neglected in the dock strike. But the 1990s are not 1984, still less 1979 or 1972. One of the saddest sights of the 1980s, a clear token of the times, saw one of the Pentonville 5 cross a picket line at Tilbury in the 1989 Docks Dispute. It seems that in today's conditions, we have to face the strong likelihood that the legislation is as permanent as Conservative governments. For a change we shall have to look to a change of government. Even then, we may find that in terms of a return to minimal legal control of industrial relations, yesterday has gone forever.

THE LABOUR MOVEMENT ALTERNATIVE

In developing an alternative to the Conservative's Employment Legislation, the Labour Movement has faced several major problems.
1. Unlike the *Industrial Relations Act 1971*, which the incoming Labour government was able to totally repeal between 1974 and 1976, Mrs Thatcher's legislation *has worked*. By the time of the next general election, probably in 1992, its foundation stones will have been on the statute book for a decade. The essentials of the legislation, despite initial doubts, are accepted by *employers*. No matter what they may *think* about some of Norman Fowler's extensions, they have used the legislation's main weapons and they would oppose any repeal which strengthened union bargaining power and workers' rights. Compare this with 1974 when Campbell Adamson, the Director General of the CBI, accepted the need to repeal the Industrial Relations Act.
2. Unlike the *Industrial Relations Act 1971* key aspects of the legislation of the 1980s have been accepted in practice by *the unions*. Compare the successful boycott of the registration provisions of the legislation in the 1970s with the failure of the TUC boycott in the 1980s. The unions have accepted injunctions, participated in ballots on industrial action and the political fund, and changed their rules to meet the requirements of the legislation. Amongst certain trade unionists there is the view that certain parts of the legislation, particularly the balloting

provisions, are not merely acceptable but useful.

3. The industrial world and the economy and society have been drastically changed by the years of Thatcherism. The challenges facing the unions in terms of shifts in the industrial structure, the labour force, the economic and political framework, as well as changes in trade unionism itself, mean that the recipes for legal reform of 1979, 1983 or 1987, may no longer be viable in the 1990s. The Labour Party has gone a long way in adapting to Thatcherism in terms of its policies, and wants to integrate any programme for the repeal of employment legislation with its economic and industrial strategy. In this context, and after three electoral defeats, the trade union leaders are in a weaker bargaining position and more distanced from the Labour Party leadership than their counterparts in 1974.

4. Whilst in 1974 there was a strong public perception of the Industrial Relations Act as a divisive piece of legislation, the essentials of Mrs Thatcher's legislation are seen rather as putting the unions in their proper place. Whilst there has been concern as the 1980s progressed that the government was going too far and producing a lop-sided legal framework unfair to the unions, the Labour Party leadership and many in the trade union movement see too strong an attachment to wholescale repeal of the laws as electorally damaging.

5. These problems have to be related to the greater intensity and expression of differences within the TUC in the 1980s compared with the 1970s. Differences over how to respond to Thatcherism spilled over, as we have seen, to weaken any united front against the employment laws. These divisions also produced differences over what should take the place of those laws.

6. By the end of the 1980s the sheer amount of law, its impact on industrial relations practice and the degree of political acceptance it had achieved, made many question whether it was possible to go back to the traditional position of excluding the law from collective industrial relations and simply using it to establish a floor of rights. Many in the Labour Movement were suggesting that the unions should reject their traditional stance of legal exclusion in favour of using the law to establish a programme of positive rights for collective organisation and individual protection.

How has the Labour Movement reacted to these difficulties? How has it gone about the task of producing an alternative to the Conservative employment laws?

Repeal and Replacement Legislation 1983

This document was adopted by the TUC General Council as the essential complement to the Wembley declaration. Produced at a time when non-compliance with the legislation was still a runner, when Labour had swung leftwards and the TUC still had a strong voice in its counsels, it followed the pattern of the early 1970s by simply calling for the repeal in their entirety of the 1980 and 1982 Acts and ancillary measures. They would be replaced by the re-establishment of the immunities against common law action suitably extended to take account of their erosion by the judges 1977-79. The floor of employment protection rights would be restored and expanded. This document formed the basis for Labour commitment on repeal in its 1983 election manifesto.

Ballots and Positive Rights

By 1985, the three new factors in play were the disintegration of union opposition to the legislation, the emphasis on ballots embodied in the 1984 Act, and the Labour Party's 'new look', with a leadership dedicated to electoralism seeing the unions as a potential embarrassment in this arena. The suggestion that the immunities which excluded the use of the common law against the unions, crucially in the field of industrial action, should be replaced by a system of positive *rights* had been floated, in a not very serious fashion, in the 1981 Green Paper *Trade Union Immunities*. This change would mean that instead of the courts being excluded from using the common law liabilities against unions when a strike or industrial action fell within the definition of a trade dispute, unions would, for the first time, be given a positive *right* to strike, to take industrial action, and to picket. This could be extended to cover rights to organise and bargain. It would bring Britain closer to the system in other countries where employment law uses this positive approach rather than the negative immunities.

In early 1985 there were suggestions from prominent Labour Party leaders that replacement of the Conservative legislation should involve at least some shift from immunities to positive rights. Against this, it was argued that the final definition of the precise meaning of any right to strike or take industrial action would still be in the hands of the courts. Judicial innovation might even be stimulated by the creation of a new positive form. And any such rights would have to possess qualifications. The immunities might, therefore, remain a better bet.

The point about the rights approach was that it dovetailed with — and its advocacy was related to — support for the maintenance, suitably refined, of the 1984 balloting provisions in any Labour government's replacement of the Conservative legislation. It was argued by Neil Kinnock and union leaders beyond the EETPU and the AEU, such as John Edmonds of the GMB, that the ballots were popular with union members and the wider electorate and that a movement which claimed it was pledged to the extension of workers' rights would find it difficult to remove workers' rights in this important area. This demonstrated the utility of the positive rights approach in ensuring that rights to ballots remained on the statute book. It provoked the view that the advocates of changes were less interested in positive rights than statutory ballots.

The Liaison Committee statement *A New Partnership, A New Britain*, published in June 1985, simply stated that "the next Labour Government will repeal the present government's divisive trade union legislation and replace it with positive legislation". Rights to more consultation and representation in company decision making were mentioned, but the document was silent on the details of rights to organise and take industrial action. However, in September 1985, *Planning for Full Employment* produced by the Party's Employment Policy Working Group stated that rights to take industrial action would involve a mixture of reinforced immunities and new positive rights. Moreover, the 1984 Act would be repealed although there would be a need to convince voters as to the reasons for removing the rights to ballots.

The 1985 Congress accepted *A New Partnership, A New Britain* but there was a conflict between two major resolutions, one from the TGWU calling for total repeal and the other from the CPSA calling for a review to see which parts of the legislation should be removed, which should be amended, and which should be retained. As a consequence, the Congress voted both for repeal and an open-ended review of its position.

The subsequent consultative document *Industrial Relations Legislation* circulated in January 1986 requested the views of affiliates on the question of immunities — positive rights and ballots. It accepted that the unions were now in the law game to a greater degree than in the 1970s and would have to break from traditional exclusionist and abstentionist attitudes.

The 1987 General Election

The response to the TUC consultative document demonstrated the differences amongst the unions on the question of future legislation. On the question of positive rights
— The CPSA, NCU, NUM, SOGAT, UCW, supported a move to a

positive right to strike.
— The AEU, COHSE, EETPU, NALGO, and the TGWU, supported a retention of the traditional immunities.
— NUPE, TASS and UCATT wanted a mixture of both.
On the question of compulsory ballots
— COHSE, NALGO, NUM, NUPE, TASS, TGWU and USDAW were opposed.
— AEU, CPSA, EETPU, NGA, SOGAT, were in favour.
There was, thus, a majority against compulsory ballots with only a minority of those in favour supporting a hard statutory obligation. In terms of unions there was a more even division over positive rights but in terms of membership, the supporters of the immunities had it. There were of course all sorts of differences and subdivisions of opinion within the different groups. Certain unions accepted the retention of compulsory ballots because of their own internal systems whilst others such as the print unions felt that the principle was worth sacrificing in order to see the return of a Labour administration.

The conflicting results of this process were fed into the TUC-Labour Party Liaison Committee. In July, 1986, two statements *People at Work: New Rights, New Responsibilities* and *Low Pay: Policies and Priorities* were published and subsequently endorsed at the TUC and Labour Party conferences that autumn. These documents again accepted the premise that a return to the position of minimal legal regulation was simply not on. They were, however, vague and lacking in detail, pitched at electoral advantage. They formed the basis for the commitments in Labour's 1987 Manifesto *Britain Will Win.*

This platform provided for
— The introduction of a statutory minimum wage.
— The extension of employment protection to part-time workers and homeworkers.
— A Ministry for Women and reinforcement of sex discrimination legislation. "In addition Labour will take firm action to promote racial equality."
— Improving the unfair dismissal protections, particularly rights to reinstatement.
— Improving the law on Health and Safety at Work.
— Strengthening the work of ACAS.
— Restoring schedule 11 of the 1975 Employment Protection Act and the powers of wages councils.
— Promoting trade union membership and encouraging union recognition.
— Restoring the right to belong to a trade union to all employees

including those at GCHQ.

— Ensuring "the essential legal freedom of workers and their unions to organise effective industrial action".

— Laying down principles to be included in union rulebooks "based upon a right for union members to have a secret ballot on decisions relating to strikes and for the method of election of union executives to be based on a system of secret ballots".

— In consultation with the TUC establishing a new independent tribunal to deal with complaints from union members that these statutory principles have been breached.

There was no firm commitment on the repeal of many of the Conservative's measures. The positive rights-immunities argument was taken no further, reinforcing the view that it had been a stalking horse for statutory ballots. The suspicion amongst many was that this degree of imprecision — after 4 years debate — was not to be justified by flexibility or a reasonable degree of electoral caution but presaged, rather, a refusal to pledge restoration of many of the unions' essential protections by an incoming Labour Government.

Labour's Policy Review

In the aftermath of the 1987 election defeat the TUC appeared content to rest on the position it had adopted prior to the contest. The Labour Party leadership, however, were determined to intensify the process of streamlining and modernisation of the Party organisation and programme which they felt could deliver the goods at the next election. The 1987 conference approved the establishment of a Policy Review. The report of the Policy Review Group *People at Work* develops the position adopted in 1987. The switch from the TUC to the Labour Party as the initiator of legislative proposals was now almost complete.

Labour's proposals carried a strong corporatist emphasis reminiscent of the 1970s. They were placed within the rubric of *Partnership at Work*

> "the task of improving British industrial competitiveness requires good industrial relations. The achievement of good industrial relations therefore lies at the very heart of Labour's new policies ... Good industrial relations requires a commitment on the part of workers and managers to work together constructively in order to make a success of the enterprise or service within which they work. Labour believes that trade unions have a strong positive role to play in developing a constructive relation between workers and managers in order to make a success of their enterprise."

Workers and employers are seen as possessing a joint interest in efficiency and unions are seen as an instrument for employee co-operation in economic success. Economic success, in Labour's view, depended on motivating employees through giving them a secure, protected, civilised, and safe working environment. Labour's strategy is one of *progressive management*: "workers require a sense of fairness and security if they are to make their own full contribution to economic and employment change". Labour agrees with the Conservative objectives of a more efficient, flexible, productive and profitable economy. It agrees with the necessity for modernisation. The difference lies in the *means* to be employed. The Conservatives are going about things the wrong way with support for "authoritarian management", "deregulation" and "excessive legalism" intended to improve Britain's international competitiveness by "undercutting". On the contrary, the way forward for management is *to take the workforce with them* through a modified, limited "corporatism at the workplace". Kindness, and involving workers through their unions, will, in the end, serve employers better than a policy of cruelty, macho management, and exclusion. It will ultimately produce better and more lasting pay-offs for employers and the economy.

Workers and their organisations should, therefore, be given more rights not only because this is justified in itself but because this will make them better partners in increasing economic efficiency. Corporatism and consensus works better than conflict and co-operation.

The Conservative legislation has been biased towards the employers and Labour, according to the document, will not fall into the same trap by producing legislation biased towards the workers. On the contrary, the employers will be fully consulted about its detail for

> "It must also be accepted in industry generally as balanced, fair and stable, and not be seen as partisan in the way the Tory legislation undoubtedly is seen. For that reason we will undertake full consultation with all interested parties."

Labour and Rights at Work

The document now contained in *Meet the Challenge Make the Change — Final Report of Labour's Policy Review for the 1990s* suggests the creation of a "Workers Charter" strongly influenced by the EEC Social Charter (see p.165). It covers the following areas

Basic Contract: Everyone at work will have the same legal status. Qualifications for employment protection such as periods of continuous employment, hours worked per week, or size of company, will be abolished so that temporary and part-time workers, self employed and homeworkers, will be covered. It will no longer be possible to sign away legal protections. "Zero hours" and "beck and call" contracts will be outlawed and overtime will be regulated and provision made for regular rest days.

Minimum Wage: A statutory minimum will start at 50% of male median earnings or £2-80 per hour in 1989. A Fair Wages Commission will be established to implement this and promote fair wage policies generally and set the minimum rates as wages councils have done in the past. A revised Fair Wages Resolution and a revised Schedule 11 style extension machinery will also be introduced.

Discrimination: Discrimination legislation will be strengthened, particularly in relation to recruitment, promotion, redundancy and retirement. The equal value regulations will be extended and so will the maternity leave provisions. One or other parent will be entitled to 3 months parental leave. Fathers will also be entitled to 10 days paternity leave at the time of the birth.

Health Safety and Welfare: The Health and Safety Executive will take responsibility for all industrial inspectorates. The number of inspectors will be increased. Crown Immunity will be removed. All enterprises will be required to appoint a senior manager responsible for this area and all employees will be entitled to receive a copy of health and safety standards applying to their work. The system of statutory safety representatives will be extended whilst fines will be increased and "in the most serious cases we will expect employers found liable to go to prison".

Unfair Dismissal: Qualifying periods will be abolished. Workers will no longer be lawfully dismissed whilst taking industrial action — instead the contract will be suspended for the duration of the action.

Industrial Tribunals: Legal aid will be extended to the tribunals and their procedures will be made faster, and more informal. Specialist equality tribunals will deal with discrimination cases involving not only sex and racism but disability and age. More class actions enabling groups of cases to be heard together will be allowed. And in dismissal cases: "Tribunals will also have greatly enhanced powers to order compensation and we will ensure that they order reinstatement as the norm and that employers abide by the order where employees feel they can return to work".

Union Recognition: Individuals will have a right to be represented by a union on a range of individual issues such as discipline or discrimination. A statutory procedure will be introduced to resolve disputes about recognition. A future Labour government will positively encourage the extension of collective bargaining "as an act of public policy".

Ballots: The document states "As a guarantee of the democratic rights of union members we will establish a new independent tribunal empowered to hear complaints from individuals which allege that their union has breached statutory provisions on strike ballots and ballots for the election of union executives".

Aggrieved members, apparently not employers or other workers (in relation to strike ballots), are the only ones to be given these rights. According to the document they will "normally" be required to first go through union procedures. There will, however, be a right of appeal from the independent tribunal to the ordinary courts on "a point of law".

Industrial Action: Specific measures introduced by the Conservatives will be repealed. These include the right of workers to be protected from union discipline when they ignore the result of a strike ballot; rights for employers to selectively sack workers even after a successful strike ballot; the right of employers to be protected against industrial action when they transfer work from struck premises; and the acceptance by the courts of employers rights to protection when they artificially split up their company into separate units as in the Wapping dispute.

Secondary Action: The document promises to *review* the boundaries of lawful strike action. It states that all forms of sympathetic action should not be unlawful if they follow a majority vote. Moreover

> Balance requires that if workers have a genuine interest in the outcome of a dispute and democratically seek to take appropriate sympathetic action in response to those in dispute, they should be able to do so within the law.

Remedies: The use of sequestration as a penalty for contempt of court will be discontinued if Labour attains office. It is not 100% clear whether the pre-1982 position where union funds were protected against civil actions would be restored. The issue of *ex parte* injunctions where an employer is entitled to get an injunction without the union being present will no longer be allowed in industrial disputes. The issue of interim injunctions and the procedures involved will also be reviewed.

Labour Court: Since the mid-1980s discontent with the ordinary courts has prompted renewed discussion about establishing a specialist body, more informal, expert and accessible, to deal with legislation involving industrial disputes. The 1986 documents stated this was under scrutiny and the 1989 document repeats "we are therefore considering in detail the merits of establishing a specialist court to deal with such matters".

Industrial Democracy: Despite periodic bursts of rhetoric about "radical" extensions of industrial democracy, this document is as dilute as its 1987 predecessor. A section headed *Extending employee participation* states "As a minimum workers should have rights to information, consultation and representation". It then points to Labour's proposals in relation to health and safety and training and promises increased rights to consultation over plant closures, redundancy and the introduction of new technology.

The Policy Review: What's Right and What's Wrong

There is much in the 1989 Labour Party Policy Review document which is helpful. Its proposals on employment protection assault most of the deficiencies of the 1974-79 legislation and would come as a windfall and relief. The proposals on such areas as unfair dismissal, discrimination, tribunal procedure, and health and safety are extremely useful as well as the breakthrough on the national minimum wage. Moreover, the document underlines the relationship between individual rights and collective organisation. Without effective trade union organisation workers will not be able to effectively use their legal rights in practice. The primary enforcers of individual rights are not the courts or inspectorates but the unions. It is largely in the area of collective union rights that the document discloses deficiencies, raises important questions, and leaves key issues unresolved.

Secondary Action: Statements by shadow Employment Secretary Michael Meacher, prior to the publication of the policy document, which essentially repeated what the document said, provoked a small storm in the media and *The Sunday Times* headline "Kinnock to sack Meacher". Meacher said there could be no justification for limiting the freedom of workers to seek external assistance while no action at all was taken to limit secondary action by employers. He claimed that the criterion of *genuine interest* in the dispute would mean that Sealink workers supporting the Dover strikers in the P&O dispute, or miners at one pit striking to support miners at another pit, might well be protected as there would be a genuine interest in the outcome of the dispute if it *affected the terms and conditions of employment of those taking secondary industrial action.* But this test would clearly not cover miners supporting nurses or trade unionists striking over GCHQ or suppliers of suppliers taking action to support those taking primary action. Insofar as it has been explained, this test follows that applied to UK employees taking sympathetic action to support strikers overseas in the 1982 Act. It was roundly condemned then by the

TUC and the Labour Party on the grounds that, by introducing a test of benefit related to the terms and conditions of those taking sympathetic action, true solidarity action taken by those who *will not* benefit was rendered unlawful.

Of course, it is possible that the test of "genuine interest" could cover such action. It needs clarifying. But — and this is a key point — as it stands, it would leave the door open to interpretation by the judges on the lines outlined above. The avoidance of this should be a major consideration in drafting any replacement legislation. And it is important for trade unionists to know with some precision what the position on secondary action will be. In the row over Meacher's comments, the *Financial Times* reported that "The message from other members of the Labour Party leadership last night was that there could be no question of the party supporting a restoration of the powers enjoyed by trade unions before Mrs Thatcher came to power".[7] Yet such a restoration might seem preferable to many trade unionists than an open-ended test of "genuine interest" which on paper would outlaw many kinds of secondary action and in the hand of the judges would no doubt outlaw most kinds. Surely the test for Labour should be democracy, not distance or material interest. If a group of workers democratically decide they wish to take action to support their fellow workers why should it matter whether they are a third, fourth, or fifth group in relation to the workers in primary dispute, or whether they stand to benefit or not?

Picketing: The document is silent on this issue, although the existing legislation rendering unlawful effective peaceful picketing at any workplace other than your own is a legal intervention in primary disputes which not only weakens the union side in the dispute but constitutes an interference with freedom of speech and movement and weakens civil liberties. Michael Meacher appeared to suggest that secondary picketing would be subject to the same test of "genuine interest" as other forms of secondary action. But this is to open up the arena to the same problems that we have already outlined. To protect union purposes, future legislation would need to contain a statutory right to peacefully picket at *any* workplace. This would need to explicitly state that *such action would not constitute obstruction of the highway and would cover a right to stop pedestrians or vehicles for a reasonable time to make a statement about the dispute.* This would entail the abolition of the 1986 legislation on police powers and could be covered in detail in a revised *Code of Practice on Picketing.*

Union Liability: The Policy Review Document states that sequestration will be excluded from industrial disputes. Michael

Meacher seemed to imply that this would stop legal action against unions as organisations over industrial action which put their funds at risk. But sequestration has been used as a penalty for the criminal offence of contempt of court. Its removal would still leave the *Taff Vale* provisions of the 1982 Act intact with union funds open to awards of damages in the full trial of a case. Whilst such actions have been few, prudence and foresight would dictate that unions should *specifically demand that the protection against actions in tort, except for personal injuries and property which protected them between 1906 and 1982, should be restored.*

At the 1988 TUC, a TGWU motion was carried which stated that the position on union liability via its funds when civil wrongs were committed, *should return to that subsisting between 1906 and 1979* when the ambit of what was lawful and unlawful in the area of industrial action was redrawn by a future Labour government. TUC policy was now to insist that, where the employer could still take legal action, that action would have to be against individual union officers — not against the union as a corporate body.

Ballots: The statements in the document make clear that Labour intends to legislate for *compulsory* ballots over industrial action. The words "as well as in the election of union executives" are shoe-horned in, without any comment or justification. It would appear, though it is not absolutely clear, that the right of employers or others affected to take legal action will be repealed. It also appears — both are mentioned — that workplace ballots will be as acceptable as postal ballots and that the provisions of the 1988 Act prescribing the latter will be repealed.

The basic question trade unionists have to address here is whether the principled ground argued by the TUC between 1983 and 1985 should be given up in the interests of tactical expediency. It will be recalled that the original argument was that the *law should not be involved in this area, there should be no compulsion.* Union members should have a right to control their own democratic arrangements unless there was evidence of serious abuse — and this was conspicuous by its absence. The urging of tactical expediency, which is not always dishonourable, is that a commitment to repeal would alienate voters who will not, or can not, be convinced that the state should not legislate minimum protections. Most unions have now adopted the legal balloting mechanisms. They have worked without too much discomfort and their continuance is a small price to pay for a Labour victory which will safeguard other vital aspects of union autonomy and activity.

This argument requires further discussion at the grassroots. Should the question of internal elections be separated from the question of ballots over industrial action? Could the problem be overcome by a broad statutory commitment to democratic arrangements in these two areas, and a statutory right for members to be protected according to the principles of a Code of Practice which would outline *a variety* of acceptable democratic arrangements? Certainly if the rights, somewhat refined, *are* to remain on the Statute Book, then their ambit requires close scrutiny. Remember the existence of the provisions on industrial action has enabled the courts to stop strikes, because of the wording of ballot papers, and restrain the holding of a ballot. The Policy Review's attempt to insulate unions from the courts by establishing an independent tribunal to deal with these issues is praiseworthy. But if, as is suggested, an appeal is allowed to the courts on "a point of law", much of the good work will be undone. A "point of law" is an extremely wide category. Who decides on its limits? The courts of course. And 1988 and 1989 have demonstrated how inventive they can be when it comes to ballots.

The Political Fund: There is no reference in the document to the political activities of trade unions and their legal regulation. In view of the Conservative measures this is a striking omission. There would seem to be four possible paths Labour could follow here. The *status quo* could be maintained — this would require a further round of political fund ballots in 1995-96. Or the position could be returned to that obtaining before 1984 with the only requirement a once-and-for-all ballot and some changes in the definition of political objectives. Alternatively, the 1984 provisions could simply be repealed, leaving unions in the same position as employers, free to spend their money as they wish on industrial or political purposes. Finally the 1984, or the 1913, provisions could be re-enacted and *applied also to employers* who would then have to receive the consent of shareholders and/or employees before they could make political donations. Silence on this issue obviously stems from the fact that the Labour leadership finds it, as so much else, a potential embarrassment. Yet the future of trade union political activities motivated the major successful campaign of the 1980s and is so vital to the future of the unions as to demand immediate discussion at all levels of the movement.

The Closed Shop: Again this is not mentioned, presumably as it is seen as unappealing to the electorate. There is also, it might be argued, little evidence that existing legislation has adversely affected unions in this area. None the less there is no justification for the almost total exclusion of discussion of this topic by the TUC and the Labour Party in recent years. Should the position be simply returned to that subsisting in 1979? Or is this a case where Labour can genuinely improve upon Thatcherism whilst safeguarding union purposes at the same time. The 1989 Act abolishes the balloting provisions for approved closed shops allegedly enacted to give unions back to their members in the 1980 and 1982 legislation. Why cannot Labour restore the democratic mechanisms removed by the Conservatives by legislating for an optional system of closed shop ballots with a required majority of 51% voting and not 80% of those eligible to vote? That this was *not* the way the Labour leadership was thinking was made clear in December 1989. Tony Blair, Labour's employment spokesperson, simply declared in a statement to his constituency party that Labour had abandoned any support for the Closed Shop and that any future legislation would protect rights to belong and *not* to belong to a trade union.[8] This was the position taken by the EEC Social Charter and the Labour leadership felt that their support for the Charter would be untenable, or at least compromised, if they continued to oppose a right not to belong to a union.

Rights and Immunities: It seems fair to say that the question of the *form* future legislation would take was raised by Jim Prior in his Green Paper as a possible delaying tactic and diversion, and was taken up by Neil Kinnock and Roy Hattersley and, under their direction, Norman Willis, as a means of facilitating a *volte-face* over the ballots. Once the retention of the balloting provisions was accepted, the positive rights approach was quietly shelved and this was perhaps distantly related to the Labour leadership's opposition to calls for a Bill of Rights. The Policy Review document has nothing to say about it.

Many of the arguments put forward during the 1985-86 debate were untestable or cancelled each other out. It is difficult to see how the rights *form*, as distinct from an extended range of legal regulation in this form could in itself encourage judicial intervention as was suggested. The Golden Formula and the immunities at their tightest never stopped judicial intervention. On the other hand, it is difficult to see how the positive rights form could, as some of its proponents suggested, *discourage* judicial intervention. The pre-1979 picketing protections were couched in positive rights form, yet in the 1960s and 1970s the courts left them in tatters. In Britain the judges have been willing to imaginatively interpret *anything* to do with trade unions laid before them *in whatever form* it has appeared. It is just as likely that they would see a new code of positive rights as an incitement rather than a deterrent to such interpretation.

The real justification for the positive rights approach, if it informed a new employment code that was far reaching in range and content and was related to wider constitutional reform, particularly reform of the judiciary and new methods of adjudication for industrial relations disputes, is that it could assert a new social legitimacy for trade union purposes. The establishment of a right to organise, a right to bargain, a right to strike, a right to picket, anchored in the context of international conventions could constitute the spearhead of an ideological and legislative redefinition of the relevance of trade unionism, after more than a decade of Thatcherism.

It is, however, clear that the piecemeal pragmatic approach of British Labourism still holds the field. It is likely that legislation on this basis by a future Labour government would be cautious in content and in form and involve the now time honoured "mixture of immunities and positive rights".

The Judges: As we have seen, the administration and operation of the law is as crucial as its content. It appears myopic to attempt to change the provisions of legislation if its final interpretation is left in the hands of the small insulated section of the ruling class that presently constitute the personnel of the Higher Courts. Any attempt to transform employment legislation to meet to any greater degree the purposes of trade unionists, must seek to transform both its content and the processes by which it is determined in practice and enforced. A densely documented record testifies to the fact that over the last century the judges resisting the will of Parliament have attempted to reassert the common law over and against statutory protections for union activities. However, despite vociferous condemnation of the *status quo* there has been little discussion amongst trade unionists as to what should replace it. The TUC and Labour Party have traditionally accepted that whilst the law may be changed, the legal system is frozen and immuteable.

The toying, for that is what it seems to be, with the idea of a special Labour Court represents some progress here in an area which has been ignored by successive Labour governments. It is sometimes remarked that such a Court could lead to a greater degree of legal regulation and thus defeat the purpose of the exercise. The answer to this is that a greater degree of legal regulation is now inevitable. The pertinent questions are *what kind of legal regulation* and *who will do the regulating?* A Labour Court, consisting of union influenced appointees and insulated from the Higher Courts could be beneficial and demands further consideration. If it is to be taken seriously why limit its operations as the Policy Review implies to cases involving industrial action?

This should not distract trade unionists from examining ways and means of reforming the judiciary, indeed a Labour Court could go hand in hand with such reform. The document suggests, in the section *A Modern Democracy*, that recruitment to the Bar should be widened to replenish its present limited base in terms of class, sex and race. Training for judges should emphasise "for greater social awareness" and appointment of judges should be removed from the Lord Chancellor's department to an independent commission. The appointment of magistrates and Crown Court procedures should also be overhauled. This is a modest programme at one with the conservatism of the document on constitutional reform and constrained by Labour's traditional respect for the constitutional status quo. It is however a small step forward.

The Police: We have traced the increasing role of the criminal law and the police in major conflicts during the 1980s. The new statement promises to make local police forces more accountable to the local communities they are there to serve. It states that the police authorities in each area will be made up of elected members only and their powers will be defined more clearly. However, tensions between local democracy and police authoritarianism are bound to continue as this will be implemented "whilst retaining day to day operational matters firmly under the control of the police". For the Metropolitan Area an elected authority will be established for the first time and the Police Complaints Authority will be granted greater independence. Whilst these proposals are limited they provide a starting point for greater attention to be paid to the role of the police in industrial disputes and a platform for further development.

THE FUTURE OF EMPLOYMENT LEGISLATION

During the 1980s the attempts by the unions to create a viable alternative to the Conservative legislation and commit Labour to its enactment have met with limited success. Through the decade the initiative has gradually shifted from the TUC to the Labour Party leadership. The Liaison Committee has ceased as it was in the 1970s to be the arena for decision making. By 1988 proposals were being initiated by the leadership of the Parliamentary Party and concretised at the level of the National Executive. The final report of Labour's top down Policy Review *Meet the Challenge — Make the Change*, with the latest proposals for legislation, was placed before the Party Conference in 1989 on a take or leave it basis. No amendments were accepted and a separate motion committing the next Labour government to the repeal of all the Conservative's anti-union legislation was lost by 3.2 to 2.2 million votes.

Yet the programme for the future of employment legislation now on offer remains in many ways woolly and unclear. It accepts that there can be no return to the past but its prescriptions on individual rights and employment protection appear more conducive to the unions' expressed goals than its proposals on union organisation and industrial action. It has nothing to say on key issues such as picketing, the closed shop and political funds. It appears to suggest that the *Taff Vale* principle of union liability legislated for in 1982 will continue. Its proposals for strengthening the right to strike are imprecise and unclear. Important areas of the Conservative legislation such as ballots over industrial action and internal union elections appear likely to remain on the statute book.

It is not simply a matter of not crossing the "t's" or dotting the "i's". Taken as a whole, the proposals necessitate the unions leaving an awful lot to the discretion of a future Labour government. Given the performance of past Labour administrations in carrying out specific commitments, statements in the document that employers will be consulted as to the provisions of new legislation, and the central emphasis on partnership, many will feel that the proposals require an excessive degree of faith in the Parliamentary leadership and that future legislation should be spelled out with more exactitude and well in advance of a general election. Whatever their hesitations and qualifications, employers can be expected to firmly oppose even the charter of individual rights proposed, let alone changes in the law on industrial action. And the differences between Labour and important unions over key areas of legislation contain the potential for future conflict.

The major motivator in the architecture of these proposals and the whole policy review has been *electoral*: the need to adapt policy to the present perceptions, aspirations and prejudices of the electorate. Specifically, this has entailed an acceptance of the view that, for Labour, too close a relationship with the unions and too close an identification with their purposes can constitute an electoral liability. Pro-union legislation is seen in these terms as electorally dodgy. Labour is not prepared to reject the unions out of hand. But it is determined to proceed cautiously. Even Michael Meacher, too radical for Labour's leadership and soon replaced by Tony Blair, emphasised that the unions would not only have less influence on the surface — there would be no deals behind the scenes: "Trade unions will not have unjustifiable covert influence on the Labour Party's policy making in or out of government".[9]

The TUC *has* been consulted in the policy-making process. But it has increasingly accepted its scaled down role of junior partner rather than mainspring of Labour's policy making: their position has been we must have a Labour government in the early 1990s even if the price is high. On issues such as ballots and the closed shop, the TUC has thus been prepared to go along with Labour. Their reduced state was starkly illustrated by Labour's employment spokesman Tony Blair's policy-making "on the hoof" over the Closed Shop issue. Not merely did he announce an important change of position on this matter, after talks with the Labour leadership and *some* of the trade union leaders, in clear violation of the norms of Labour Party, TUC and trade union democracy. His new ordinance was quietly accepted, or indeed endorsed, by TUC and union leaders — the only opposition coming from left-wing Labour MP's. Other factors, such as Mrs Thatcher's continuing political success until 1989, the TUC's diminishing political and industrial reach, the deepening of divisions amongst the movement, and the promise of more and more Conservative legislation, intensified the unions need for political change and enabled the TUC to bring dissidents in line. The General Secretary of the NGA, for example, explained his conversion over the issue of retaining the balloting provisions by observing "If we don't get Labour in this time some of us may not be around next time".[10] And GMB General Secretary, John Edmonds, felt by the end of 1989 that the unions had wanted too much from Labour governments in the past and claimed that the unions "will not seek favours from the next Labour government".[11]

Of course, there are many in the movement who doubt whether making policy by opinion polls is the best way to get Labour in and who have strong reservations about what Labour will do if it does get in in this fashion. There are also many who will agree with us on the serious limitations of Labour's proposals on the replacement of the Conservative's employment legislation and the need for further debate. Such debate can be clarified if we return to where we began and relate employment legislation to industrial and economic policy.

As we have seen, right wing Conservatives like Mrs Thatcher dedicated to the free operation of the market, will seek to use the law to weaken union organisation, limit the right to strike, and deregulate labour markets. Socialists dedicated to the transformation of capitalism will, in contrast, use the law to strengthen trade unions, give free play to the right to strike and surround employers with a battery of legal controls. They would do this with the objective of mobilising trade unionists to challenge the controllers and owners in factories, offices, companies, and to safeguard the measures the government was taking from subversion by capital. A determined socialist government might legislate for the complete removal of the injunction from industrial disputes — workers would be free to strike at any time over any issue and utilise remedies such as sequestration to take over the assets of employers refusing to recognise and bargain with trade unions.

In similar fashion, the proposals for legislation in the Policy Review are related to the Review's wider economic framework, a framework which does not see a fundamental conflict between capital and labour does not seek therefore to transfer power and resources from capital to labour and does not seek unequivocally to strengthen workers' organisations. As we have seen, the keynote of the Policy Review is *partnership* — co-operation between unions, employers and the state, with the object of increasing economic efficiency and Britain's international competitiveness. The object of Labour's policy is not to move in the direction of socialism but to modernise British capitalism. The objective is to make capitalism more competitive and efficient, through harnessing the workforce in a way Thatcherism has failed to do, in the interests of the existing organisation of the enterprise and the economy. The creation of the new partnership will require *some* readjustment in the relationship between employers and unions, as it will in other areas such as social security and taxation if it is to be acceptable and successful. But giving too much power to the unions could upset the economic apple cart and such readjustment is likely to be mild or token.

For example, the document states that "control of inflation must be a major priority". However, in implementing such control it rejects both the policies of the Conservatives and incomes policy. "On pay generally we reject a pay policy or any form of pay norm as being unhelpful and unworkable". It states, moreover, that "the objective is a fully employed economy", that there will be increases in public spending on social services, that there will be no general rise in taxation, but that the balance of national income must be switched from consumption to investment. It is difficult to see how these policies could be successful. They imply high rates of productivity growth, and they dictate government pressure to reduce wages growth.

This would in all probability prompt a crisis resort to incomes policy — following the path of every Labour government since 1945 — if, and even then it is a big 'if', consumption is to be held down in the interests of investment, and full employment as well as increased public spending are to be brought into sight. But pay norms, formal incomes policy or whatever, Labour, particularly with the commitment to a minimum wage, *must* seek to control bargaining over pay. It is indeed difficult to see a Labour government pledged to this strategy being able to tolerate average earnings increasing at their present rate. In this context it would be suicidal to, as it were, reinflate the unions too quickly. Labour has not adopted its present approach *simply* to help it get elected. The new approach is also predicated on what it thinks it may have to do once it *is* elected. This is *the reason* for the silence on the closed shop, secondary action, picketing and so forth. For legal measures here could strengthen the bargaining power of the unions and enhance their ability to pursue policies on wages and conditions which could conflict with Labour's economic objectives.

The TUC accepts Labour's Proposals

This analysis was given some substance by the events of 1990. The Labour Party published a digest and update of its Policy Review conclusions. *Looking to the Future* endorsed "the efficiency and realism which markets can provide". There would be no "irresponsible dash for growth" but in the area of welfare and public spending in general, "advance towards our objectives will necessarily depend on achieving that growth. We will not spend nor will we promise to spend more than Britain can afford." The document repeated that there would be no statutory incomes policy. But a Labour government would negotiate public sector pay within clearly defined budget limits, whilst a national economic summit involving government, employers and unions would hammer out a national economic strategy, taking account of the needs of the competing claims of investment, exports and public spending in order to "develop a broad understanding of what is feasible in the light of economic realities". Entry into the EEC exchange rate mechanism was also viewed as a discipline for the unions. "Management and trade unions will know that if their production costs rise faster than those of other European countries they will not be able to compete successfully within the single market." A *voluntary* incomes policy was clearly on the agenda.

In order to placate electoral opinion and make it tougher for the union rank and file to bust through such strategies, the document repeated the line of its predecessors: key parts of the Conservative legislation would remain on the statute book. There was now a clear commitment to a new Industrial Court which would be headed by a High Court Judge sitting with lay members. Sequestration would now remain but would stop short of total confiscation of a union's assets. The Conservative legislation on ballots would be modified but its essentials would remain. Pure solidarity action would remain outlawed. Secondary picketing would be permitted only where the second employer was "directly assisting the first employer to frustrate the dispute". Sympathy action would be lawful only where the second employer was taking over the work of the first employer; or was an immediate customer or supplier; or where the outcome of the primary dispute would "necessarily or probably" affect the terms and conditions of the second employer's workforce; or where, as in the Wapping dispute, corporate legal identity was used to make secondary action unlawful. The freedom not to join a trade union was now officially recognised.

The 1990 TUC represented another watershed. A resolution supporting the Labour Party proposals was carried by a large majority. An alternative composite moved by NALGO calling for the repeal of the Tory legislation was narrowly defeated by 4.4 million to 3.5 million votes. Despite significant opposition centred around NALGO, MSF, NGA and the TGWU, the issue was fudged, with unions like the TGWU voting for both resolutions. None the less, at a Congress which also saw support for a National Economic Assessment and moves towards centralised pay bargaining — moves in which many saw the seeds of a TUC enforced incomes policy — the TUC had accepted that central aspects of the Conservative legislation — which they had spent most of the 1980s excoriating — should remain in business under a Labour government.

The Future and the Unions

Is this what trade unionists want or isn't it? Labour's proposals constitute a programme for a rerun of the social contract if in a different, and in some ways, diluted form. As in the 1970s, the reach of the programme in terms of any significant distribution of income and wealth to the working class and in terms of the transfer of any real economic stake in the enterprise, or any measure of control over its organisation and operation, is severely limited. In the legal sphere the EC influenced programme of individual rights is an improvement on the 1970s but the weakening of organisational rights and immunities represents a retreat which could impair the effective articulation of individual rights. The proposals for refurbishment of institutions, such as the judiciary and the police, have their attractions, but the proposals for constitutional reform, while a step forward, are half hearted and unintegrated taken as a whole compared with the more radical programme proffered by Charter 88.

The proposals are a carefully calculated offer to the unions based upon what the Labour leadership feels it can get away with and what EC developments will require. They are a recipe for trade unions which will continue as weaker sectional organisations, bearing, in the future, the wounds of the Thatcher years. The crisis in the unions with 8.3 million trade unionists affiliated to the TUC in the 1980s compared with more than 12 million in 1979, structural factors limiting any significant change for the better, divisions within the movement and political impotence is reflected in the fact that there has been little effective opposition to Labour's programme. But there has been very little real discussion. The exercise in developing an alternative to Thatcherism has been firmly top-down. Acceptance represents the war weariness and the desire to see a return of a Labour government in the union ranks, the constituencies and the ranks of Party activists.

By the end of the 1980s there were no real signs of a reversal of the decline in trade union membership or, despite the massive upheavals characterized by extended coercive state intervention — most notably the Miners' Strike — of any radicalisation within the unions. The renewed strike activity and militancy at the end of the decade, whilst encouraging, was firmly economistic and sectional — in itself inadequate to transform the situation. It is clear that, in present circumstances, the processes of socialist renewal will be slow and painful and will require patience in a situation where Labour's policies represent, not simply bureaucratic manoeuvring or the interests of the Party and TUC leaders, but reflect the ideological position and overall balance of forces within the Labour Movement. In these circumstances, grandiose alternatives are untimely and futile. But this should not inhibit debate as to alternatives which can both help to change the current position and provide a more realistic and inspiring programme for the betterment of the working class in the 1990s.

It remains clear that, despite its limitations in practice, the legislation constitutes a significant barrier to the development of efficient trade union action. This can be seen not only from the 164 claims brought against trade unions in 1989 under the "unjustifiable discipline" provisions of the 1988 Act — which would go under Labour — but from the use of the legislation on ballots and secondary action in major disputes — key essentials of which would *remain* if Labour were elected. And opinion polls commissioned by NALGO prior to the 1990 TUC raised interesting doubts about the degree of public support for the legislation and the degree of opposition to its repeal. Yet clarion calls for the total repeal of all the Conservative legislation may appear at once too abstract, too all embracing, too insensitive to the overall balance of forces. In tactical terms it may appear more propitious to bargain for the complete repeal of the legislation on secondary action, whilst accepting, perforce, Labour's position on ballots. A return to the 1979 position on the former can be justified in terms of democracy, freedom of movement and freedom of speech — as well as in terms of the vital conception of trade unionism as a *movement* and in terms of the enhanced *strength* of that movement. The problem with wholescale repeal of the balloting provisions is the extent to which it appears to many trade unionists as an attack upon democracy and fundamental rights.

It seems, to this author at least, that many problems would be minimised were the unions to give clearcut and unequivocable support to a positive programme of rights, discarding once and for all the "immunities" approach. This would make it very difficult for opponents of secondary action to argue, in a supposedly free society, against the right to withdraw one's labour in support of workers in another industry if such a decision was democratically arrived at. It would mean that the requirement that collective decisions should be democratically arrived at, could lead to the codification in a charter of positive rights of a number of methods by which decisions could be made — not only via postal ballot. It is many years since Keir Hardie rationalised the immunities approach in terms of removing the unions beyond the range of their enemies' guns. That approach has failed to do this over the last century. The enemies' guns have almost continuously pursued the Labour Movement and require spiking and dismantling. A positive Code of Rights coupled with an essential reform of the judiciary could lend a new legitimacy to trade unionism in the twenty-first century and provide the impetus for a fresh start.

However, what is most vital is that discussion should take place amongst the grassroots of the Labour Movement about the proposals for change put forward by the Labour Party — and about alternatives. Thus far, the exercise has been too top-down. It is hoped that this book will encourage that process, a process in which the future of Employment Law *has* to be related to its wider political and economic context. For the projection of new employment laws in isolation from the projection of a new framework for industry and the economy, is a relatively fruitless exercise. The future of employment legislation is intimately bound up with the future of social and economic policy. Employment law is an instrument for making economic and industrial policy work by helping to give you the kind of unions and kind of industrial relations you want.

Discussion on its future cannot proceed in a vacuum. We have to relate it directly to the kind of working relationship and unions we want to see in the kind of society we want to see. And, as ever, these decisions are far far too important to be left to the leadership of the trade unions and the Labour Party.

Discussion Questions

1. Make a list of the major changes that have taken place in the unions since 1979. Make an assessment of the strengths and weaknesses of British trade unionism after more than a decade of Thatcherism.
2. Produce a report on the lessons your union should draw from the *The White Collar Workers' Tale*.
3. Would the unions be better off with a new system of positive rights or a re-enactment of the immunities?
4. What kind of laws should the unions want on:
   — the closed shop
   — secondary action
   — political funds.
5. Do you think the proposals in the Labour Party Review, looked at overall, represent a reasonable package of new employment laws?

References

Chapter 1 **Before the Flood**

1. O. Kahn-Freund, 'Legal Framework' in A. Flanders, H.A. Clegg, *The System of Industrial Relations in Great Britain*, Basil Blackwell, 1967, p.44.
2. *Rv. Druitt* (1867) 10 Cox 592.
3. 0. Kahn-Freund, 'Introduction' to K. Renner, *Institutions of Private Law and their Social Functions*, Routledge and Kegan Paul, 1949, p.28.
4. Malins VC in *Springhead Spinning Co. v. Riley* (1868) LR6 Eq 551:638.
5. *Duport Steels Ltd. v. Sirs* (1980), IRLR 112, 161.
6. Quoted in Lord Wedderburn, *The Worker and the Law*, Penguin Books 1986, p.17.
7. Lord Diplock in *Duport Steels Ltd. v. Sirs* (1980), IRLR 112, 161.
8. S. Pollard, *The Wasting of the British Economy*, Croom Helm, 1982, p.6.
9. Lord Diplock in *Duport Steels Ltd. v. Sirs*, op cit.
10. Lord Salmon in *Duport Steels Ltd. v. Sirs* op cit.
11. F.A. Hayek, *Law Legislation and Liberty*, Vol III, Routledge, Kegan Paul, 1979, p.89-90.
12. Lord Keith, 'Industry, the City of London and our Economic Future' (Ernest Sykes Memorial Lecture) in D. Coates, J. Hillard, eds, *The Economic Decline of Modern Britain* Wheatsheaf Books 1986.
13. F.A. Hayek, *1980s Unemployment and the Unions*, Institute of Economic Affairs, 1980, p.52.
14. ibid p.58.
15. W. Hutt, *The Theory of Collective Bargaining 1930-1975*, IEA, 1975, p.119.
16. A. Shinfield, *What Right to Strike?*, IEA, 1983.
17. House of Lords Debates 358 column 27.
18. House of Commons Debates, Vol 894, 37-8, 23 June 1975.
19. Norman Tebbit, *Upwardly Mobile*, Weidenfeld and Nicholson, 1988, p.153-4.
20. D. Barnes, E. Reid, *Government and Trade Unions: The British Experience 1964-79*, Heinemann, 1980, p.x.
21. Sir Keith Joseph, 'Solving the Union Problem is the Key to Britain's Recovery', Centre for Policy Studies, 1979, reproduced in D. Coates, J. Hillard, op cit, p.99.
22. Sir Keith Joseph, *Reversing the Trend*, Centre for Policy Studies, 1975, p.4.
23. Hugo Young, *One of Us*, McMillan, 1989, p.45.
24. ibid p.75.
25. Norman Tebbit, op cit, p.153-4.
26. Sir John Hoskyns, 'First Steps to Freeze Out Unions', letter, *The Guardian*, September 13, 1988.
27. Department of Employment, 'Employment Secretary Explains Government Approach to Industrial Relations in the 1980s' *Press Notice*, 20th December, 1979, p.5.

28. ibid, p.5.
29. Norman Tebbit, *Upwardly Mobile*, p.184.

Chapter 2 **Softly Softly Turn the Key**

1. Conservative Party, *Conservative Manifesto 1979*, p.6-9.
2. CBI, *Comments on Government's Legislative Proposals*, December 1980, p.6.
3. Industrial Relations Review and Report, *Industrial Relations Legal Information Bulletin*, 150, 1980.
4. Incomes Data Services, *Brief* 166, October, 1979.
5. TUC Circular 282 'Comments on the Proposed Industrial Relations Legislation' 1980.
6. S. Dunn, J. Gennard, *The Closed Shop in British Industry*, McMillan, 1984.
7. TUC Circular 212 'Employment Bill — Provision of Public Funds for Certain Union Ballots' 1980.
8. Central Arbitration Committee, *Annual Report*, 1979, para 4.5; L. Dickens, M. Hart, M. Jones, B. Weekes, *A Response to the Government Working Papers on Amendments to Employment Protection Legislation*, Industrial Relations Research Unit, University of Warwick, 1979; M. Jones 'CAC and Schedule 11: The Experience of Two Years', *Industrial Law Journal*, March 1980.
9. J. McMullen, *Employment Law Under the Tories*, Pluto Press, 1981, p.105.
10. House of Lords Debates, Vol 401, Col 1942-3, 25 July 1979.
11. W. Daniel, E. Stilgoe, *The Impact of Employment Protection Laws*, Policy Studies Institute, 1978, p.20.
12. R. Clifton, C. Tatton-Brown, *Impact of Employment Legislation on Small Firms*, Department of Employment, 1979.
13. 'Maternity Leave — The IRRR Survey', *Industrial Relations Review and Report*, February 1980, p.2.
14. *Working Paper for Consultations on Proposed Industrial Relations Legislation: Picketing*, p.16.

Chapter 3 **The Second Cut is the Deepest**

1. TUC, *Report*, 1982, p.379.
2. Len Murray interviewed in 'The Thatcher Decade' *Radio 4*, April 11, 1989.
3. TUC, *Report*, 1980.
4. TUC, 'Employment Bill: Provisions of Public Funds for Certain Union Ballots', Circular 212, 1980.
5. TUC, *Report*, 1980, p.236. A video was eventually produced presented by Colin Welland dealing with the 1982 Act.
6. ibid, p.237.
7. ibid, p.390 — UCATT resolution.
8. *Trade Union Immunities*, Cmnd 8128, HMSO, 1987, p.1.
9. Incomes Data Services, *Brief* 209, July 1981, p.5.
10. TUC, *Report*, 1981, p.74-82.
11. TUC, *Report*, 1981, p.74.
12. TUC, *Report*, 1982, p.360.
13. TUC, *Report*, 1982, p.358.
14. P. Wintour, 'Will Norman have his own Pentonville 5?' *New Statesman*, 29 January, 1982; J. McIlroy, 'The TUC — Ten Years for the Locust' in D. Cox, W.J. Morgan, eds. *Facing the Future: Issues for Industrial Education*, University of Nottingham, 1991.
15. TUC, *Report*, 1982, p.405.

16. TUC, *Report*, 1982, p.379.
17. TUC, *Report*, 1982, p.387-388.
18. *The Guardian*, 7 April 1982.
19. *Industrial Relations Legislation: The Employment Act 1980 and Employment Bill 1982, Report by the TUC General Council adopted by the Conference of Executives of Affiliated Unions at the Wembley Conference Centre April 5th, 1982*, p.17.

Chapter 4 **Bullets and Ballots**

1. R. Undy, R. Martin, *Ballots and Trade Union Democracy*, Blackwell, 1984, p.167.
2. *Employment News*, February 1983, p.2-3.
3. Department of Employment, *Democracy in Trade Unions*, Cmnd 8778, HMSO, 1983, p.3.
4. ibid, p.20.
5. *Labour Research*, February 1983, p.43. The 1981 Green Paper *Trade Union Immunities* had earlier raised this issue.
6. TUC Press Release, 12 July 1983, 'Government Proposals Threaten Democracy'.

Chapter 5 **Heroes and Villains**

1. N. Millward, M. Stevens, *British Workplace Industrial Relations 1980-1984*, Gower Press 1986.
2. Lord Wedderburn, *The Worker and the Law*, Penguin, 1986, p.247.
3. Ibid, p.247.
4. L. Dickens, D. Cockburn, 'Dispute Settlement Institutions and the Courts' in R. Lewis, ed. *Labour Law in Britain*, Blackwell, 1986, p.558.
5. N. Tebbit, *Upwardly Mobile*, Weidenfeld and Nicholson, 1988, p.207.
6. News International document circulated by SOGAT, February 1986.

Chapter 6 **Another Brick in the Wall**

1. Incomes Data Services, *Brief*, No.341, January, 1987, p.11.
2. *Labour Research*, October 1985, p.26.
3. TUC, *Report*, 1987, p.30-31.
4. Ibid, p.31-32.
5. *Employment Gazette*, April, 1987, p.162.
6. Industrial Relations Review and Report, *Legal Information Bulletin*, No.330, June 1987, p.16.
7. Ibid, p.16.
8. Department of Employment, *The Employment Act 1988 — A Guide to its Industrial Relations and Trade Union Law Provisions*, p.10.
9. Incomes Data Services, *Brief*, 349, May 1987, p.17.
10. *Financial Times*, 1st February 1988.
11. *P&O European Ferries (Portsmouth) Ltd. v. NUS, The Independent*, March 28, 1988.
12. *The Guardian*, May 4, 1988.
13. *The Guardian*, July 7, 1988.
14. *Labour Research*, July 1989, p.2.

Chapter 7 **Wider Still and Wider**

1. *Labour Research*, December 1989.

2. Conference of Catholic Bishops, Committee For the World of Work, *A Threefold Cord*, Catholic Truth Society, 1989.
3. S. Deakin, F. Wilkinson, *Labour Law, Social Security and Economic Inequality*, Institute of Employment Rights, 1989.
4. Social Trends 19, 20, 1989, 1990, HMSO; *The Guardian*, February 15th 1990.
5. A. Leonard, *Pyrrhic Victories: Winning Sex Discrimination and Equal Pay Cases in the Industrial Tribunals 1980-84*, EOC, 1987.
6. S. Deakin, F. Wilkinson, op cit.
7. *Labour Research*, January 1990, p.4.
8. *Financial Times*, May 6th 1989.
9. National Association of Port Employers, *Repeal of the Dock Labour Board Scheme: Industrial Action — An Analysis*, p.5, 6, 1987.
10. Quoted in *Tribune* May 12th 1989.
11. *The Guardian*, June 8th 1989.
12. *The Guardian*, June 9th 1989.
13. *Financial Times*, July 8th 1989.
14. *Financial Times*, October 11th 1989.
15. Department of Employment, *Unofficial Action and the Law*, 1989.
16. *Financial Times*, October 13th 1989.
17. M. Stevens, N. Millward, D. Smart, 'Trade Union Membership and the Closed Shop in 1989', *Employment Gazette*, November 1989.
18. D. Metcalfe, *Water Notes Dry Up*, Centre for Labour Economics, London School of Economics, Discussion Paper 314, 1988. N. Crafts, 'The Assessment: British Economic Growth Over the Long Run', *Oxford Review of Economic Policy*, 4, I, 1988. These views are criticised in P. Nolan, P. Marginson, *Skating on Thin Ice; David Metcalfe on Trade Unions and Productivity*, Warwick Papers in Industrial Relations 22, University of Warwick, 1988.
19. Quoted in John Hendy, *The Conservative Employment Laws: A National and International Assessment*, 1989, Institute of Employment Rights, p.35.

Chapter 8   **Yesterday's Gone**

1. S. Nickell, S. Wadhwani, M. Wall, 'Unions and Productivity Growth in Britain 1974-86'; S. Wadhwani, M. Wall, 'The Effects of Unions on Corporate Investment'; S. Wadhwani, 'The Effects of Unions on Productivity Growth, Investment and Employment: A Report on Some Recent Work'; S. Machin, S. Wadhwani, 'The effects of unions on organisational change, investment and employment' — Working Papers, Centre for Labour Economics, London School of Economics. These papers conclude that the legislation had little impact on weakening unions in unionised firms — differential productivity growth in these firms was the result of management bargaining away restrictive practices in the recession. See also P. Nolan, 'Walking on Water? Performance and Industrial Relations under Thatcher', *Industrial Relations Journal*, 20, 2, Summer 1989.
2. Department of Employment, *Removing Barriers to Employment*, 1989, p.1. See Reference in Note 1 and review by W. Brown, S. Wadhwani, in *National Institute for Economic and Social Research Review*, 131, February 1990.
3. BBC TV, *9 o'clock News*, 10th August 1989.
4. H. Young, *One of Us*, p.211. She replied however: "You know I would rather go down than do that so forget it" ibid.
5. H. Beynon, ed, *Digging Deeper: Issues in the Miners' Strike*, Verso, 1985, p.36.
6. 'Which way forward for the Unions?' in 'Socialist Policy Review', *Interlink: Special Issue*, Summer 1989, p.41.
7. *Financial Times*, September 4, 1989.
8. *Financial Times*, December 18, 1989.

9. *Financial Times*, March 22, 1989.
10. Quoted in A. Wilson, 'The Future of Trade Union Law: Positive Rights and Immunities', *The Industrial Tutor*, 4, 3, Spring 1986, p.29.
11. *Financial Times*, November 6th, 1989.

Further Reading

If you want to go further into the historical background and the details of the present legal position then Lord Wedderburn's book *The Worker and the Law*, Penguin, 1986, first published in 1965 and now in its third edition is your best bet. Originally intended as a brief introduction it is now a pretty exhaustive 1,000 page classic covering all aspects of the law. Another good detailed book is Roy Lewis, ed, *Labour Law in Britain*, Blackwell, 1983. Jeremy McMullen's *Rights at Work*, Pluto Press, 2nd edition, 1983, is now out of date but still carries interesting information, whilst J.A.G. Griffith *The Politics of the Judiciary*, Fontana, 3rd edition, 1985, is excellent on the role of the judiciary.

Two recent popular books on Thatcherism well worth consulting are Peter Jenkins, *Mrs Thatcher's Revolution*, Pan, 1989 and Hugo Young, *One of Us*, MacMillan, 1989; see also, Stuart Hall and Martin Jacques, eds. *New Times: The Changing Face of Politics in the Nineties*, Lawrence and Wishart, 1989.

For brief analysis of recent developments in the trade unions see John McIlroy *Trade Unions in Britain Today*, Manchester University Press, 1988 and Ken Coates, Tony Topham, *Trade Unions in Britain*, Fontana, 1988, whilst David Coates, *The Crisis of Labour*, Phillip Allan, 1989, is a stimulating analysis of the situation since 1945.

A very good account of the *Messenger* dispute is in Mark Dickinson, *To Break a Union*, Booklist Ltd., 1984. On the miners' strike there is Huw Beynon, ed. *Digging Deeper: Issues in the Miners' Strike*, Verso, 1985; Bob Fine, Robert Millar, *Policing the Miners' Strike*, Lawrence and Wishart, 1985, which both deal with the legal aspects of the strike.

Jon and Ruth Winterton, *Coal, Crisis and Conflict: The 1984-85 Miners' Strike in Yorkshire*, Manchester University Press, 1989, is an engrossing, rounded account of wider relevance than its title suggests. On the Wapping dispute there is Linda Melville, *The End of the Street*, Methuen, 1986, whilst Ken Coates, Tony Topham, *Trade Unions and Politics*, Blackwell, 1986, deals with the background to the political fund ballots and the successful campaign.

Finally, a rather journalistic but accessible account of recent changes in the Labour Party which provide the background to the Policy Review is to be found in Colin Hughes, Patrick Wintour, *Labour Rebuilt*, Fourth Estate, 1990.

Glossary

Act A written law passed by the House of Commons and the House of Lords and then assented to by the Queen.

Additional Award Sum of money awarded to a successful applicant by an industrial tribunal when a recommendation of re-engagement/reinstatement has been made by the tribunal but not complied with by the employer.

Applicant Person taking a case to an industrial tribunal.

Arbitration The process when two sides to a dispute agree that a third party, such as ACAS, will give a decision on the case.

Associated Employer Two employers are 'associated' in law if one is a *company* of which the other directly or indirectly has control or if both are *companies* of which a third party has control.

Basic Award Sum of money awarded to all successful applicants in unfair dismissal cases. It is based upon the calculation of a statutory redundancy payment but can be reduced to nil in consideration of the applicant's conduct.

Bill A draft law introduced into Parliament, usually by the government, although there are Private Members' Bills. If it passes successfully through Parliament it becomes an Act.

Bridlington Agreement The set of rules governing disputes between unions agreed at the 1939 TUC in Bridlington.

Central Arbitration Committee The committee is made up of a legally or academically qualified chair and 2 lay members selected from panels nominated by the CBI and TUC. It hears complaints made by unions about disclosure of information and can make binding awards on terms and conditions.

Certification Officer An official who grants union certificates of independence; keeps records of union's members, accounts, etc.; supervises political funds and amalgamations; and hears complaints from union members.

Check-off The practice by which an employer deducts the union dues of workers directly from wages or salary.

Civil Law Legislation and common law which covers issues deemed not to be sufficiently serious to attract the criminal law so that it is left up to legal persons, individuals, companies, trade unions, who suffer damage to take legal action themselves. The system of courts, procedure and remedies differs from the criminal law and the usual remedies are damages or the imposition of a court order. The most important divisions within the civil law are the law of *contract* and the law of *tort* and it is more important than criminal law in the industrial relations field.

Code of Practice A document produced by ACAS, the Department of Employment, or another official body such as the Health and Safety Executive. It is intended to guide management and trade unionists and its provisions will be taken into account by courts and tribunals in legal action.

Commissioner for the Rights of Trade Unionists An official appointed to advise and assist trade unionists in bringing to court an increasing range of legal actions against trade unions.

Common Law The law made directly by the judges through hearing cases and establishing precedents — as distinct from legislation made by Parliament and interpreted by the courts. But legislation takes precedence.

Compensatory Award The sum of compensation the employer must pay a worker in an unfair dismissal case to compensate for wages and other benefits lost through the dismissal.

Conciliation The process by which a third party such as ACAS tries to stimulate both sides to a dispute to come together and reach their own agreement.

Conspiracy An agreement by two or more people to behave in such a way as will necessarily involve the commission of an offence if the agreement is carried out as the parties intended. Both the tort of conspiracy and criminal conspiracy have been important in the development of Labour Law.

Contempt of Court A criminal offence arising out of failure to comply with the directions or order of a court. The penalty for contempt is in the discretion of the court and can involve a fine or sequestration.

Contract Written or verbal agreement which is legally binding. The courts and Parliament denote the legal relationship between employer and employee as a Contract of Employment.

Contract Out The right of individual trade unionists under the 1913 Trade Union Act to refuse to pay the political levy.

Costs Refers to the rules by which the courts can order one side in a legal action to pay all or a proportion of the costs incurred by the opposing side in pursuing the action. In industrial tribunals costs are limited to certain situations, e.g. where a case is brought or defended in a frivolous, vexatious or unreasonable fashion.

Court of Appeal The court, usually made up of three judges, which hears appeals from the High Court, County Court or Employment Appeal Tribunal on points of law, and from the Crown Court on points of law or fact.

Court of Session Scottish equivalent of High Court (Outer House) and Court of Appeal (Inner House).

Criminal Law Contrasts with civil law and is concerned with wrongs regarded by Parliament as sufficiently threatening to society to merit direct state intervention. So, as distinct from civil law, where the legal process is started by the legal person, the state usually initiates *prosecutions* through the police or the Health and Safety Executive and pursues penalties and enforcement through *fines* and *imprisonment.* Criminal law affects industrial relations usually in the areas of health and safety, industrial action, particularly picketing, and discipline.

Crown Court Local criminal court which hears appeals from magistrates courts and hears serious criminal cases with a jury. It also hears some civil cases.

Crown Employment Employment by the state.

Crown Immunity The exclusion of government departments from the ambit of Acts of Parliament. The ability of the crown to do unlawful things.

Damages The sum of compensation awarded by a court to the winner in a legal case and paid by the loser to restore the winner to the position he or she would have occupied had the unlawful act not occurred.

Directive An Order of the European Community to be translated into law by each of the member states.

Employment Appeal Tribunal A body which hears appeals from industrial tribunals and the certification officer on points of law. Consists of a High Court judge and 2 lay members from panels nominated by the TUC and employers' organisations.

European Commission The body appointed from member states to formulate proposals for EC policy for consideration and decision by the Council of Ministers and to supervise the day-to-day administration of the European Community.

European Court of Appeal The court consists of eleven judges with four Advocates-General whose job is to put forward cases in an impartial way reflecting the public interest, rather than the interests of the parties, to a case. The court adjudicates on the meaning of the basic treaties and measures introduced by other EC bodies and its rulings are binding on member states.

Ex parte injunction An injunction issued by a court after hearing only one party to the case.

Fixed Term Contract A contract of employment which terminates on a specified date even if it can be terminated by either party to it giving notice before that date.

Green Paper A document which details the possibilities for legislation in a particular area; it is issued by the government and circulated to interested parties for consultation.

Guarantee Payment A sum of money to be paid on a daily basis by employers to workers laid off.

High Court This court usually consists of one judge and hears civil cases where compensation claimed is more than £5,000, as well as appeals from magistrates.

House of Lords This term is used to cover both the second chamber of Parliament and the supreme court in the UK which hears appeals from the Court of Appeal. The court normally consists of five to seven judges. They are usually promoted from the Court of Appeal but then become Law Lords.

Independent Trade Unions Unions which have received a certificate of independence from the certification officer. The importance of this is that many of the positive rights granted in legislation in the 1960s and 1970s to unions and their members only apply to unions which possess this certificate, demonstrating their freedom from domination, control or interference by an employer.

Inducement to Breach of Contract An important tort which has been central to the law on industrial conflict, it is perpetrated where you knowingly and intentionally induce any person to break his or her contract without lawful justification. The technical requirements of 'knowledge' and 'intention' are often minimally explored in hearings for interim injunctions.

Industrial Tribunals Each tribunal consists of a legally qualified chair and two lay members nominated by employers and the TUC. These tribunals normally deal with cases involving the individual worker such as dismissal, redundancy or discrimination, although they also hear appeals against health and safety notices.

Injunction A court order requiring a party to a case to do or stop doing something which is or may be unlawful.

Insolvency The situation where a company is bankrupt through inability to pay its debts and is put in the hands of a receiver to be wound up.

Interdict An injunction in Scotland.

Interim Injunction A temporary injunction intended to preserve the *status quo* issued by the court sometimes on an *ex parte* basis at an interim hearing, pending the full hearing of the case. The standard of proof required by the court has been lower than that required at the full hearing and this has caused problems for trade unionists.

Interim Relief This usually refers in industrial cases to the orders available to trade unionists dismissed for union activities or non-unionists dismissed for non-membership of a union, maintaining wages until a full hearing of the case.

Law Lords The judges in the House of Lords who, as life peers, are also entitled to sit in the 'political' House of Lords.

Legislation Acts of Parliament as distinct from Common Law which legislation takes precedence over.

Magistrates Courts Courts presided over by unpaid lay magistrates, known as Justices of the Peace, which hear less serious criminal cases and decide whether there is enough evidence to commit more serious cases for trial at Crown Courts.

Political Fund The fund (which must be quite separate from the *general* fund) which under the 1913 Trade Union Act unions can resource only via a specific *political levy* on their membership. A union's political objects can only be financed from its political fund and the establishment of the fund requires a ballot of all members which must be repeated every ten years.

Post-entry closed shop The position prevailing where a worker must become a member of a union, or a particular union, after taking up employment.

Pre-entry closed shop The position prevailing where a worker must be a member of a union or a particular union *before* being hired.

Pre-Hearing Assessment A hearing conducted by industrial tribunals to assess whether doubtful cases should go on to a full hearing.

Protective Award A sum of compensation awarded by tribunals to employees when an employer has failed to carry out legal requirements to consult over proposed redundancies with union representatives.

Qualifying Period The period of service which employees must have worked with their employer before they are entitled to bring certain legal cases to tribunals. The periods differ according to the legal right pursued.

Redundancy The situation where an employee is dismissed because the business closes, or the business moves, or where the employers' need for workers to do work of a particular kind has ceased or diminished.

Redundancy Consultation The requirement laid down in legislation for employers to consult with union representatives prior to making workers redundant.

Redundancy Payments The statutory minimum payments the state requires employers to pay redundant employees based upon the employees' wages and length of service with the employer.

Reinstatement/Re-engagement Orders made by an industrial tribunal in unfair dismissal cases requiring the employer to take back a successful applicant. As they cannot be directly enforced they are in reality recommendations rather than 'orders'.

Secondary Action Sympathy strikes or other industrial action, such as a refusal to handle goods, taken by a group of workers who are not directly concerned in a dispute but are in solidarity with a group of workers who are.

Secondary Picketing This phrase has been popularised by the press to refer to the situation where a group of workers picket a workplace, other than their own, in order to persuade workers there to join a dispute. It is used to apply to the situation where the secondary group of workers is directly involved in the dispute but inactive - as well as the situation where the secondary group has no direct connection with, or immediate interest in, the primary dispute.

Sequestration The device by which courts order the take-over of all or part of the assets of a party in contempt of court.

Special Award Extra compensation awarded by an industrial tribunal where a worker is found to be dismissed in violation of legislation for membership or non-membership of a trade union.

Statute An Act of Parliament.

Statutory Instrument A Law made by a Minister authorised to do so by legislation, eg tribunal regulations. Statutory instruments are *delegated legislation.*

Tort A civil wrong which, as distinct from a criminal wrong, is left up to the party suffering damage to remedy by going to court. But some wrongs, eg assault, can be both civil and criminal.

TUC Dispute Committee Body consisting of senior trade unionists which decides on disputes between trade unions under the Bridlington Agreement.

Union Membership Agreement A legal form of the closed shop by which all workers in a particular grade or category are required to be or become members of a union(s).

Wages Councils Bodies established by legislation with power to establish minimum wages, holidays, and other terms of employment for workers in poorly organised low paid industries. They consist of representatives of employers and workers as well as 'independents'.

White Paper Proposals for legislation, normally outlined in more specific form than in a Green Paper, circulated to interested parties for consultation.

Index

The
SOCIAL CHARTER
and the
SINGLE EUROPEAN MARKET

John Hughes

We can hardly understate the importance for the future political economy of Europe of the wide-ranging developments and changes being set in motion in the course of constructing a single market for the European Community. At the same time, the debate about the Social Charter and the Action Programme embodies two interlinked dimensions of social and political concern following from this development. In this luminous text, John Hughes shows how the new needs of equity require a rapid evolution of new norms of social and political practice.

Addressing social partners such as trade unionists and consumers' groups, he argues that the Community's emphasis on social dialogue and the equitable extension of social rights need to go hand in hand with large-scale programmes of expenditure to help disadvantaged reqions, to combat discrimination against part-time workers, reflected so starkly in women's inferior pay for work of equal value, to tackle long-term unemployment, and to meet the needs of young people entering the labour market. In this way, and with persistent effort, we can constitute the social dimension of the single European market.

Hugh McMahon MEP contributes a checklist on how the Social Charter is faring from the viewpoints of the Commission's Action Programme and that of the European Parliament.

John Hughes is consultant to the Trade Union Research Unit (TURU), Ruskin College, Oxford.

ISBN 085124 524 2 £6.95 paper
ISBN 085124 523 4 £20.00 cloth

Elf Books 1   SPOKESMAN
                                   for European Labour Forum

European Union: Fortress or Democracy?

Towards a Democratic Market and a New Economic Order

MICHAEL BARRATT BROWN

1992 is not only the year when the European Community becomes a single market, with all the economic implications for associated countries as well as for the twelve members. It will also be the crunch year for Eastern Europe's transition to a market economy, and perhaps most important of all the year when bridges will have to be built from Europe to the peoples of the Third World of developing countries, whose hearts and minds were never won for a military settlement of the Gulf crisis. This book is inspired by the fear that preoccupation with purely European questions will lead to neglect of Europe's responsibility for the desperate situation in the Third World countries, which are almost without exception one-time European colonies.

The author, who is an international economist, examines some of the problems involved in preventing the emergence of a fortress mentality in Europe as a response to the catastrophic situation outside. He raises fundamental questions about the failure of economic command systems in the East to deliver the goods, the equal failure of the capitalist world market to meet the needs of more than a small minority of the world's people, and the disastrous results for all from rising debts and falling incomes in the consequent recourse to internecine struggle and military adventure. In doing so, he offers some suggestions for new forms of economic development, new ways of making the market democratic, and new types of trade relations which are both fairer and more environmentally sustainable.

Michael Barratt Brown is a director of the Bertrand Russell Peace Foundation. He was the founding Principal of Northern College. Now he is the Chairman of Third World Information Network and Twin Trading Ltd.

ISBN 0 85124 521 8   £7.95   paper
ISBN 0 85124 520 X   £20.00   cloth
Elf Books 2

SPOKESMAN
for European Labour Forum

Against a Rising Tide

Racism, Europe and 1992

MEL READ MEP and ALAN SIMPSON

*A*gainst a Rising Tide considers how racism and xenophobia form increasingly prominent threads in the tapestry of European economies and societies. At one level, the authors argue, little has changed. European industry has always required cheap labour, and has usually drawn it from former colonies and the Third World. And domestic racism has helped keep this labour mainly poor and forever foreign (irrespective of what it says on your passport or birth certificate). But 1992 will bring contradictions of its own. "Freedom of Movement" will not apply equally throughout the Community. It will depend on citizenship status. Clandestine meetings of foreign ministers are tightening immigration rules and procedures, specifically in relation to Third World countries. Business has found a new source of cheap labour in Eastern Europe. And the extreme Right has found new converts to old prejudices in the crevices of faltering European economies.

The authors explore ways in which those with a different vision — that of a "people's" Europe — might work to move beyond the divisions of prejudice, discrimination, exploitation, and intimidation. Pooling their experience of anti-racist work at local, national, and international levels, and taking Nottingham as an example, they offer practical ways in which local authorities and local people can combat racism, setting this work in a European context. Perhaps most significantly, they challenge us to look at racism in a less fragmented way — seeing citizenship rights, economic exploitation, and the threat of physical attack as inter-related aspects of the new European racism.

Mel Read is the Labour Member of the European Parliament for Leicester, Nuneaton and North Warwickshire. She is also Chair of the European Parliamentary Labour Party. Formerly, she was Employment Officer at the Racial Equality Council in Nottingham. She is a lifelong trade union activist and former national executive member of MSF.

Alan Simpson is Research Officer for the Racial Equality Council in Nottingham. He is author of several works dealing with racial discrimination in housing, economic policy and the inner cities, community development, and policing policy.

ISBN 0 85124 526 9   £6.95   paper
ISBN 0 85124 525 0   £20   cloth
Elf Books 3

SPOKESMAN
for Nottingham Racial Equality Council
and European Labour Forum